THE
UNITED STATES
IN THE
TWENTIETH CENTURY

DEMOCRACY

Edited by Richard
Maidment

Hodder & Stoughton

in association with

The Open
University

This text forms part of an Open University Second Level Course D214 *The United States in the Twentieth Century.* If you would like a copy of *Studying with the Open University*, please write to the Central Enquiry Service, PO Box 200, The Open University, Walton Hall, Milton Keynes MK7 6YZ, United Kingdom.

British Library Cataloguing in Publication Data

Democracy. — (US in the Twentieth Century Series)

I. Maidment, R.A. II. Series
321.8

ISBN 0 340 59686 4

First published 1994

Impression number	10	9	8	7	6	5	4	3	2	1	
Year			1998	1997	1996	1995	1994	1993			

Edited, designed and typeset by the Open University.

Printed in Great Britain for the educational publishing division of Hodder Headline Plc, 338 Euston Road, London NW1 3BH by Thomson Litho Ltd, East Kilbride.

7667C/D214 Book 3/

UNIVERSITY COLLEGE
WINCHESTER

Martial Rose Library
Tel: 01962 827306

To be returned on or before the day marked above, subject to recall.

CONTRIBUTORS TO THIS VOLUME

Christopher Bailey, Department of American Studies, University of Keele

John Clarke, Faculty of Social Sciences, The Open University

Richard Hodder-Williams, Department of Politics, University of Bristol

Desmond King, St. John's College, University of Oxford

Robert McKeever, Department of Politics, University of Reading

Richard Maidment, Faculty of Social Sciences, The Open University

Guy Peters, Department of Political Science, University of Pittsburgh

Jon Roper, American Studies, University College of Swansea

Alan Ware, Worcester College, University of Oxford

John Zvesper, School of English and American Studies, University of East Anglia

Cover

Lincoln Memorial, Washington, DC

Photo: United States Travel & Tourism Administration

CONTENTS

PREFACE

The five volumes in this series are part of an Open University, Faculty of Social Sciences course *The United States in the Twentieth Century*. In many respects the course has been a new venture — it is the first time that the Open University has entered the field of American Studies and it did so at a time when resources were not abundant. So the development of this course is due, in no small part, to the enthusiasm and support of many colleagues in the Faculty of Social Sciences. There are too many people to thank individually, but my appreciation must be recorded for some of them.

The United States in the Twentieth Century would not have been made without my academic colleagues, Anthony McGrew, Jeremy Mitchell and Grahame Thompson. Their role was central to the conception and planning of the course and their presence made the production of it an intellectually stimulating as well as an enjoyable experience. Mike Dawson, the Course Manager, took all the tension out of a process that is normally fraught and difficult. His calm efficiency, common sense and good humour got the rest of us through the production process with few anxieties. Jeremy Cooper of the BBC not only ensured that the course has an excellent audio-visual component, but made a very important contribution to its overall development. The Course Team owes a substantial debt to the editorial work of Stephen Clift and Tom Hunter who did all that was asked of them plus a great deal more. The designs for the covers, and indeed for the entire course, by Sarah Crompton were immediately and enthusiastically welcomed by everybody. David Wilson of the Book Trade Department was always available and his advice was both appreciated and heeded. Our colleagues in Project Control and in the Operations Division of the university were unfailingly supportive and helpful. However, none of these books would have seen the light of day without Anne Hunt who, along with her colleagues Mary Dicker and Carole Kershaw, typed successive drafts of the manuscripts of all five volumes without complaint and with remarkable accuracy and speed.

These books owe an enormous debt to our Americanist colleagues in institutions other than the Open University. This series has drawn on their scholarship and expertise, and above all on their generosity in being willing to participate in this project. The Course Team owes a particular debt to Professor David Adams, Director of the David Bruce Centre at the University of Keele, the external assessor of *The United States in the Twentieth Century*. His tough advice and wise counsel assisted us greatly. We incurred a similar obligation to Professor Ian Bell, also of the University of Keele, who helped us far beyond the call of duty. Doctor Ronald Clifton, who has done so much for American Studies in Britain, was enormously helpful and supportive in making sure this course came to fruition.

Finally there were moments when it might have been easier for Margaret Kiloh, the Dean of the Faculty of Social Sciences, to have been less than enthusiastic about *The United States in the Twentieth Century* but her support never wavered.

Richard Maidment, Course Chair
Milton Keynes, December 1993

I would like to thank all the contributors to this volume for their enthusiasm and generosity with their time and effort. In particular I would like to thank Professor David Adams whose advice greatly improved the final draft. Norma Sherratt was extremely helpful and made several valuable suggestions. Stephen Clift edited this volume, as usual, with meticulous efficiency. Finally, I would like to thank all the members of the Course Team whose collective advice was invaluable.

Richard Maidment, Course Chair
Milton Keynes, January 1994

★ ★

INTRODUCTION

Richard Maidment ★

In May 1831 Alexis de Tocqueville arrived in the United States. He returned to France in February of the following year but this relatively brief experience of the United States allowed de Tocqueville to write *Democracy in America*, a book that has endured since its publication in 1835. Interestingly his observations and analysis of early nineteenth century American life, which were strikingly incisive and revelatory when they first appeared, continue to illuminate our understanding of the United States as this century draws to a close. Several of de Tocqueville's concerns and insights into the society and polity of the United States in the 1830s retain our interest, most notably his view of America's democratic character.

Nothing struck de Tocqueville more forcibly 'than the general equality of condition among the people ... The more I advanced in the study of American society, the more I perceived that this equality of condition is the fundamental fact from which above all others seem to be derived ... '. The egalitarianism of American society, according to de Tocqueville, was matched by a commitment to majority rule and democracy. 'The people reign in the American political world as the Deity does in the Universe.' (de Tocqueville, 1966, vol.1, p.7.) Equality and democracy, he believed, were the keys to understanding the United States. Of course, de Tocqueville was only reporting that which he observed. He certainly did not endorse either of these American traits, because he was no advocate for egalitarianism or majority rule. Indeed, he did not attempt to conceal his distaste. However, in the intervening century and a half since the book was written, enthusiasm for democracy and equality have become all but universal, while very serious questions have been raised over the condition of American democracy at the end of the twentieth century. Alexis de Tocqueville's concerns, as it were, have been reversed. There is little debate that all societies and polities should be, or at the very least seek to be, democracies, though there is a great deal of discussion over whether there is democracy in America.

This volume of essays reflects on the democratic credentials of the key institutions and processes of the American political system at a time when there is a profound degree of unease about the political process. This unease pervaded the 1992 presidential campaign when all the major candidates, including the incumbent George Bush, shared the view that the political process in the United States was not functioning satisfactorily. In fact the political system was frequently described as being in a state of 'gridlock' — in other words, locked or frozen — and all but unable to function. The phenomenon of 'gridlock' is evident in several of the chapters of this book and the emphasis is appropriate because it brings into focus some key issues about the operation of politics in the United States. Also it illustrates one of the central tensions of contemporary American democracy. It is a tension that is rooted in the history of the United States.

The reference and context of late twentieth century American democracy is provided by a Constitution that is the product of the eighteenth century. The concerns of the Founding Fathers, those remarkable men who assembled at the Constitutional Convention in Philadelphia in May 1787, were not those of twentieth century democrats. They did not share the values of contemporary democracy. The Founding Fathers did not embrace majority rule nor did they want to see the enactment of the wishes of the majority into legislation at least with any rapidity. They did not value effective and efficient government. Quite the contrary, they had a profound fear and concern of how a majority would rule. James Madison, the 'father of the Constitution', made these fears absolutely clear in *The Federalist Papers*. In *The Federalist* No.10, Madison gave voice to his concerns. He believed that all societies unfortunately have to deal with factions or interests. In Madison's view, factions are endemic to the social condition and all of them are a potential danger to 'the permanent and aggregate interests of the community'. But are all factions equally dangerous or is there one that poses a particular threat to the body politic? According to Madison, there is indeed a faction which is dangerous above all others, the majority faction. 'When a majority is included in a faction, the form of popular government, on the other hand, enables it to sacrifice to its ruling passion or interest both the public good and the rights of other citizens. To secure the public good and private rights against the danger of such a faction, and at the same time to preserve the spirit and the form of popular government, is then the great object to which our inquiries are directed.'

The Constitution that emerged at the Convention in Philadelphia was designed to achieve Madison's objectives. It sought to restrain and control the majority faction in order to ensure the liberty of all Americans. The Framers of the Constitution were ingenious in the way they attempted to fulfil this goal. The principal strategy that they deployed was to disperse power within the political system. The Constitution created two distinct levels of governmental institutions, one for the states, and the other set of institutions was at the national level. Moreover, the national or federal institutions were given specific and limited responsibilities and powers, and those powers which were not designated to the federal government were reserved for the states. The Constitution then went on to subdivide the powers allocated to the federal government on the broad lines indicated by the doctrine of separation of powers, with the executive, legislative and judicial powers the responsibility of the presidency, the Congress and the federal courts respectively. But just in case this dispersal of power was insufficient to stop a majority faction from gaining control of all the key levers of government, the Convention added the notion of checks and balances, which is perhaps the only wholly original contribution to the art of constitution making that has emerged from the United States.

The Constitution established an independent base of authority for the presidency, Congress and the courts, but it also created a degree of interdependence. The presidency, for instance, was not designed solely as an executive institution, it was also allocated a legislative role. The President was given the power of veto over bills passed by the Congress. Similarly, the Congress was permitted to intervene in matters which were traditionally within the domain of the executive. These checks and balances, of which there are several in the Constitution, were designed to be points of friction and barriers to a sense of comity and goodwill between President and Congress. But just in case these points of friction did not succeed in developing a sufficient degree of institutional antagonism, the Founding Fathers added a further ingredient into the constitutional mixture. They insisted that the political branches of the federal government, the presidency, the Senate and the House of Representatives, represented different constituencies and have different modes of election. The Framers believed that this combination would ensure that the President, Senators and Representatives would not share the same ambitions and goals and consequently view each other with a suspicion that bordered on hostility.

The overriding objective of this elaborate and complicated construction was to bring about 'gridlock' or a position as near to 'gridlock' as possible. The Framers did not want a governmental system that was characterized by co-operation and that acted with dispatch. They hoped for conflict and believed that they had made that conflict an integral element of the American constitutional structure. The current complaints about 'gridlock' would be a source of satisfaction for them.

'The American Constitution', wrote William Gladstone in 1878, 'is ... the most wonderful work ever struck off at a given time by the brain and purpose of man'. Gladstone's admiration was understandable and the admiration would no doubt be even greater a hundred years later, because the Constitution has provided the political framework for a society that has been in constant state of change over the past two centuries. Yet, remarkably, during that time there have only been 27 amendments to the Constitution and ten of those were adopted in 1791. The Constitution has endured but, interestingly, some of the principal values and beliefs that animated the generation that wrote the Constitution have not endured at least to the same extent. The Constitutional Convention recognized the importance of establishing a government by the people but they very much wanted to channel and control popular views and emotions. But this fear of majorities, even if it had not disappeared, certainly had diminished by the early nineteenth century and by the closing decades of that century the democratic principle was completely dominant. The discourse of politics in America was aggressively democratic. The politics of the United States had become assertively populist. It was an imperative for politicians that they paid homage to their electorates, the wishes of the people were paramount. The fears expressed by Madison no longer found any significant resonance. The twentieth century only confirmed the triumph of democracy. The late nineteenth and early twentieth century reforms of the primary election and the referendum derived their strength and impetus from the acceptance of the majoritarian principle. The people must be in control has been the irresistible cry of politics in America during this century. But throughout the triumph of majoritarianism the Constitution has remained essentially intact. The democratic principle has had to coexist with Madison's Constitution. Moreover the Constitution has worked rather well.

The American constitutional system by comparison with virtually all the other major liberal democracies has an unparalleled number of points of access both in Washington and in the states' capitals. This access enables the extraordinary array of diverse interests that exist in the United States to make their views known and more importantly to affect the decisions that are made. They have been able, over the past two centuries, to use this access to great effect. They have blocked or postponed proposals, either legislative or administrative, which they believed were unhelpful to themselves. The slow and cumbersome decision-making process both in the Congress and in the executive branch has allowed interests, however small and peripheral, to intervene and have a voice and an impact. However, when the interests have been powerful and substantial, although unable to command majority support, their influence has been very significant and frequently able to hinder the wishes of the electorate. This ability has continually frustrated those Americans who have wished to use the political system for the purposes of reform.

So what is the nature of American democracy? The portrait that emerges from this book is of a very distinctive constitutional democracy. This emerges very strongly both in Chapter 1 by Jon Roper and in the final chapter by Richard Hodder-Williams. Roper examines America's democratic heritage while Hodder-Williams considers the claims for a new constitution. In Chapter 5 Robert McKeever looks at the role of the courts. The federal courts and in particular the United States Supreme Court have had and continue to have an enormous impact on the policy-making process. The judiciary in the United States play a critical role in the making of public policy, a role which is far greater than their judicial colleagues in any other liberal democracy. McKeever evaluates this very distinctive feature of American constitutionalism and reflects on the democratic implications, which are considerable. The chapters by Guy Peters and Christopher Bailey deal with the difficulties of the policy-making process and the problems confronting both institutions and politicians in formulating public policy. This book examines several instances where reform has not been easy to achieve in part because of the capacity of minorities to block action. Alan Ware looks at the party system and the rather unique character of American parties, which contribute to the elongated and laboured process of making public policy. In Chapter 8, John Clarke discusses the nature of the American welfare state and the struggle over its creation and development, which still does not reach European levels of provision. One of the key debates in the

1990s will be over the extent and funding of the public provision of health care. In Chapter 7, John Zvesper examines ethnicity and race, which brings into focus a number of similar but also related issues over the ability of the political system to limit discrimination and guarantee a level of equality. Desmond King looks at city government and the problems that confront the cities.

The discourse of American politics in the twentieth century leaves little doubt that the electorate and their political representatives see themselves as democrats and that the United States is the pre-eminent liberal democracy in the world. Politicians take this for granted. They often proclaim it but rarely feel obliged to justify it. Democracy, they assert, is an American value and their constituents agree. However, this collection of essays does make it clear that the reality of American democracy is somewhat more complex and less clear-cut than the triumphalist language that is occasionally used. These essays raise collectively a very substantial set of questions over the demo-cratic character of the polity and interestingly several of these questions are rooted in the American historical experience. They emerge from tensions that have always existed over democratic beliefs and values and these ten-sions have not entirely dissipated.

REFERENCE

Tocqueville, A. de (1966) *Democracy in America*, 2 vols, London, Fontana.

A DEMOCRATIC POLITY?

Jon Roper ★

1 INTRODUCTION: DEMOCRACY AND THE END OF HISTORY

> And if we are now at a point where we cannot imagine a world substantially different from our own, in which there is no apparent or obvious way in which the future will represent a fundamental improvement over our current order, then we must also take into consideration the possibility that History itself might be at an end.
>
> (Fukuyama, 1992, p.51)

> I think I see the destiny of America embodied in the first Puritan who landed on those shores, just as the whole human race was represented by the first man.
>
> (de Tocqueville, 1945, vol.1, p.301)

Democracy rules. Fukuyama's suggestion, that the 'end of history' has been reached, is based upon the apparent triumph of an idea: an ideology. So 'a remarkable consensus concerning the legitimacy of liberal democracy as a system of government' has 'emerged throughout the world over the past few years, as it conquered rival ideologies like hereditary monarchy, fascism, and most recently communism'. Liberal democracy is the 'end point of mankind's ideological evolution' (Fukuyama, 1992, p.xi). And if history is seen as an account of the conflict between ideas, expressed in terms of political and social struggle, then because ideological consensus now has been achieved, history itself has come to a full-stop.

Is this, then, the rendezvous with the destiny that Alexis de Tocqueville saw embodied in the American landfall of the first Puritan settler? To critically challenge the 'end of history' thesis, it is necessary to explore the development of the idea of democracy in America. This chapter, then, considers the nature of America's liberal democratic polity through an examination of its historical development. The 'idea of America' expressed by Thomas Jefferson in the Declaration of Independence (1776) is taken as a starting point. The practical implications of that idea, which incorporated America's basic democratic values, are traced, first in the newly independent states, and in the framing of the American Constitution. It was then that the 'idea of America' was embedded in the 'idea of the United States', creating a powerful ideology of democratic nationalism.

American democracy, however, has been marked by the tension that is created by the procedures of majority rule conflicting with the need to preserve minority rights. Constitutional and institutional safeguards have addressed this problem: federalism, a separation of powers, a Bill of Rights and the existence of a Supreme Court which has annexed to itself the power of judicial review. James Madison, in No.10 of a series of articles known as *The Federalist Papers* — perhaps the most famous exposition of the political thought of those who framed the Constitution — argued persuasively that America could preserve minority rights within a majoritarian political system. But de Tocqueville later argued that the 'tyranny of the majority' might have a social as well as a political dimension, influencing ideas, attitudes and the opportunity for diversity of opinion within the nation's democratic polity.

With the Civil War, democracy in America broke down. The Union fought the Civil War to maintain the geographical and the ideological integrity of the United States. In so doing, it demonstrated that the 'idea of America' as a democratic polity was to be expressed through the preservation of the 'idea of the United States'. The Union victory in the Civil War also confirmed to many that America's democratic experiment was now destined to succeed. It was, indeed, a turning point.

Alexis de Tocqueville's observation that America's purpose could be seen in the desire of its first Puritan settler to build the 'City Upon a Hill' is illustrative of a recurrent theme in American political thought. Manifest destiny, and America's mission to re-create the world in the image of its democratic polity are ideas that have resonated through the nineteenth and twentieth centuries. Surviving the challenges of the economic Depression of the 1930s, America's democratic polity emerged from the Second World War to meet the further test of Cold War confrontation. And it has been the collapse of communism in the former Soviet Union and elsewhere that has resulted, in Fukuyama's view, in the 'end of history'. It is but another version of the argument that the 'idea of America' in the shape of its democratic values can transcend the geographical boundaries of the United States.

But history continues. Nowadays what confronts Americans is a seductive myth of national identity: theirs is a democratic polity that has been fashioned over two centuries in the changing images of the ideas that gained popular support during the struggle for independence from Britain. To understand their enterprise, and the nature and character of democracy in the United States is to appreciate the power of those ideas. It is also to realize that the 'end of history' is merely a pause to draw breath: that ideological debate can provide a creative impetus to fresh political and social development. And it is to admit that a world fashioned in the reflection of America's democratic polity might be but a pale imitation of what has been, after all, a unique experiment and a remarkable achievement.

2   THE HISTORICAL EXPERIENCE OF DEMOCRACY

The animating spirit of American democracy is distilled in the spare and elegant prose of the Declaration of Independence (4 July 1776). 'We hold these truths to be self-evident, that all men are created equal, that they are endowed by their Creator with certain unalienable Rights, that among these are Life, Liberty and the pursuit of Happiness.'

The fundamental values of modern America's democratic polity are here. 'All men' in Thomas Jefferson's partial language of the time, have a God-given equal right to liberty. The struggle to extend that right to everyone, irrespective of their ethnic origin, or their gender, would become a defining theme in the historical and political experience of the United States. But understanding the development of Jefferson's thought in the Declaration is just as crucial to an appreciation of the nature of American democratic ideas.

He went on to suggest that in order to 'secure these rights, Governments are instituted ... deriving their just powers from the consent of the governed'. If governments abused the peoples' rights, then their legitimate ultimate sanction was to change things. Such an assertion allowed Jefferson to conclude, after cataloguing the various objections that Americans had to the conduct of George III's government in the colonies, that 'a Prince whose character is thus marked by every act which may define a Tyrant, is unfit to be the ruler of a free people'. America's rebellion against British rule was elevated through measured political argument into what would be regarded as a justifiable and principled act of revolution.

The Declaration of Independence 'has become the classic democratic manifesto of modern history' (Warfel et al., 1937, p.133). It illustrates 'the dramatic proposition that all men are created equal with natural liberties which, if taken away at all, cannot be justly taken without consent' (Lynd, 1973, p.3). It expresses the values — principally equality and liberty — which continue to define the nature of American democracy. American government should protect and promote in equal measure the liberty of each individual. Furthermore, Jefferson argues, government exists solely to 'secure' rights. It does not rule over people: rather, it establishes the framework within which the individual's 'unalienable rights' can be expressed and preserved. That was a revolutionary thought, a radical idea. It became an American democratic ideal.

The image of a democratic polity may have been glimpsed in the crucible of America's War of Independence. The challenge to create it remained. Jefferson cast the mould in 1776 when he wrote the Declaration of Independence. It was set when 55 delegates, George Washington, James Madison, Alexander Hamilton and Benjamin Franklin among them, fashioned the Constitution of the United States in 1787. Discussion of the nature of modern American democratic thought thus starts inevitably with a consideration of the political origins of the United States. Indeed, 'it is a common characteristic of modern political systems that their legitimizing myths are derived from the rhetoric of their founding revolutions' (Grimes, 1976, p.1). Political ideas in America are informed by a profound nostalgia. Contemporary agreement on democratic values relies still on a widespread conviction that Jefferson's inspiration remains valid and that the Founding Fathers arranged things well.

Eleven years separated the writing of the Declaration and the construction of the Constitution. Political ideas and events during that time shaped modern America's democratic polity. Initially, therefore, the common cause of the thirteen American colonies was to rid themselves of British rule. The co-ordination of that effort was a considerable achievement. John Adams wrote in 1818 that it was 'perhaps a singular example in the history of mankind. Thirteen clocks were made to strike together — a perfection of mechanism, which no artist had ever before effected' (quoted in Warfel *et al.*, 1937, p.204). Nevertheless, the intent was not necessarily to create the United States of America from the wreckage of British imperial influence.

The colonies became states, independent of one another as well as of Britain. Following the Declaration, however, Jefferson's genie of republicanism was out of the bottle. Equality, liberty, government resting on consent; a free people who might rule themselves: all these were imaginative possibilities at

The Constitutional Convention, Philadelphia, 1787. George Washington, the convention's president, is standing at the centre of the podium. (George F. Mobley, National Geographic Society photographer, courtesy United States Capitol Historical Society)

the end of the eighteenth century. Ideas prompted experiments. State constitutions were devised in attempts to structure these novel political aspirations within a coherent framework of government.

It is in the newly independent states that some of the basic features of modern America's democratic polity first appear. Republicanism was an uncontested principle. It meant the conscious rejection of rule by a hereditary monarch on the prevailing European pattern. It implied popular sovereignty: the people were to be the ultimate source of all political authority. So they should elect their representatives to public office, either to the legislature, charged with passing laws, or to the executive, which ensured such laws were carried out. There might also be a judicial function of government, designed to monitor these constitutional processes. It was a government structured through a separation of powers. As John Adams put it in 1775: 'a legislative, an executive and a judicial power comprehend the whole of what is meant and understood by government. It is by balancing each of these powers against the other two, that the efforts in human nature towards tyranny can alone be checked and restrained' (quoted in Vile, 1967, p.133). The state constitutions were written — in itself another principled innovation — in an attempt to reflect such constitutional wisdom.

SUMMARY

The core values of American democracy are to be found in the Declaration of Independence (1776). This document also defined an idea of government which rationalized and justified America's rejection of British rule.

American government was based upon the idea of popular consent, and existed primarily to guarantee the people's 'unalienable rights'. In democratic terms, the Declaration argued the importance of the preservation of an individual's equal right to liberty.

Following the War of Independence, the creation of governments in the newly independent states was inspired by the revolutionary rhetoric of the Declaration. The states became republics, founded upon principles of popular sovereignty and representation, and incorporating the idea of a separation of powers between the executive, legislature and judiciary. Their constitutions were also written down in order to define the structure of government within each state.

3   DEMOCRACY IN THE STATES

The mood was democratic. The issue was power. And the problem of distributing political power within a republican community, of achieving Adams's balance, in turn seemed often intractable. Suspicion of executive power, fuelled by a popular disgust at the prior antics of Britain's unelected chief executive, George III, resulted in a reluctance to delegate too much political responsibility to a person alone. State constitutions emphasized the primacy of legislative power rather than executive authority. It was thought that the popular will could be expressed best through representation in a properly elected assembly.

Yet mistrust of delegating power to representatives for longer than was judged absolutely necessary led to frequent, often annual, legislative elections, with unanticipated results. Taking such rapid snap-shots of changing popular political sentiment meant that control of the state legislature might be passed between shifting majority factions. Majorities ruled. People changed their minds. Laws passed became laws repealed. James Madison, who saw that such practice, however democratic in aspiration, offended against order and political stability, summed up: the lack of *'wisdom* and *steadiness'* in legislation was proving to be 'the grievance complained of in all our republics' (quoted in Wood, 1969, p.405). Could the people — or their representatives — be trusted to use democratic power responsibly?

The political instability that was increasingly apparent in some of the state republican experiments justified a gamble. The Articles of Confederation, agreed between the states in 1781, committed them only to 'a firm league of friendship with each other'. Madison, among others, became convinced that they should be replaced by a plan for a more coherent national government, which might encourage the development of a political order between the states that they had been unable to establish from within. The challenge now became to write a Constitution for the United States.

The idea of the United States of America, however, turned conventional political wisdom on its head. The Founding Fathers were attempting something unique. Democracy as a form of government was thought to work only when small groups of people could come together — the classic American example was the New England town meeting — to decide on issues of common concern. Republican government, where power was delegated to representatives, as the state experiments with it had shown, need not achieve political order and social stability. Now, the proposal was to create a national government, on republican principles, and extending its authority over thirteen different and disparate states. With each state jealous of its local sovereignty, the difficulties faced by those Americans in favour of union in the late eighteenth century are reminiscent of those encountered by Europeans of a similar persuasion some two centuries later.

But union was also inspired by fear. If there was no common cause, what would be the result? Independence itself might be lost. Alexander Hamilton outlined the likely course of events if individual states rejected the need to unite. There would be domestic division and rivalry: that was the lesson of history. 'To look for a continuation of harmony between a number of independent unconnected sovereignties, situated in the same neighbourhood, would be to disregard the uniform course of human events, and to set at defiance the accumulated experience of ages'. Again,

America, if not connected at all, or only by the feeble tie of a simple
league offensive and defensive, would by the operation of such
opposite and jarring alliances be gradually entangled in all the per-
nicious labyrinths of European politics and wars; and by the
destructive contentions of the parts into which she was divided
would be likely to become a prey to the artifices and machinations
of powers equally the enemies of them all.

(*The Federalist Papers*, 1787–8, No.9)

In other words, America would become like Europe itself.

There was not simply a need to create a national government in order to
achieve political stability. There was also the sense that if America did not
unite, it would fall apart: that perhaps the thirteen states would begin to
resemble thirteen different nations, fighting amongst themselves for land,
resources, and advantages of trade. The United States of America needed a
Constitution which would establish its territorial integrity. And it also had
to preserve the republican and democratic values expressed in the Declaration of Independence. Indeed, 'the doctrine of the consent of the governed
as it evolved in the 1780s stipulated, at least implicitly, that a government
would be evaluated largely on the basis of how it improved the well-being
and protected the natural rights of its citizens' (Cronin, 1989, p.12). How
were those who constructed the Constitution to achieve these aims?

Remember Jefferson. Governments gathered 'just powers from the consent
of the governed'. If the democratic principle is implicit in the need for popular consent, the democratic problem is what constitutes 'just powers'. The
state experiments had demonstrated that often the impolitic distribution of
power, with too much given to one institution — the legislature — offended
against an ordered society. An organized majority in a legislature could
enact laws which threatened the interests of others. Republican government
in and of itself had proved to be no guarantor of individual rights. Majorities might oppress minorities. Could a democratic republic be created which
both took account of, and solved that problem? That was the issue which
the Founding Fathers were to tackle.

SUMMARY

The state constitutions proved often to be maladroit in the distribution
of power between the various functions of government. Concentration
of power in the legislature, combined with frequent elections, led to
political instability.

To preserve the experiment in republican government, some became
convinced that a federal constitution was necessary. The move towards
union was also inspired by the fear of increasing political division and
rivalries among the states.

> The state experiments had shown that republican principles did not guarantee the practical preservation of individual rights. How to balance majority rule and minority rights was a critical question that confronted the Founders as they designed a democratic republican constitution for the United States.

4   THE FEDERAL CONSTITUTION

It would, as Madison realized, 'decide forever the fate of republican government' in America (quoted in Wood, 1969, p.467). And it did. The Constitution incorporated two main principles which aimed to prevent majorities, or their representatives elected to legislative and executive office, from abusing political power, through frustrating its use. The doctrine of a separation of powers, which in the state governments had proved too weak a constitutional theory to stand alone, was joined to the concept of federalism. Together, these ideas created opportunities to distribute power between state and national governments, and among political institutions, in innovative ways.

Federalism, the 'accidental lucky division of this Country into distinct States' permitted power to be divided between the states and the central government. Within the legislature of the United States, federalism allowed the powers of the House of Representatives, 'the grand depository of the democratic principle of the Government', to be balanced by those of the Senate, where each state had equal representation (Tansell, 1927, pp.143, 125). The separation of powers between the legislature (Congress), executive (President) and judiciary (Supreme Court) further incorporated a system of checks and balances between institutions to limit the constitutional autonomy of each. No single institution or layer of government could gain too much power for too long.

Federalism and the separation of powers, and the design of the United States Constitution, wove together ideas and experiment to sketch the outlines, visible at a distance of over two centuries, of America's contemporary democratic polity. In the words of the document's preamble, it would: 'establish Justice, insure domestic Tranquility, provide for the common defence, promote the general Welfare, and secure the Blessings of Liberty to ourselves and our Posterity'.

The idea of liberty, so prominent in the Declaration, here is relegated: a lower priority than the need for justice, tranquility, defence and welfare. That is a reflection of the experience of the state constitutions, which focused the Founding Fathers' attention on issues of political power, order and stability.

The genius of the Constitution lies in the way in which it tears up the political rule-book and creates something new. The idea of a republican democracy which owed its strength to the union of the states was, in the context of its times, revolutionary. A federal republic imagined on such a scale was uncharted territory. As Thomas Jefferson wrote, 'the full experiment of a government democratical but representative was and is still reserved for us'. Furthermore: 'the introduction of this new principle of representative democracy has rendered useless almost everything written before on the structure of government, and in a great measure relieves our regret if the political writings of Aristotle or of any other ancient have been lost or are unfaithfully rendered or explained to us' (quoted in Frisch and Stevens, 1973, pp.35–6). The future American prospect was instead to be a new contribution to the art and science of governance.

The Constitution aims to provide a structure of government which will respect each individual's natural rights to life, liberty and the pursuit of happiness. It attempts to prevent governmental authority from infringing or impinging on those rights. In 1776, the colonies had not only declared their opposition to British rule; Jefferson had written a manifesto which effectively argued that to maintain an individual's independence, the role of government must necessarily be restricted. The state experiments had shown, however, that power in a republic was as open to abuse as it was in any political system. There was nothing magical about the principle of popular sovereignty that dispelled the tendency of those who gained public office under its rules from interpreting their powers to their own advantage, and from acting in their own interests, rather than to benefit the community, or to promote the equal advantage of each individual.

If the Declaration of Independence outlines the values of American republican democracy, the Constitution thus seeks to preserve them through embedding them in the foundations of the United States. Indeed, the future of the republic rests upon the survival of the union. Individual state governments may have had republican democratic aspirations, but they had been unable to establish stable political institutions which could guarantee the survival of such principles. The 'idea of America' itself, expressed by Jefferson in 1776, is contained in the idea of the United States, constructed in its Constitution of 1787. The historical experience and development of America's democratic polity has built upon such origins. When the elderly Benjamin Franklin emerged from the Constitutional Convention in Philadelphia, he was asked what the meeting had achieved. 'A republic, if you can keep it'. That challenge continued.

SUMMARY

The United States Constitution aims to prevent the abuse of power through frustrating its use. It does this through combining the idea of a separation of powers with the principle of federalism.

The Constitution was a revolutionary form of government. It was an attempt to preserve the values of the Declaration within the framework of a workable system of republican government. Along with the Declaration it became the foundation of America's modern democratic polity.

5 MAJORITY RULE AND MINORITY RIGHTS

Franklin's remark reflects not so much a prevailing pessimism, as a cautious realism. The American Constitution was a step into the political unknown: those responsible for it were under no illusions. 'All the Founding Fathers — Jefferson as well as Hamilton, Madison along with John Adams — shared a deep-seated fatalism about the ultimate instability of republican government' (Lynd, 1973, p.3). Their lack of confidence in the political system which they had imagined and designed was due to their enlightened view of human nature. They believed that power had a corrosive impact on individual morality: that tyranny of some form was the likely outcome if personal ambition conspired with political opportunity.

What then, had they achieved? In the intricate structure of the federal design, by dividing power between institutions and among levels of government, the Founders had attempted to constrain and confine the powers of republican government. Their success has been reflected in the modern recognition of 'gridlock': the inability of executive and legislature to work together in political harmony. Such antagonism between the institutions of the government of the United States is not a surprising phenomenon. It was the intention of those who planned the Constitution to make government difficult, although not impossible. And indeed, America's democratic polity has been 'informed and conditioned by a fundamental apprehension of government and a fear of the uses to which government can be put' (Foley, 1991, p.81).

Fear of governmental power, however, was part of a larger concern to prevent one section of the community dominating national politics. The Constitution was designed to avoid the problem that had dogged the newly independent states: factionalism. In particular it attempted to deal with the problem of a majority faction, which, through the electoral rules of republican democracy, could gain power legitimately, yet which might be tempted to use it in ways that rode roughshod over the rights of minorities. The most famous exposition of the Founders' thought, Madison's *Federalist* No.10, gives an informative glimpse into contemporary views of republicanism, democracy, political power, majority rule, and the sources of social division.

Factions, according to Madison, cause 'instability, injustice and confusion' and in turn, these have been 'the mortal diseases under which popular governments have everywhere perished'. Removing the causes of faction in society is impossible. Such divisions are 'sown in the nature of man'. Madison argues indeed that 'the most common and durable source of factions has been the various and unequal distribution of property'. Furthermore, 'those who hold and those who are without property have ever formed distinct interests in society'. And it is government's task to arbitrate between these interests.

But any government is ill-equipped for this purpose. Madison asks: ' ... what are the different classes of legislators but advocates and parties to the causes which they determine?' Once government has the final say in the regulation of differing interests in society, then the race is on between competing groups to gain control of the legislature, to use governmental power to their own advantage. Madison concludes: 'The inference to which we are brought is, that the *causes* of faction cannot be removed, and that relief is only to be sought in the means of controlling its *effects*' (*The Federalist Papers*, 1787–8, No.10).

The 'republican principle' of majority rule, prevents minority factions from being voted into positions of power. The object of the Constitution thus becomes to prevent a fixed majority dominating the processes of government. Madison puts his faith in the United States: its size and the system of representation which would determine its government meant that a successful majority would have to be composed of a coalition of interests which, over time, would inevitably form and reform in different combinations. The essence of American republican democracy would lie in competition between groups: the idea of pluralism. Madison introduced American politics to market forces.

At least, that was the theory. In *The Federalist* No.51, the point was re-emphasized. 'Different interests necessarily exist in different classes of citizens. If a majority be united by a common interest, the rights of the minority will be insecure'. So in the federal republic of the United States: 'Whilst all authority ... will be derived from and dependent on the society, the society itself will be broken into so many parts, interests, and classes of citizens, that the rights of individuals, or of the minority, will be in little danger from interested combinations of the majority' (*The Federalist Papers*, 1787–8, No.51). Checking, balancing and dividing power between institutions and layers of government, the federal Constitution in effect held a mirror up to reflect the Founders' view of America: factions would be controlled through forcing them to compete for power within a fragmented political system.

To critics, however, despite Madison's reassurances, and the powerful arguments of *The Federalist Papers*, the new Constitution still implied a concentration of political power which threatened individual liberty. The response to such fears lay once again within the document itself. Pragmatic politicians rather than Delphic oracles, the Founders had provided for their work to be amended when necessary through a mechanism that required the initial support of either two-thirds of the Congress or two-thirds of the states. This process was used to add to the Constitution its most significant codicil: the Bill of Rights.

The importance attached to the Bill of Rights as an integral part of America's democratic experiment illustrates the continuing suspicion that political power threatens individual liberty. These first ten amendments to the Constitution, agreed in 1791, seek to extend the concept of natural rights, expressed in the Declaration, to an equally important definition of the stockade of each individual's civil rights in relation to the powers of government. Freedom of religion, speech, the press, and assembly are guaranteed. So too is the right to silence to avoid self-incrimination (the fifth amendment, made most famous during the congressional anti-communist investigations of the McCarthyite 1950s). Various other rights are established which aim to ensure the equal application of due processes of law. The attempt is made to define the frontiers which determine the relationship between individual liberty and governmental authority in the United States.

The meaning of the Bill of Rights, and indeed of the Constitution and of the other amendments to it, is, however, open to reinterpretation. And this is where the power of judicial review, exercised by the Supreme Court, meshes directly with the majoritarian impulse of American democracy. For it is the Court which can decide whether laws passed and decisions made violate the spirit and intent of the Constitution. The popular acceptance of the role of the Supreme Court within America's democratic polity, where legislative action is decided by majority rule but remains subject to the scrutiny of unelected judges is an apparent paradox in the political life of the nation. Yet it is understandable in terms of the fundamental beliefs which shape American attitudes towards the role of government in society.

'It is emphatically the province and duty of the judicial department to say what the law is ... the courts are to regard the Constitution [as] superior to any ordinary act of the legislature, the Constitution and not [the] ordinary act must govern' (quoted in Maidment and McGrew, 1986, pp.45–6). Chief Justice John Marshall, in the case of *Marbury v. Madison* (1803), established this most important principle of American constitutional law with neither fuss nor fanfare. He merely asserted the Court's right to judge the constitutionality of the nation's laws, and thus placed it subsequently often on the side of individuals or minorities otherwise dispossessed of political influence under the majoritarian rules of America's democratic game. The Supreme Court's role in defining the limits of governmental authority and of individual liberty, and also the meaning of political equality, through its interpretation of the Constitution and the Bill of Rights, has been of critical importance in establishing the prevailing ethos of America's democratic society.

'It is no accident that preoccupation with the rights and wrongs of majority rule has run like a red thread through American political thought since 1789' (Dahl, 1956, p.4). When, in the 1830s, Alexis de Tocqueville travelled from France to observe American democracy in action, he publicized the phrase, 'the tyranny of the majority' as a potential problem within the nation's political system. And in so doing, he focused renewed attention on the way in which the American democratic polity sought to reconcile the procedure of majority rule and the principle of preserving minority rights. But unlike Madison, de Tocqueville argued that the 'tyranny of the majority' might be a democratic phenomenon which was beyond constitutional and institutional control.

Once again it was a question of power. Alexis de Tocqueville pointed out that the majority had not only political legitimacy but also the moral authority to shape the attitudes and beliefs of a democratic society. 'The very essence of democratic government consists in the absolute sovereignty of the majority; for there is nothing in democratic states that is capable of resisting it'. Individuals deferred to the majority, believing that, as equal citizens, the collective wisdom of the greater number was more likely to be correct than their own idiosyncratic beliefs. Moreover, it was accepted that 'the interests of the many are to be preferred to those of the few'.

Alexis de Tocqueville confessed: 'I know of no country in which there is so little independence of mind and real freedom of discussion as in America'. It was a place where 'the majority raises formidable barriers around the liberty of opinion' (de Tocqueville, 1945, vol.1, ch.15). Such comments point to a paradox in America's democratic polity. While groups could compete for power in the competitive market-places of national or state politics, they did so within an agreed framework of fundamental ideological belief. Dissent from the basic 'idea of America' represented a challenge to the political and moral authority of the majority.

In a way, de Tocqueville was mistaken to blame the majority for such tyranny over opinion. The states were united in cherishing their democratic values. As Louis Hartz observed, 'at the bottom of the American experience of freedom, not in antagonism to it but as a constituent element of it, there has always lain the inarticulate premise of conformity' (Hartz, 1955, p.67). That sense of moral and political agreement on the fundamental principles of American democracy was the ideological glue which joined the 'idea of America' to the 'the idea of the United States' as a republican democracy. Ideological conformity has contributed to the stability and the continuity of America's democratic society. And indeed, when that political consensus broke down, the result was Civil War.

SUMMARY

The Constitution attempts to constrain and confine the use of governmental power in a republican democracy. In that sense, 'gridlock' is a possibility that is built into America's democratic system. The Founders were concerned that the rights of minorities might be threatened by majority factions. Madison, in *The Federalist* No.10, argues that the Constitution will control such factions by creating a competitive, pluralist political system in which no one group or interest will be able to dominate the government.

The Bill of Rights further defines the individual's civil rights in relation to the sphere of government authority. The Supreme Court, through the power of judicial review, has been able to define and redefine the meaning of constitutional power and of individual rights in the context of the changing character of America's democratic polity.

Alexis de Tocqueville suggested that the 'tyranny of the majority' had a moral as well as a political dimension. Individuals would find it difficult to dispute the collective wisdom and consensus of majority opinion. As such, there was a tendency towards conformity of beliefs in American society, which, while it encouraged stability, remained a threat to liberty of opinion.

6 DEMOCRACY, SLAVERY AND THE CIVIL WAR

Despite the concern with the preservation of both natural and civil rights, the toleration of slavery within the newly formed nation left another fundamental paradox at the core of the democratic republican experiment. This tension, which the Founding Fathers thought had been accommodated through the compromises of the Constitution, eventually proved to be an irreconcilable difference between the states. The South seceded from the Union. To resolve the argument over slavery, which by then transcended politics and raised basic issues of philosophy and morality, Americans finally ignored democratic procedures, and appealed to a court of last resort: they fought a Civil War.

It was both catalyst and catharsis. It punctuates the historical experience of democracy in America. Before the Civil War (1861–5) the creation of a democratic republic was undertaken in the spirit of an experiment: afterwards, its preservation could be presented as the fulfilment of the nation's providential destiny. But while slavery existed, it made America's experience of democracy provisional. For the question that haunted the nation's politics remained the same: how could a democratic community tolerate this most illiberal of institutions in its southern states? In an attempt to resolve that dilemma, the meaning of American democracy itself became open to redefinition and reinterpretation.

What was the proper relationship that should exist between state and national sovereignties within a federal system? 'The 1787 Constitution mapped out a broad division of jurisdictions, allotting primary powers to the federal government in areas like foreign policy. But the frontier between national and state power was unavoidably indistinct' (Cunliffe, 1977, p.534). The state rights argument, adopted by the South to justify and preserve its 'peculiar institution' of slavery, asserted that individual states retained a sphere of sovereign power that could not be infringed by the federal government. But if democracy was about values — if it was to claim superiority over competing systems of government on moral grounds — then slavery remained a scar on the face of American idealism.

Southern states, seeing democracy as a process of government, argued that their rights derived from a strict construction of the Constitutional settlement of 1787. Those who wished to force the issue of the abolition of slavery, however, took a moral high road which led them forward from the principled position taken in the Declaration of Independence. Democracy was not simply a mechanistic relationship between institutions and spheres of governmental authority; it incorporated a desire to create an equitable and free society. Slaves were by status unequal, and by definition unfree. It was a matter of rights versus right (Roper, 1989, pp.86–93).

So 'the question of whether the national or state governments possessed ultimate authority to determine the status and enforce the rights of American inhabitants produced a national political and constitutional debate that centered on slavery and culminated in the South's secession in 1861'

(Kaczorowski, 1987, p.50). But that fact of secession had political implications that went beyond the proximate issue of slavery. The 'idea of America' articulated in the Declaration had found practical expression within the constitutional arrangements of the United States. If the nation was now to disintegrate, could such democratic values as equality and liberty be preserved? It was the fear of political divisions leading to permanent partition, and of the rivalry and instability that might result from it, which had promoted the idea of union in the first place. There is a sense in which the North fought the Civil War to keep the United States united and the 'idea of America' alive. Afterwards, indeed, 'the war between the states became commemorated as both a victory for the American nation and for American democracy' (Foley, 1991, p.74).

Abraham Lincoln played the decisive rhetorical role in rededicating the nation to its democratic purpose. In the Gettysburg Address in 1863, he drew upon the spirit and the promise of 1776. 'Four score and seven years ago our fathers brought forth, on this continent, a new nation, conceived in Liberty and dedicated to the proposition that all men are created equal'. Now the nation had declined into Civil War: it was a test of 'whether that nation or any nation so conceived and so dedicated, can long endure'. Lincoln concluded with a vow and a prophecy, reaffirming the 'idea of America' in perhaps its most often-quoted form. In dedicating the battlefield at Gettysburg as a military cemetery, he said: 'we here highly resolve that these dead shall not have died in vain — that this nation, under God, shall have a new birth of freedom — and that government of the people, by the people, for the people, shall not perish from the earth'.

The speech is a compelling articulation of the democratic ideal and the idea of American nationalism at a time when internal divisions — and war — threatened the continued existence of the United States and the future of its republic. Had the sovereignty of the United States remained divided between North and South as a result of the Civil War, then the Gettysburg Address would have become the throwaway lines of a failed President. Lincoln's words endure, and find such contemporary resonance, because they were ultimately endorsed by the outcome of the war itself.

D.W. Griffith was right to call his epic silent movie of the Civil War and its aftermath *The Birth of a Nation*. For the Union victory resolved finally the issue of competing state and federal authority within the United States, emphatically in the latter's favour. And yet, although it cured such constitutional problems, and indeed led to the abolition of slavery, the Civil War could not obliterate the heritage of racism that would continue to give the lie to the democratic rhetoric of equality in American society, particularly in its southern states.

'Ambiguity, ambivalence, tension, paradox, irony, tragedy, contradiction, and schizophrenia have always governed the status of the black man in the American political system and process' (Dubois Cook, 1976, p.276). The nature of that status was not resolved by the Civil War, nor, some would argue, was it profoundly affected by the heroic impact of the Civil Rights movement on American society a century later. The black community's struggle for acceptance at all levels, political and economic, social and cultural, within America's democratic polity, continues to trouble the course of twentieth-century American politics. It remains an issue which a nation proclaiming itself democratic in Lincoln's terms cannot for long ignore.

SUMMARY

The existence of slavery in the southern states was a clear contradiction of America's democratic idealism. The Constitution failed to bring about a lasting compromise: the republic collapsed into Civil War.

The 'idea of America' which the Constitution had sought to safeguard was threatened by the South's secession. The North fought the Civil War in part to preserve the United States as a democratic republic.

Lincoln's Gettysburg Address represents a rededication of the United States to the purposes of its democratic polity. Yet despite the Union victory in the Civil War, the heritage of racism within the United States still confronts the ideal of a democratic community, in which each individual is proclaimed to have an equal right to liberty.

7   DEMOCRACY AS EXPERIMENT: DEMOCRACY AS DESTINY

Modern America's democratic polity has been shaped thus by the forces of realism and idealism, of experiment and destiny. That is why the creation of the United States as a democratic republic and the watershed of the Civil War are events which retain such a significance in any understanding of the contemporary course of American democratic thought. Before the Civil War, the themes of experiment and destiny ran through the American historical experience in tandem. Since 1865, however, the idea of America's democratic destiny has predominated, particularly as the nation has increasingly projected its political and cultural values towards the wider world.

As the United States survived the Civil War, therefore, it did so with a growing national sense that its great experiment with democracy was destined to succeed. So 'experiment gave ground to destiny as the promise of national life' (Schlesinger, 1977, p.518). Such belief in a special, providential purpose imparted a particular significance to the idea of democracy in America. In so far as it incorporated the values expressed in the Declaration, and embedded in the Constitution, American democracy became not only the animating spirit of the nation itself, but also a model to be exported elsewhere. The history of America hence became the story of triumphant democracy: a mythical account, to be sure, but nevertheless one which has crucially defined the nation's political culture and self-image.

In this version of events, the stirrings of destiny are seen in the pre-revolutionary era: in seventeenth-century Puritan New England. Escaping the religious and feudal restrictions of Europe, the Puritans came to America with a plan. In John Winthrop's powerful imagery, they would create in the wilderness the 'City Upon a Hill', an 'idea of America' which has resonated through the history of the United States (Winthrop quoted in Boorstin, 1966, pp.8–25). From settlement to colony, from state to union, from continent to globe, the Puritans' mission, to redeem the world they had left behind, was transformed into America's secular purpose: to re-create that world in the image of its democratic republic.

The documents which symbolize America's democratic polity
— the Declaration of Independence and the Constitution —
are preserved on public display in the National Archives,
Washington, DC

That sense of special destiny is a constant refrain. John Adams wrote in 1768: 'I always consider the settlement of America with reverence, as the opening of a grand scene and design in Providence for the illumination of the ignorant and the emancipation of the slavish parts of mankind all over the earth' (quoted in Sumner, 1874, p.54). More recently, there was Ronald Reagan: 'I have always believed that this land was placed here between the two great oceans by some divine plan. ... We can meet our destiny and that destiny can build a land here that will be for all mankind a shining city on a hill' (quoted in Smith, 1986, p.26). The echoes of Puritan idealism in American democratic rhetoric are never far away.

American democracy in this context is thus not a passive political process; a form of government, an abstraction of political institutions. It was imbued with the spirit of an energetic and dynamic enterprise which would carry its ideals rapidly beyond the frontiers of the original thirteen states. Prior to the Civil War, in 1845, John O'Sullivan, in the *Democratic Review*, wrote of ' ... the fulfilment of our manifest destiny to overspread the continent allotted by Providence for the free development of our yearly multiplying millions'. In a later issue that year, the *Review* predicted that 'the whole of this vast continent is destined one day to subscribe to the Constitution of the United States'. For European powers in the nineteenth century, territorial expansion overseas was admitted to be imperialism. For the United States in the same period, expansion across the contiguous continent was the fulfilment of a democratic design.

Once again the genius of the Founders was apparent. A federal republic allowed new states to be organized and to enter the union as equal partners with the others, and not as territorial additions to existing states. Expansionism could march together with democracy. Jefferson confessed in 1809, 'I am persuaded that no constitution was ever before as well calculated as ours for extensive empire and self-government' (quoted in Williams, 1980, p.61). And as President James Polk argued in his inaugural address in 1845, 'it is confidently believed that our system may be safely extended to the utmost bounds of our territorial limits, and that as it shall be extended the bonds of our Union, so far from being weakened, will become stronger'. An 'empire of liberty' could be created with each new addition both conforming to federal republican principles, and, as the United States expanded, endorsing the providential progress of the democratic idea.

'In no other country in the world was expansion conceived to be as natural and as inevitable a part of the fulfilment of a nation's destiny as it was in America' (Kern, 1983, p.239). In the nineteenth century the democratic republic of the United States was not defined by its fixed border, but by its changing frontier. As the geographical limits of the continental United States were reached — in 1890, the national census proclaimed the frontier closed — it was the idea of democracy which, for Americans, transcended territorial restrictions, and which became an ideal with world-wide implications.

In the 'American Century', therefore, democratic rhetoric has addressed not only a domestic, but also an international audience. Following the First World War, President Woodrow Wilson had no doubts: 'the stage is set, the destiny disclosed. It has come about by no plan of our conceiving, but by the hand of God who led us into this way. We cannot turn back. We can only go forward, with lifted eyes and freshened spirit, to follow the vision. It was of this we dreamed at our birth. America shall in truth show the way. The light streams upon the path ahead, and nowhere else'. America would teach the world about the virtues of a democratic polity. So 'Wilson has a central importance as one who practically and symbolically integrated all the elements of empire as a way of life' (Williams, 1980, p.134). And the world might become America's democratic dominion, even though the isolationist sentiment of the inter-war period delayed the nation's progress towards the President's goal.

SUMMARY

The idea that its providential destiny is to create a democratic polity has been a consistent theme in American political thought. The belief in the nation's special and separate purpose to act as a model for imitation elsewhere may be traced back to Puritan New England, and it remains part of contemporary political rhetoric.

The aftermath of the Civil War marked the birth of the United States as a nation in which democracy was no longer seen as an insular experiment. The idea of America's 'manifest destiny' had justified territorial expansion across the continent in the nineteenth century. Following the First World War, President Wilson in particular was in no doubt that America should project its democratic values to a wider, international audience.

8 DEMOCRACY IN DEPRESSION AND COLD WAR

The Wall Street Crash had a seismic impact upon the American political system. It brought Franklin Delano Roosevelt to the White House in 1933, where he was to remain until his death in 1945. Not the least of his legacies would be to provoke a constitutional reaction to his unique achievement in winning four consecutive presidential elections. Future tenants of the White House would be limited to two terms in office (to Ronald Reagan's chagrin: as he left office, aged 77, he announced he would campaign for the amendment's repeal). What was more significant, however, was the use to which Roosevelt put presidential power.

The New Deal was government activity on an unprecedented scale. Roosevelt's flurry of domestic legislation, whatever its ultimate success in dealing with the Depression — and much was initially deemed unconstitutional — nevertheless proved symbolic in shaping American political attitudes for a generation. For many, government power was now to be welcomed rather than mistrusted. And of the achievements of the New Deal, as Hugh Brogan points out, 'unquestionably the most important was the preservation of American democracy, the American Constitution and American capitalism'. To preserve meant to change. The significance of the New Deal was in its re-writing of the accepted rules of American political activity. So Roosevelt 'enabled the American government to assume the responsibility of safeguarding the welfare of the American people in a sense far more radical than that envisaged by the Founding Fathers, but not in a fashion inconsistent with what they most valued — republican government' (Brogan, 1986, p.566).

Roosevelt thus brought Madison's system into the twentieth century. He responded to the demand for government activity in the face of economic collapse, and capitalizing on such popular support, forged a powerful co-operative link between executive and legislature in which the White House seized and retained the political initiative. American government worked. Legislation was passed. 'Gridlock' was avoided in a manner not seen again until Lyndon Johnson implemented his 'Great Society' programmes of the 1960s. Yet in so altering popular perceptions of the role of government in American society, Roosevelt also accelerated the trends within national politics which led to the increase in executive power and the growth of the 'imperial presidency' (Schlesinger, 1973).

Under Roosevelt, executive autonomy was used in a generally constructive manner. However, as the presidency came to dominate the American political process, the intricate system of constitutional checks and balances designed to prevent abuses of power appeared to break down. Two events — the foreign policy debacle of Vietnam and the domestic scandal of Watergate — in separate but related ways, revealed what was happening to America's democratic polity. As Richard Nixon became the first President to be forced to resign the office, America could reflect on Jefferson's prediction to Madison, made in 1789: 'the tyranny of the legislature is really the danger most to be feared, and will continue to be so for many years to come. The tyranny of the executive power will come in its turn, but at a more distant period' (quoted in de Tocqueville, 1945, vol.1, p.280).

Richard Nixon leaves Washington for the last time as President (1974). The Watergate scandal demonstrated the abuses of power that might result from the development of the 'imperial presidency'

Jefferson's prophecy became self-fulfilling during the era of the Cold War. In this highly-charged political atmosphere, America's commitment to popular sovereignty, individual rights and opportunities for political participation could be contrasted favourably with the absence of such democratic principles in the Soviet Union. At the same time, however, the nature of American democracy might still be a matter of debate. Pluralist and élitist interpretations of the political system offered competing insights into the character of contemporary political life.

Pluralist theories of the distribution of political power argued that Madison's ideal of a free-wheeling, dynamic, competitive system of group politics — modified slightly to take account of industrial and economic development, social change and growth — had become the reality of twentieth-century American democratic activity. As it emerged during the 1950s, however, this idea of democracy increasingly 'took on the role of an "ideology", designed to explain and to justify the system of government found in the United States. Pluralism became not only an account of what is, but an outline of what ought to be' (Nicholls, 1974, p.25). Robert Dahl, for example, in *A Preface to Democratic Theory* (1956) argued that 'so long as the social prerequisites of democracy are substantially intact in this country', the American political system 'appears to be ... relatively efficient ... for reinforcing agreement, encouraging moderation, and maintaining social peace in a restless and immoderate people operating a gigantic, powerful, diversified, and incredibly complex society' (Dahl, 1956, p.151).

Despite such reassurances, others argued that the true nature of American politics was somewhat different. In *The Power Elite* (1956), the sociologist C. Wright Mills suggested that those who controlled the levers of political, economic and military power in America, through their influence over the channels of mass-communication, effectively set the national political agenda, moulding it to their own aims and objectives (Mills, 1956). Instead of an open, pluralist society, where power flowed from the people to their government, the 'power élite' had hijacked the republic. It had taken advantage of a structural weakness of a democratic polity. The potential erosion of communal life in a notional society of equals — the 'lonely crowd' (Riesman, 1950) — had been a problem raised too in the nineteenth century. It was also Mills' concern. 'Following the analysis of de Tocqueville, he pointed to the danger of a mass society where effective communal bonds have been broken down, or have never really existed, and where a collection of dissociated individuals is dominated by a small élite' (Nicholls, 1974, p.26).

The Madisonian ideal of a democratic polity in which political authority was fragmented, controlled and restrained was compromised too as a result of the political pressures exerted by Cold War confrontation. If pluralist politics operated at local and even state level, élitist theorists could still argue that effective power was concentrated among those who now defined and defended the national interest. For the perceived ideological challenge which communism offered to the 'idea of America' had to be met. Political, economic and military power had thus to be co-ordinated to preserve the ideal of democracy not just nationally but internationally as well. Wilson's perception of American destiny was now enshrined in Truman's doctrine.

And yet, on occasion, even members of an élite could reflect on the demo-cratic contradictions implied by their policies. In Eisenhower's farewell address to the nation, the retiring President worried about the 'conjunction of an immense military establishment and a large arms industry' which had grown up in the country. Its influence, he suggested, was 'economic, politi-cal, even spiritual' and was felt 'in every city, every State house, every office of the Federal government'. And this had consequences for America's demo-cratic polity. Eisenhower warned that 'we must guard against the acquisition of unwarranted influence, whether sought or unsought, by the military industrial complex. The potential for the disastrous use of power exists and will persist' (Eisenhower, 1961, pp.1035–40). It was an argument that sub-sequent events such as Vietnam and Watergate were to illustrate.

So when Nixon resigned, what had gone wrong? Despite Eisenhower's mis-givings, the military-industrial complex was presented to the nation by his contemporaries and his successors as the guardian of the 'idea of America' in a hostile world. Told that there was an imperative to defend the United States from both external threat and internal corruption, symbolized in the Cold War commitment to 'containment' overseas and the conduct of anti-communist investigations at home, Americans were persuaded to condone an extension of governmental authority, with its accompanying commitment of economic resources to the build-up of military power. The traditional fear of such a concentration of power was countered by the larger — if irrational — fear that the 'un-American' ideology of communism might subvert American democracy. And as the 'imperial presidency', the political architect of the military-industrial complex, was shattered by defeat in Vietnam and the scandals of Watergate, critics could suggest that in order to save Ameri-ca's democratic polity it had almost been necessary to destroy it.

SUMMARY

The New Deal saved America from the economic collapse which threa-tened in turn the survival of its democratic polity. As a result, however, there was an unprecedented concentration of political power in the hands of the executive.

During the Cold War, pluralist theorists argued that the reality of American democracy could be seen in political competition between groups. In many ways it was a prescriptive as well as a descriptive analysis. Critics suggested that America's democratic polity had become dominated by a 'military-industrial complex' which sustained an élite group in power.

The Cold War encouraged an atmosphere in which government activity was further extended in order to defend American democracy from a perceived ideological threat. This period also marked the devel-opment of the 'imperial presidency', which unravelled in the aftermath of the Vietnam War and the revelations of Watergate.

9   CONCLUSION: AMERICA'S DEMOCRATIC POLITY

One's-self I sing, a simple separate person,
Yet utter the word Democratic, the word En-Masse.

(Walt Whitman)

Whitman's lines dramatize the tension in America's democratic polity that can be seen in the conflict which arises between the desire to preserve the rights of a person and the determination to express the power of the people. Senator Eugene McCarthy has suggested that it is 'the most difficult problem of democracy: that of reconciling freedom and authority, of striking a balance between personal liberty and the demands of the common good'. Yet he also admits that 'American political thought from the beginning of our national existence has been strongly influenced by a negative and pessimistic concept of the nature and function of government' (McCarthy, 1960, p.23).

In America's democratic polity, therefore, the preservation of individual autonomy often has been preferred to the endorsement of government action. Franklin Roosevelt's 'New Deal', Lyndon Johnson's 'Great Society' and even the idea which Bill Clinton referred to in his successful election campaign as the 'New Covenant', may represent attempts to allow individual aspirations to be fulfilled through a sense of community, rather than in opposition to it. But the obstacles that reform-minded Presidents repeatedly have to confront are the institutional structures which deliberately divide and separate powers. In the twentieth century thus far only Roosevelt and Johnson have achieved the creative synthesis between the executive and Congress which is necessary to pass a coherent programme of domestic legislation. It is no surprise that the 'imperial presidency' was largely defined in the sphere of foreign policy, away from Congressional scrutiny, and where, in the Cold War era, the executive assumed political autonomy.

Democracy in America thus attempts to preserve a sphere of individual liberty in the face of possible intrusions of government activity. Whatever the achievements of the 'New Deal' and the 'Great Society' the reaction against them is never far away. The Watergate scandal dramatized the dangers of an unprincipled use of power. Its aftershocks contributed to the political climate of the 1980s, when Ronald Reagan and George Bush were Presidents who successfully campaigned 'against government'. In so doing they articulated a consistent theme that has historically shaped America's democratic polity and one which indeed may claim to represent in various guises the nation's dominant and enduring public philosophy.

In the 1960s, President Kennedy charged a commission with considering contemporary 'Goals for Americans'. Its conclusions reiterated the idea that has characterized the nature of American democracy: 'the status of the individual must remain our primary concern. All our institutions — political, social, and economic — must further enhance the dignity of the citizen, promote the maximum development of his capabilities, stimulate their responsible exercise, and widen the range and effectiveness of opportunities for individual choice' (American Assembly, 1960, p.3). American democracy has been seen consistently as the apotheosis of such individualism; an individualism expressed politically in terms of the equal rights accorded to the nation's citizens.

In an important sense the 'idea of America' has also remained constant. The essential values of a democratic polity were impressed upon America's conscience in 1776, and became the defining force of American nationalism in 1787. The survival of a democratic republic depends upon the existence of the United States. That idea, dramatized in the circumstances of the founding of the federal republic, and given further impetus by the Civil War, has been a consistent theme in American political thought. As the other great federation of modern times, the Soviet Union, has fallen apart, it is worth emphasizing how the progress of the democratic idea became a self-referential national myth which sustains the idea of the United States itself. Democracy as destiny is God's design for the United States. Indeed, 'even in a secular age, a sense of manifest destiny is not deduced from sociological laws but treated as part of a providential plan' (Wright, 1974, p.283).

The idea of democracy thus defines the nation's purpose: the 'first new nation' as the 'last best hope for mankind'. The strength of the democratic ideal in the United States lies in its capacity to create a unity of ideological attitude out of the diversity of political interests which continue to jostle in the market-place of American society. The result is that Americans ' … are a pluralistic, pragmatic people openly living in a dream, bound together by an ideological consensus unmatched by any other modern society' (Bercovitch, 1981, p.6). Democracy has become the dominant ideology which defines America to itself, and profoundly affects the nation's perspectives on the wider world.

'Our fate' as Richard Hofstadter observed of America, 'is not to have an ideology but to be one' (quoted in Cunliffe, 1974, p.19). At the beginning of the Cold War, the wagons of America's democratic consensus were circled. To combat the monolithic ideology of international communism, the United States offered the world an example of an undifferentiated ideology of democracy, based upon the values articulated by Jefferson in 1776. The providential progress of the democratic idea, as it defined the nation's historical experience, was the antithesis of Marxist determinism, which saw society's progress towards a different ideological destiny. The idea of America as a democratic polity sustained the nation in the face of the perceived threat from international communism.

In this atmosphere, the historiography of American democracy emphasized the continuity of the nation's historical and constitutional experience in contrast to the continuous revolutionary disruptions which had affected the rest of the world. The case for American exceptionalism, and a critical interpretation of its consequences, was made in particular by Louis Hartz in his influential work, *The Liberal Tradition in America* (1955). He argued that the American experience made internal philosophical and ideological debate redundant. The absence of a feudal past contributed to the creation of the 'liberal tradition' which distinguished America's political development from that of Europe, and made it unique among nations. And at a time when America was assuming its role as the international standard-bearer of democratic values, Hartz appreciated the fact that, held in a philosophical time-warp, the United States was ill-equipped to enter into rational discussion with other nations on issues of ideological concern.

Unchallenged by serious domestic ideological divisions — in the United States it was sufficient to call an ideology 'un-American' to remove it from serious political discussion — the nation had achieved a liberal democratic consensus. The cost of such agreement was intolerance. Hartz suggested that 'when a liberal community faces military and ideological pressure from without it transforms eccentricity into sin, and the irritating figure of the bourgeois gossip flowers into the frightening figure of ... a Senator McCarthy' (Hartz, 1955, p.12). It was an appropriate metaphor for American democracy during the early years of the Cold War.

Senator Joseph McCarthy gained political power and notoriety in the 1950s through allegations and investigations of communist activity in the US. His methods often abused the civil liberties preserved in the Bill of Rights

'Can a people "born equal" ever understand peoples elsewhere that have to become so? Can it ever understand itself?' In 1955 Hartz concluded his work with two questions that are as relevant to the United States at the end of the Cold War as they were at its beginning. For the history of America's conduct during that period of sublime international tension suggests that the nation has problems in appreciating not only the force of revolutionary change in the world — from China to Cuba, from Vietnam to Iran and also perhaps in the 'evil empire' of the former Soviet Union itself — but also in realizing that the cultural myths defining its own sense of national democratic purpose have hampered genuine domestic philosophical and ideological debate. And in a world moving 'beyond containment' it may be even more necessary for America to understand itself in order to begin to understand others.

In a later work, Hartz pointed out that 'the simplification of American political alignments, which led to the burgeoning triumph of democracy, was a simplification also of cultural experience' (Hartz, 1964, p.45). The version of American history which sees a nation moving ever forward towards a rendezvous with its democratic destiny, while it creates a powerful sense of national identity, is a partial and partisan construction. And while America looks 'beyond containment', new domestic challenges to this dominant 'idea of America' may emerge as the threat from international communism apparently recedes. The identification of Jefferson's Declaration and Madison's Constitution as the foundations of a unifying ideology of democratic nationalism tolerating no competitors may be questioned in a country which can admit the imaginative possibilities implied by a heightened sense of ethnicity. The pursuit of multi-culturalism can engender competing 'ideas of America' which confront the ruling dogmas of America's democratic inheritance in both a dramatic and a compelling way.

For the moment, however, that 'simplification of cultural experience' continues to influence American political ideas. It has led many, like Woodrow Wilson, to think that America can teach others the nature of a democratic polity. It has also rendered the nation reluctant to learn from the world in return. Instead the belief is that America's democratic values must retain a transcendent, and universal appeal. Benjamin Franklin's challenge continues. The democratic republic survives through gaining new recruits and fresh support for its ideals. It is the imperialism of an idea.

Clinton Rossiter, contributing to Kennedy's commission, wrote: 'What Jefferson said of us in 1802 is every bit as true in 1960. We are "acting for all mankind" as well as for ourselves and our posterity. The failure of American democracy would bring democracy everywhere down into ruins' (Rossiter, 1960, p.78). It is that assumption which illustrates the importance of the democratic ideal in America's political culture and the extent to which it shapes contemporary attitudes. Other Americans, however, remain self-critical or sceptical about the extent to which this self-referential idea of democracy is realized within the national political process. Although ideals of equality and liberty were articulated in the Declaration, by permitting the persistence of slavery within the Union, the Constitution immediately compromised those values. To the extent that contemporary America continues to struggle to define its citizens' civil rights within the context of its multicultural society, it still fails in its democratic purpose.

Furthermore, the system of government which frustrates the use of power in the belief that it will thereby avoid political corruption has, in recent years, tempted some Presidents and their advisers to pursue their individual conceptions of the national interest in covert ways. The result has been an American democratic polity that has had to come to terms with the constitutional crimes and misdemeanours of Watergate and Irangate. As Jefferson wrote in a more pessimistic moment still, 'I tremble for my country, when I reflect that God is just' (Jefferson quoted in Peden, 1954, p.163).

And yet American democratic thought has been characterized instead by its continuing and resilient optimism: that ultimately the nation can and will live up to the political wisdoms which Jefferson so eloquently expressed in the Declaration of Independence. The 'idea of America' which is embodied in the idea and the institutions of the United States itself, has survived the War of Independence, Civil War, World War and Cold War.

In 1841, Ralph Waldo Emerson, in an essay called simply 'Politics', quoted Fisher Ames, another scholar from Massachusetts, contrasting the system of government which America had rejected in 1776 with that which the United States had adopted in 1787. 'A monarchy is a merchantman, which sails well, but will sometimes strike on a rock, and go to the bottom; whilst a republic is a raft, which would never sink, but then your feet are always in the water' (Emerson, 1907, p.345). America's democratic polity, after more than two hundred years of political change and development, is resolutely still afloat.

SUMMARY

America's democratic polity tries to reconcile the potentially conflicting demands of governmental authority and individual rights. It aims to construct a stockade of individual liberty into which government activity should not advance. A dominant theme in American democratic thought has been the fear of the uses to which governmental power may be put.

The idea of a democratic polity is the defining force of American nationalism, at the cost of simplifying the nation's cultural experience. Domestic challenges to the historical consensus may yet be found among those whose ideas are shaped by a different political consciousness, as members of minority groups within America's multi-cultural and multi-ethnic society.

The system of government which attempts deliberately to frustrate the use of power has not always prevented its abuse. Yet despite its faults, America's modern democratic polity retains much of the optimism which first inspired the idealism of the Declaration of Independence in 1776.

REFERENCES

American Assembly (1960) *Goals for Americans: the Report of the President's Commission on National Goals*, Englewood Cliffs, Prentice-Hall.

Bercovitch, S. (1981) 'The rites of assent: rhetoric ritual, and the ideology of American consensus' in Girgus, S. (ed.) *The American Self*, Albuquerque, University of New Mexico Press.

Boorstin, D. (ed.) (1966) *An American Primer*, Chicago, University of Chicago Press.

Brogan, H. (1986) *The Pelican History of the United States of America*, Harmondsworth, Penguin Books.

Cronin, T. (1989) *Direct Democracy*, Cambridge, Mass., Harvard University Press.

Cunliffe, M. (1974) 'New world, old world: the historical antithesis' in Rose, R. (ed.).

Cunliffe, M. (1977) 'American thought' in Welland, D. (ed.) *The United States — a Companion to American Studies*, London, Methuen.

Dahl, R. (1956) *A Preface to Democratic Theory*, Chicago, University of Chicago Press.

Dubois Cook, S. (1976) 'Democracy and tyranny in America: the radical paradox of the bicentennial and blacks in the American political system' in Havard, W. and Bernd, J. (eds).

Eisenhower, D. (1961) 'Farewell Address, January 17, 1961' in *Public Papers of the Presidents of the United States: Dwight D. Eisenhower 1960–1961*, Washington, DC, US Government Printing Office.

Emerson, R. (1907) 'Politics' in *Essays and Other Writings*, London, Cassell & Co., Ltd.

Foley, M. (1991) *American Political Ideas*, Manchester, Manchester University Press.

Frisch, M. and Stevens, R. (eds) (1973) *The Political Thought of American Statesmen*, Ithaca, F.E. Peacock Publishers Inc.

Fukuyama, F. (1992) *The End of History and the Last Man*, New York, Free Press.

Grimes, A. (1976) 'Conservative revolution and liberal rhetoric: the Declaration of Independence' in Havard, W. and Bernd, J. (eds).

Hartz, L. (1955) *The Liberal Tradition in America*, New York, Harcourt Brace Jovanovich.

Hartz, L. (1964) 'The rise of the democratic idea' in Schlesinger, A. Jr. and White, M. (eds) *Paths of American Thought*, London, Chatto & Windus.

Havard, W. and Bernd, J. (eds) (1976) *200 Years of the Republic in Retrospect*, Charlottesville, University Press of Virginia.

Kaczorowski, R. (1987) 'To begin the nation anew: Congress, citizenship, and civil rights after the Civil War', *American Historical Review*, vol.92, no.1, pp.45–68.

Kern, S. (1983) *The Culture of Time and Space 1880–1918*, London, George Weidenfeld & Nicolson.

Lynd, S. (1973) *Intellectual Origins of American Radicalism*, London, Wildwood House.

McCarthy, E. (1960) *Frontiers in American Democracy*, Cleveland, World Publishing Co.

Maidment, R. and McGrew, A. (1986) *The American Political Process*, London, Sage.

Mills, C. Wright (1956) *The Power Elite*, New York, Oxford University Press.

Nicholls, D. (1974) *Three Varieties of Pluralism*, London, Macmillan.

Peden, W. (ed.) (1954) *T. Jefferson, Notes on the State of Virginia*, New York, W.W. Norton.

Riesman, D. (1950) *The Lonely Crowd*, New Haven, Yale University Press.

Roper, J. (1989) *Democracy and its Critics*, London, Unwin Hyman.

Rose, R. (ed.) (1974) *Lessons from America: an Exploration*, London, Macmillan.

Rossiter, C. (1960) 'The democratic process' in American Assembly, *Goals for Americans: the Report of the President's Commission on National Goals*, Englewood Cliffs, Prentice-Hall, pp.61–78.

Schlesinger, A. Jr. (1973) *The Imperial Presidency*, Boston, Houghton Mifflin.

Schlesinger, A. Jr. (1977) 'America: experiment or destiny?', *American Historical Review*, vol.82, no.3, pp.505–22.

Smith, H. (1986) 'Symbol and idea in *Virgin Land*' in Bercovitch, S. and Jehlen, M. (eds) *Ideology and Classic American Literature*, Cambridge, Cambridge University Press.

Sumner, C. (1874) *Prophetic Voices Concerning America*, Boston, Lee & Shepherd.

Tansell, C. (ed.) (1927) *Documents Illustrative of the Formation of the Union of the American States*, Washington, DC, US Government Printing Office.

Tocqueville, A. de (1945) *Democracy in America*, 2 vols, New York, Vintage Books edn.

Vile, M.J.C. (1967) *Constitutionalism and the Separation of Powers*, Oxford, Clarendon Press.

Warfel, H., Gabriel, R. and Williams, S. (eds) (1937) *The American Mind*, New York, American Book Company.

Williams, W.A. (1980) *Empire as a Way of Life*, Oxford, Oxford University Press.

Wood, G.S. (1969) *The Creation of the American Republic*, Chapel Hill, University of North Carolina Press.

Wright, E. (1974) 'America: the end of the dream' in Rose, R. (ed.).

FURTHER READING

See Foley (1991), Hartz (1955), Maidment and McGrew (1986) and de Tocqueville (1945) in the references.

Boorstin, D. (1953) *The Genius of American Politics*, Chicago, University of Chicago Press.

Madison, J., Hamilton, A. and Jay, J. (1987) *The Federalist Papers*, Harmondsworth, Penguin Books.

THE POLITICS OF DEADLOCK

Christopher Bailey ★

1 INTRODUCTION

Periods of coherent, programmatic action have been rare in the United States during the twentieth century. The bursts of legislative activity that characterized the New Deal (1933–4), the liberal reforms of the Great Society (1964–5), and the first year of the Reagan Administration (1981), stand in stark contrast to the deadlock that has otherwise seemed to typify the American political system. All too often government has appeared incoherent, lacking in direction, and incapable of responding to domestic challenges or fulfilling international responsibilities. Presidents have rarely been able to provide effective leadership, and Congress has all too often seemed excessively preoccupied with parochial concerns. The political system, in short, does not appear to work. In the words of James MacGregor Burns: 'The ultimate test of a political system is performance, and it is the failure of the American system to produce that has most alienated leaders and followers alike, whether the liberal left seeking social justice and economic equality, or conservatives seeking a lean and parsimonious government' (Burns, 1984, p.14).

Deadlock does not mean that no laws are produced. Although legislative production has declined from the high of 1,028 new laws enacted by the 84th Congress (1955–6), an average of some 600 new laws have been produced by almost every Congress since the late 1960s. The main exception was the 97th Congress (1981–2) which produced 473 new laws. Measured in terms of the length of enactments, legislative production might even be argued to have increased during this period. The 1,028 laws produced by the 84th Congress totalled 1,848 pages while the 664 laws produced by the 99th Congress (1985–6) totalled 7,198 pages. Even the 473 new laws enacted by the 97th Congress totalled 4,343 pages. Evidence for deadlock based on such data would seem to be lacking. Deadlock should not be viewed, however, simply in terms of legislative production. Outcomes need to be distinguished from outputs (Cooper and Brady, 1981, p.999). Proponents of deadlock argue that much of the legislation produced by Congress is inconsequential. Commemorative laws which establish commemorative days, weeks, months, years, and decades, or name federal buildings after prominent Americans, constitute approximately half of the laws produced by Congress. Even when laws do address pertinent problems they tend to do so on an *ad hoc* or piecemeal basis, and not as part of a programme of governmental action. Deadlock should be viewed, in short, as the absence of coherent, timely governmental action to address the problems confronting the United States.

Critics have usually pointed to the Constitution as the main source of the deadlock that appears to dominate American politics. The Constitution, some critics contend, provides the US with a set of eighteenth-century political institutions which are ill-suited to responding to the problems of the twentieth century. 'A government is an organism with work to do', Donald Robinson has noted, 'It must be judged according to its fitness to perform the tasks we assign it. A horse is fit to pull a carriage, but it cannot take a man to the moon.' (Robinson, 1986, p.40.) In other words, antiquated government is the cause of deadlock. Taking a slightly different line, Michael Mezey has suggested that the Constitution should be 'properly viewed as a constitution against government' (Mezey, 1989, p.44). The Founding Fathers so feared government that they deliberately produced a political system that would not work under normal circumstances. Deadlock is inevitable, in this view, because the political system was designed to produce deadlock.

Although acknowledging that the Constitution does not promote efficient government, some observers have argued that the deadlock in the American political system is also a consequence of the nation's pluralistic political culture. 'The absence of a unified élite and the presence of a cacophony of groups and interests ... ', Roger Davidson has argued, make ' ... a fragmented, open decision-making system virtually inevitable' (Davidson, 1988, p.19). In other words, the diversity of America magnifies the fractures generated by constitutional arrangements. Deadlock is commonplace, in this view, because achieving a consensus on the aims and means of government action is well nigh impossible.

Locating the sources of the deadlock that appears to characterize the American political system is important. If deadlock is a consequence of the constitutional arrangements that were made some 200 years ago, all that needs to be done to promote efficiency is to modernize government. Constitutional reforms that would bring government out of the age of the horse-and-carriage and into the space-age would eliminate deadlock. If deadlock is also a consequence of a pluralistic political culture, efficiency is not so easily promoted. Reforms designed to promote majoritarian rule will either not work, or else will severely limit the representation of minority interests in the governmental process.

2   SOURCES OF DEADLOCK

Two potential sources of the deadlock that appears to characterize American politics have been identified. First, constitutional arrangements which divide power between a President and a Congress have produced a system of government that is replete with veto points. With the central institutions of American government deliberately designed to check and balance each other, co-operation is necessary to overcome stasis. Secondly, the heterogeneity of American society serves to atomize political life. Regional, cultural, and ethnic diversity makes it difficult to organize and sustain unifying institutions such as strong political parties that might overcome the divisions created by constitutional arrangements.

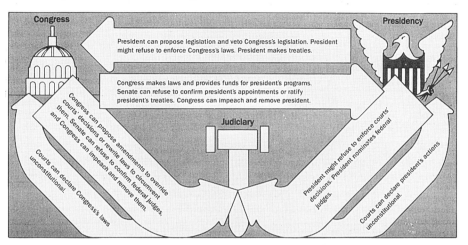

Figure 2.1 *Checks and balances between the branches of government makes political leadership very difficult. Co-operation and compromise are required if deadlock is to be broken*
(Source: Welch *et al.*, 1992, p.34)

The framers of the Constitution divided power between a President and a Congress in an effort to forestall the emergence of a tyrannical form of government in the US. Fearful that tyranny was most likely to occur when executive and legislative power were concentrated in the hands of a single individual or institution, the framers ensured that executive and legislative power were distributed among independent institutions. The President was given legislative power in order to act as a check upon the legislature, and Congress was given executive power in order to act as a check upon the actions of the executive. Legislative power was checked even further by the decision to divide Congress into two independent chambers. With legislation required to pass both the House of Representatives and the Senate, each chamber was effectively given the power of veto over new laws.

Article I, Section 8 of the Constitution provides Congress with an impressive array of legislative powers. Congress is granted unambiguous authority to 'lay and collect Taxes' and 'provide for the common Defence and general Welfare of the United States'. Further powers include the right to coin money, regulate commerce, incur debts, undertake public works, provide for a militia, raise armies, and declare war. To ensure that such powers may be exercised effectively, the final clause of Article I, Section 8 gives Congress the power 'To make all Laws which shall be necessary and proper for carrying into Execution the foregoing Powers, and all other Powers vested by this

Constitution in the Government of the United States, or in any Department or Officer thereof.' The 'necessary and proper' clause, sometimes known as the 'elastic' clause, provides the basis for assertions that Congress has implied legislative powers in addition to those enumerated.

Although Article I, Section 1 of the Constitution claims that 'All legislative Powers herein granted shall be vested in a Congress of the United States', some legislative power is also given to the President. Article II, Section 3 gives the President the power to recommend legislation to Congress, and 'on extraordinary Occasions' convene or adjourn either or both chambers. The President is also granted the power to veto enactments passed by Congress. Article I, Section 7 states that the President must either sign a bill, in which case it becomes law, or else return it unsigned to Congress within ten days, in which case it is vetoed. Congress may overturn a presidential veto with a vote of two-thirds majorities in both chambers.

The Constitution divides executive power in much the same way that legislative power is divided. Article II, Section 1 states that 'The executive Power shall be vested in a President of the United States'. Section 2 establishes the President as Commander-in-Chief, and gives him or her the power to appoint 'Ambassadors, other public Ministers and Consuls, Judges of the supreme Court, and all other Officers of the United States'. The President is also given the power to negotiate treaties and issue pardons. Many of these powers, however, are shared with Congress. The Senate must confirm presidential appointments and ratify treaties. The ability of the President to wage war is circumscribed by Congress's power to 'raise and support armies'.

Often overlooked in discussions of the executive is the role that Congress plays in defining what is meant by executive power. The basic design of the executive branch is determined by Congress. Cabinet departments and other agencies are created by statute not presidential fiat. Congress also defines much of the workload of the executive branch. Statutes set a goal, perhaps cleaner water, better highways, or improved civil rights, which the departments and agencies are expected to transform into reality. To ensure that the executive branch works to achieve these goals, Congress may use a number of devices to secure compliance with legislative intent. Congressional appropriations often contain precise instructions as to how and where the executive branch is to spend money, and on a few occasions money has been withheld from uncooperative agencies. Executive officials are also regularly called to give evidence about their work before congressional committees.

A controversial method of controlling the executive branch has involved inserting provisions into laws that give Congress the right to veto executive action. Known as the legislative veto, Congress first used this technique in 1932 when it gave President Hoover the right to reorganize the executive branch, provided neither the Senate nor the House of Representatives disapproved of the way that the reorganization was implemented. Congress made increasing use of the legislative veto over the next 50 years. During the 1970s, the legislative veto, as James Sundquist has noted: 'found its way into laws dealing with railroads, education, financial aid for New York City, election finance, the disposition of President Nixon's tapes and papers, the call-up of military reserve units or members, and advance payments or loans to military contractors' (Sundquist, 1981, p.350). Doubt about the constitutionality of the legislative veto, however, has existed almost as long as the device has been used. Presidents have certainly viewed the legislative veto as infringing upon executive prerogatives. In 1983 the Supreme Court in *Immigration and Naturalization Service v. Chadha* declared one particular version of the legislative veto to be unconstitutional, but it is not clear whether the Court's decision is applicable to all legislative vetoes.

The division of legislative and executive power between two independent branches of government profoundly affects the way that the political system functions. With each branch possessing the potential to veto the actions of the other, co-operation is essential if legislation is to be enacted and administered. Without co-operation the potential for legislative and executive action is greatly reduced. Legislation will be impossible to enact unless the super majorities that are necessary to overturn a presidential veto can be obtained, and congressional opposition will severely impede executive action. In short, deadlock is likely to result when co-operation between the branches is absent.

Strong political parties have long been regarded as providing a means of bridging the gap between the branches of government. Even the Founding Fathers, who were generally hostile to political parties, soon realized that some extra-constitutional institution was needed to bring a degree of unity to the system of government that they had created. In 1800, just over a decade after the Constitution had been written, two embryonic political parties were already competing to win control of the entire system of government. Three decades later and political parties had become an established feature of the American political landscape.

The need for strong political parties has been recognized by political scientists as well as politicians. In 1900 Henry Jones Ford argued that parties were created as a means 'to establish a control over the divided powers of government'. In Ford's opinion, parties were 'a necessary evil' (Ford, 1900, pp.297–8). Some 50 years later the necessity of party government had become a dominant paradigm of American political science. In 1950 the Committee on Political Parties of the American Political Science Association published a report which stated that a strong majority party was an 'indispensable instrument' in a political system where power was divided. A strong majority party, the report suggested, was needed to provide both direction and harmony to American government (American Political Science Association, 1950).

Two conditions must be met if a political party is to serve as a means of bridging the gap between the separated branches of government. First, the party must win control of each institution of government. Incomplete conquest of government will result in an incapacity to govern. Secondly, the party must be unified. Control of government will mean little if party discipline is lacking. Periods when both of these conditions have pertained, however, have been rare during the twentieth century. American political parties have not only tended to be fragmented, but periods of unified party control of government have become increasingly infrequent.

American elections have created or continued a condition of divided government, where one party controls the presidency and another at least one chamber of Congress, for 34 of the 94 years since 1900. Although unusual in the period before 1952, divided government has become particularly evident over the last 40 or so years (see Table 2.1). The most common pattern has been for Republican Presidents to confront a Democratic Congress.

Table 2.1 Years of divided government, 1900–94

	Unified years	Divided years	Percentage of divided years
1900–52	44	8	15%
1952–94	16	26	62%
1900–94	60	34	36%

Sundquist has argued that the persistence of divided government since 1952 has made the American political system unworkable (Sundquist, 1988). Not only has a vital instrument for co-ordinating action between the branches been removed, but divided control has meant that partisan rivalries have reinforced institutional rivalries to magnify the difficulties created by the country's constitutional arrangements. Finding an answer to problems such as the budget deficit is made impossible, Sundquist suggests, because discourse between the branches degenerates into partisan bickering when government is divided. The need to secure partisan advantage leads to posturing and leaves problems unsolved.

The suggestion that divided government has magnified the problems that are inherent in American constitutional arrangements has many supporters (Cutler, 1988; Mezey, 1989; Ginsberg and Shefter, 1990). Separate studies by David Mayhew and Roger Davidson have found little evidence, however, to support such a thesis (Mayhew, 1989, 1991; Davidson, 1991). After examining the historical record, Mayhew concluded that divided government has made little difference to the enactment of important legislation in the period since 1946. Davidson also found little connection between legislative activity and party control of government. Important legislation was just as likely to be enacted during a period of divided government as during a period of unified government. The period of divided government during the Nixon and Ford Administrations, for example, produced some of the most important statutes of the post-Second World War era. Included among these statutes were the National Environmental Policy Act of 1969, the Occupational Safety and Health Act of 1970, the Clean Air Act of 1970, the Equal Opportunity Act of 1972, and the Consumer Product Safety Act of 1972. Other statutes revised the tax code, regulated campaign finance, and improved welfare programmes. The mathematics of party control, in short, has simply not been a significant factor in explaining legislative output.

One reason why divided government has made little difference to the enactment of important legislation lies in the fact that the executive and legislative branches have different power bases and institutional needs. Even when a member of Congress and the President belong to the same party, agreement on an issue may not be automatic because of the different constituencies that each serves, the different election cycles that each faces, and the different perspective that each gains from working within their particular institution. So important and profound are these differences that Burns has suggested that both the Democratic Party and the Republican Party are divided into presidential and congressional 'wings' that constitute 'separate though overlapping parties' (Burns, 1963, p.196). The result, in Burns' opinion, is a 'four-party system that compels government by consensus and coalition rather than a two-party system that allows the winning party to govern and the losers to oppose' (ibid., p.7). To secure the enactment of legislation, the presidential party must negotiate with the congressional party, or vice versa even when both share the same label.

The 'four-party system' developed by Burns identifies some of the cleavages generated by American constitutional arrangements, but over-estimates the coherence of the congressional party in particular. Party unity in Congress has never been strong. Both the Democratic Party and the Republican Party have always tended to encompass a variety of different interests, and finding a unified party position on a particular issue has never been easy. In recent years, such difficulties have been compounded by the development of candidate-centred campaign techniques which have tended to depress partisan appeals. Similarly, the notion that there is a single, unified, presidential party may also be misplaced. The executive branch speaks with so many voices that identifying a single position on a particular issue is often difficult.

Describing the federal government as being dominated by two, or even four parties is misleading. The lightness with which party labels are worn in Washington DC means that, in many respects, a no-party system operates. Parties remain essential to the organization of government, particularly Congress, but are of limited importance when it comes to determining the content of legislation. For legislation to be enacted and administered coalitions need to be negotiated on an issue by issue basis. Party labels may provide a basis for such coalitions but are neither sufficient nor necessary. Each individual will have his or her own set of preferences and needs. Coalitions will be formed only when the variety of preferences and needs can be accommodated.

The weakness of political parties explains why the production of important legislation has not varied significantly during the periods of unified and divided government. In a no-party system, factors other than party largely account for the production of legislation. Needed is an analysis of the factors that facilitate coalition-building in the absence of party. Presidential leadership qualities, congressional electoral incentives, catalytic events, and public opinion are some of the factors that Mayhew suggests might explain legislative production (Mayhew, 1991, chs.5, 6).

A consequence of the no-party system is that no permanent, stable institution exists to bridge the gap created by the separation of powers. As Richard Neustadt has observed: 'What the Constitution separates our political parties do not combine' (Neustadt, 1980, p.33). Establishing the links necessary to enact and administer legislation, as a result, is a time consuming and difficult operation. Presidents and congressional leaders must negotiate with a wide variety of political actors, each with different preferences and needs, to create the coalitions needed to pass legislation. Bridges can be constructed to link the executive and legislature, but they will be short-term structures that are unable to carry much heavy traffic.

SUMMARY

Constitutional arrangements divide power between the President and Congress, and make co-operation between the two branches a prerequisite for government action.

Parties can act as a bridge between the divided branches of government, but in the US the parties are too weak to fulfil this function.

With the failure of parties, bridges must be negotiated on an issue to issue basis. Negotiating such co-operation is time-consuming and difficult.

3   THE POSSIBILITY OF PRESIDENTIAL LEADERSHIP

Presidential leadership has often been viewed as the *sine qua non* for effective government in the United States. No other government institution is as well positioned to provide both direction and co-ordination to American political life. Not only does the President occupy a central position in the political system, but as the only politician with a national constituency no person other than the President may claim to speak for all Americans. Sectional interests may be aggregated in Congress, but only the President can attempt to offer an expansive definition of the national interest based on factors other than particularism. 'Only the President represents the national interest' declared John F. Kennedy in 1960 (quoted in the *New York Times*, 15 January 1960).

Expectations that the President should provide something more than symbolic leadership did not become firmly established until the New Deal. The combination of a deep national crisis and the long tenure of President Franklin D. Roosevelt served to transform both the role and the structure of the presidency. In less than a decade, President Roosevelt firmly established the principle that the President had a duty to initiate and seek support for a legislative programme that advanced the interests of the nation. Additional resources were made available as presidential responsibilities grew. The Executive Office of the President (EOP) was created in 1939 to provide the President with more help.

The President can persuade the 'congressional snail' to run like a 'rabbit' on very few occasions. The New Deal under Roosevelt was one such occasion

Roosevelt has cast a long shadow over the presidency (Leuchtenburg, 1985). In the 50 years since his death each of his successors has had to respond to increased public expectations about the role of the President. Even Presidents who have advocated a reduced role for the federal government have found their room for manœuvre limited by the weight of public expectations. In the words of one noted commentator: the President ' … nowadays … cannot be as small as he might like' (Neustadt, 1980, p.6). The institutions created under President Roosevelt have also continued to develop. The EOP has expanded into a presidential branch of government employing approximately 2,000 staff (Hart, 1987). Taking into account the protection provided by the Secret Service, a special communications system provided by the Pentagon, and the other personnel seconded from the Executive Branch, the total cost of the presidential office in 1992 has been estimated to be close to $1 billion.

The fact that the President has more resources and may be better positioned than any other politician to provide direction and co-ordination to American political life does not mean that leadership is easily exercised. Considerable obstacles exist within the political system which must be overcome if the President is not to be frustrated. Congress, bureaucrats, and the courts all possess sufficient power to check presidential leadership. Leadership will only be effective if the President can obtain some form of control over the structures and processes of American government. Without such control presidential efforts to provide direction to American political life will amount to little. Claims to define the national interest will have no more impact that empty campaign promises.

The ability of the President to obtain control over the structures and processes of American government is constrained by constitutional arrangements which share power between separate institutions. The President has no means of exercising control over Congress, little authority over the Supreme Court, and incomplete command of the federal bureaucracy. Confronted with the reality of shared power, the President has three possible courses of action. First, the President may exploit ambiguities in the Constitution to maximize presidential power. Secondly, the President may seek to persuade others that their interests will be furthered by what he or she wants to do. Thirdly, the President may act extra-constitutionally and seek to circumvent the limitations on his or her power.

The only unilateral power given to the President in the Constitution is the power of pardon. Article II, Section 2 states that the President 'shall have Power to Grant Reprieves and Pardons for Offences against the United States, except in Cases of Impeachment'. All other enumerated powers are shared. Presidents since George Washington have sought to expand their ability to act unilaterally, however, by exploiting ambiguities and gaps within the Constitution. Presidents have often claimed that certain powers are 'inherent' in the Constitution. Proponents of 'inherent' power argue that presidential power is derived not only from the enumerated powers which are clearly outlined in Article II, but also from inferences that may be drawn from the Constitution.

'Inherent' powers may be claimed when the Constitution is either ambiguous or silent. The lack of precision in phrases such as 'The executive Power shall be vested in a President of the United States', 'The President shall be Commander in Chief of the Army and Navy of the United States', and '[the President] shall take Care that the Laws be faithfully executed', provides a determined President with an opportunity to define those terms to suit his or her purpose. The President may also claim power in areas where the Constitution is silent. If the Constitution does not specifically enumerate a power, the President may seek to claim it as his or her own.

The successful assertion of 'inherent' power by the President requires acquiescence from the other branches of government. Acquiescence is not only important in allowing the President to achieve short-term goals, but may also have a long-term significance because of the precedent it establishes. Presidential assertions of 'inherent' power are more difficult to dispute if they have been institutionalized through custom and precedent. Unsuccessful assertions of 'inherent' power will have the opposite effect. So important has the success or failure of past assertions of 'inherent' power been that Richard Pious has coined the term 'prerogative government' to illustrate the source of much presidential power (Pious, 1979, p.49).

Both Congress and the Supreme Court may deny presidential claims of 'inherent' power. In 1952 President Truman issued an executive order to take control of the American steel industry based on the authority vested in him as President 'by the Constitution and laws of the United States and Commander-in-Chief of the armed forces of the United States'. President Truman's claim that he had 'inherent' power to nationalize the steel industry was overturned, however, by the Supreme Court in the case *Youngstown Co. v. Sawyer* (1952). The Court determined that the President had usurped the legislative power of the Congress in ordering the seizure of the steel industry. In the Court's opinion, only Congress could have ordered such a seizure. The Court denied further presidential claims of 'inherent' power during the Nixon Administration. In *United States v. US District Court* (1972) the Court rejected claims that the President has the 'inherent' power to order wiretaps in domestic security matters without judicial authorization. In *United States v. Richard M. Nixon* (1974) the Court rejected claims that the President could define what was covered by executive privilege and what was not. For most of the twentieth century, however, the Supreme Court has generally acquiesced when Presidents have claimed 'inherent' power. Efforts to restrict presidential power have tended to come from Congress.

Acquiescence to claims of presidential power during the twentieth century have been most notable in foreign affairs. In *United States v. Curtiss-Wright Corp.* (1936) the Supreme Court declared the President to be ' ... the sole organ of the federal government in the field of international affairs' (299 US at 320, 1936[1]). Congress was also prepared to give the President considerable freedom to conduct foreign affairs. Partly out of recognition that the President was better able to make the quick decisions that foreign affairs during the Cold War demanded, and partly because Senators and Representatives did not wish to be held responsible for issues of national security, claims of presidential power to conduct foreign affairs were rarely challenged by Congress between 1940 and the late 1960s. Congress was even willing to delegate additional power to the President. From the National Security Act of 1947 to the Gulf of Tonkin Resolution of 1964 Congress enacted a series of measures that enhanced presidential power in foreign affairs.

Congressional acquiescence to claims that the President had 'inherent' power to conduct foreign affairs began to end in the early 1970s as concern grew about the course of the Vietnam War. The Case Act of 1972 sought to limit the President's power to enter into secret agreements with foreign countries. All international agreements to which the United States was a party were required under the terms of the Act to be transmitted to Congress within 60 days. The War Powers Resolution of 1973 sought to restrict the President's power to wage war. Under the terms of the Resolution, the President was required to consult Congress before committing troops to combat, to report to Congress afterward, and to withdraw the troops if congressional approval for their deployment was not obtained within 60 days. Other enactments sought to restrict the President's power both to wage 'covert' war and sell arms to foreign nations.

[1]That is US law report (1936), vol.299, p.320.

Congress has traditionally been far less willing to acquiesce to presidential claims of 'inherent' power to conduct domestic affairs. The fact that Senators and Representatives have strong electoral imperatives to maintain some control over domestic matters has meant that they have tended to defend their enumerated powers in this area. Particular attention has been paid to maintaining congressional control of the appropriations process. Persistent efforts by President Nixon to reduce or eliminate funding for programmes with which he disagreed, for example, led to passage of the Congressional Budget and Impoundment Act of 1974. The Act required the President to inform Congress of any decision to rescind (cancel) or defer (postpone) appropriations. The approval of both the House of Representatives and the Senate became necessary to rescind funds, while the disapproval of either chamber became sufficient to veto deferrals.

Although Congress has tended to resist presidential claims of 'inherent' power to conduct domestic affairs, considerable discretionary power has been delegated to the President during the twentieth century. Power has been delegated in two ways. First, Congress has enacted statutes which establish general goals but leave the details to be determined by the President. An illustration of the amount of discretion that Congress has been willing to give to the President is provided by the Economic Stabilization Act of 1970. The Act authorized the President 'to issue such orders and regulations as he may deem appropriate to stabilize prices, rents, wages, and salaries at levels not less than those prevailing on May 25, 1970'. Secondly, Congress has enacted statutes which give the President power to act in an emergency. President Roosevelt used emergency powers to close banks, seize railways and relocate Japanese-Americans during the Second World War. President Johnson invoked statutory emergency powers in 1968 to restrict the amount of American capital that could be invested abroad. President Nixon used similar powers in 1970 to call out troops to deliver the mail during a postal strike. A congressional study carried out in the mid-1970s revealed no less than 470 emergency statutes that gave the President authority to act without reference to Congress (cited in Koenig, 1981, p.162).

Grants of delegated power may be reclaimed at any time. Congress may determine that too much discretion has been given to the President and seek to legislate details rather than just general goals. The power of the President to influence the implementation of legislation will be reduced if statutes specify precise standards that must be met by certain deadlines. Congress may also remove the statutory authority which enables the President to assert emergency powers. The National Emergencies Act of 1976, for example, removed all the accrued emergency powers of the President. Future claims of emergency power by the President were also made subject to a congressional veto under the terms of the 1976 Act.

Implied and delegated powers do not provide the President with sufficient power to control all the structures and processes of American government that are necessary to exercise consistent leadership. Incomplete command of government means that the President must secure the support of other actors in the political system. President Harry Truman summed up the nature of presidential power when he said: 'I sit here all day trying to per-suade people to do the things they ought to have sense enough to do with-out my persuading them … That's all the powers of the President amount to' (quoted in Neustadt, 1980, p.9). Without the co-operation of others the President will achieve little: presidential orders will not be followed, nor will presidential wishes be fulfilled. 'Presidential *power*', Neustadt observed, 'is the power to persuade' (ibid., p.10).

The constitutional arrangements of the United States means that to exercise leadership the President must secure the co-operation of Congress above all other institutions. Unable to introduce legislation or appropriate money, the President must obtain the support of Congress if new laws are to be enacted and existing programmes properly implemented. Co-operation, however, is not easily secured. The President has no formal means of forcing Congress to do his or her bidding. Not only does the Constitution prohibit the Presi-dent from introducing a bill in Congress, but he or she also has no explicit agenda-setting powers. Nor does the President have any formal power over congressional careers. Fixed electoral terms mean that the President cannot dissolve Congress and call fresh elections, and promotion within the Senate and House of Representatives is determined by party rules over which the President has no control.

The absence of formal methods of control means that the President must use informal methods of persuasion. Presidential use of patronage and projects are two means by which congressional favour might be courted. The Presi-dent might make an appointment to the executive branch at the behest of a Senator or Representative, or else might encourage construction projects in particular constituencies, in order to win votes. Considerable doubt has been cast, however, upon the efficacy of patronage and projects as persuasive tools. Few examples can be cited of a Senator or Representative changing their vote to obtain jobs or projects. A number of observers have suggested that the President is better served, in fact, if he concentrates upon establish-ing good general relations with Congress (Kellerman, 1984; Bowles, 1987). Providing Senators and Representatives with signed photographs, presiden-tial memorabilia, and other favours creates an atmosphere of co-operation which will work to the advantage of the President in the long term. The legislative success enjoyed by the President, in this view, is determined largely by his or her skill in creating the conditions necessary for success.

The suggestion that the skills of the President make a difference to legislat-ive outcomes has been attacked by George Edwards (1980, 1989). In studies which analysed roll-call data from 1953 to 1986 he found little evidence that legislative skill made any difference to legislative outcomes. 'Presidential legislative skills are not closely related to presidential support in Congress; on close examination a president's legislative skills reveal themselves to be limited in their potential for obtaining support from Senators and Represen-tatives' (Edwards, 1989, p.211). Edwards argues that ideology, personal pref-erences, and constituency pressures have a far more important influence on how a legislator casts a vote than appeals from the President. The legislative skills of the President may have an impact at the margins of coalition-building, but are of little consequence at the core. Legislative success will come to a President if his or her proposals are congruent with the wishes of a core coalition in Congress. No amount of bargaining will generate success if such congruence is lacking.

Implicit in Edwards' arguments is the idea that Presidents are powerless to impose an agenda upon Congress. A similar argument has been advanced by Charles Jones (1991). He suggests that Presidents are constrained by the policy agenda that exists when they assume office, and that the important factor in explaining legislative success is whether the President and members of Congress can agree on the specific policy alternatives necessary to deal with existing problems. The choice of policy and not legislative skill, according to Jones, is the key to success. The legislative success enjoyed by Roosevelt, Johnson, and Reagan occurred because those Presidents chose policy alternatives that addressed existing problems and were acceptable to Congress. The partisan composition of Congress may have made agreement easier to obtain, and the legislative skills of Roosevelt, Johnson, and Reagan may have made a difference at the margins, but the main reason why dead-

Counting the votes at the margin is important to a President.
Here President Johnson studies a congressional voting record

lock was broken during the New Deal, Great Society, and the first year of the Reagan Administration, lies in the fact that President and Congress agreed not only on what problems should be addressed, but also on how to address those problems. Given the different imperatives driving Presidents and Congress, periods of agenda congruence have been very rare. Jones suggests that electoral returns or significant events such as the assassination of President Kennedy may promote congruence, but that any unity of purpose will be short lived.

The fact that Presidents have few formal or informal means of exercising control over the structures and processes of American government has led several Presidents to take extra-constitutional action to circumvent limits on their power. During the Civil War, for example, President Abraham Lincoln issued a number of orders that exceeded his constitutional authority. In defiance of Article I, Section 8 of the Constitution, which gave Congress the power 'To raise and support Armies', one order issued by Lincoln increased the size of the armed forces beyond that mandated by Congress. Another order suspended the writ of habeas corpus even though Article I, Section 9 of the Constitution appeared to reserve that power to Congress. When asked to justify his actions, Lincoln responded with the question: 'Was it possible to lose the nation and yet preserve the Constitution?'

Opposition to the extra-constitutional actions taken by President Lincoln was muted because of the circumstances prevailing at the time. Other Presidents have not been so fortunate. Evidence that President Nixon had been aware of the break-in at the Democratic Party headquarters in the Watergate complex in 1972 led to his resignation two years later. President Reagan survived the scandal that resulted when news emerged in 1986 that he had authorized arms sales to Iran and funding to the Contra guerrillas in Nicaragua despite the fact that both actions appeared to contravene the laws of the United States. Several of his aides, however, were found guilty of acting illegally.

The temptation for the President to act extra-constitutionally is immense. Expected to provide both direction and co-ordination to American political life, but lacking the formal or informal power necessary to exert control over the structures and processes of government, the President must constantly seek methods of circumventing the limits on his or her power to act. In the words of Theodore Lowi:

> ... mass expectations about presidential power are so great that presidents must, as in Watergate, attempt to control their environment to the maximum, especially those aspects of it that might tend to be barriers in the way of meeting presidential responsibilities. Those responsibilities are so pressing and so close to unmeetable that presidents must have vast contingency plans to make up the differences between expectations and realities.
>
> (Lowi, 1985, p.178)

Effective and consistent presidential leadership, in short, is rarely possible under the constitutional arrangements of the United States.

SUMMARY

The President is expected to provide both direction and co-ordination to American political life.

The Constitution does not provide the President with sufficient power to control the structures and processes of government. As a result, Presidents are tempted to act extra-constitutionally to circumvent the limits on their power.

Presidents will fail to deliver what they have promised or what the American people expect from them.

4 THE POSSIBILITY OF CONGRESSIONAL LEADERSHIP

Congress, like most legislatures in the Western world, has experienced problems in coping with the twentieth century. Changing public expectations about the role of government have led to demands for action which Congress has seemed unable to meet. Designed at a time when government involvement in social or economic affairs was minimal, if not non-existent, Congress has often appeared to struggle when dealing with the issues of twentieth-century America. Unlike most other Western legislatures, however, Congress has managed to retain both power and independence. Protected by constitutional arrangements which reserve certain powers to Congress and guarantee Senators and Representatives a power base that is independent of the executive branch, the legislature of the United States has managed to maintain a significant role in the American political system.

A widespread belief that congressional power exceeds congressional competence has meant that Congress has often been cited as the main cause of the deadlock that appears to plague the American political system. Critics have suggested that Congress has proved incapable of producing policies that address the problems of twentieth-century America, and has also proved far too willing to obstruct presidential initiatives. In contrast to other Western democracies in which legislatures have generally ceded power to the executive, the ability of the President to find solutions to the problems of American society have remained circumscribed by the power and independence of Congress. In other words, the charge against Congress is not just that it has failed to provide leadership, but also that it has consistently obstructed presidential efforts to provide leadership.

The central thrust of most criticisms of Congress is that Senators and Representatives lack both the incentives and means that are necessary to provide national leadership. Critics suggest that members often seem to be motivated primarily by the desire to improve their prospects of re-election and of paying excessive attention to parochial issues. Not only do they devote considerable time and resources to constituency services, but the perceived views of constituents will have an influence on how they cast their votes. Both factors will affect the possibility of congressional leadership. First, time and resources devoted to constituency service means less time available for national issues. Secondly, concern for the perceived views of constituents may circumscribe the development of a national perspective. A lack of motivation, however, is usually regarded as only half the story. Critics suggest that even when members are willing to respond to national concerns, the procedures of Congress normally frustrate such efforts. The legislative process is complex and contains many opportunities for obstruction. A well-placed minority in Congress can frustrate the wishes of the majority for a considerable period of time.

Concern that a lack of interest in local issues might have adverse electoral consequences has caused Representatives and Senators to devote considerable time and resources to serving their constituents. Members are not only spending more time in their constituencies, but they are also sending constituents more mail, and locating more staff in local offices. The result has been a change both in congressional work patterns and in congressional workloads. In terms of work patterns, the legislative schedules of the Senate and the House of Representatives have been changed to accommodate the increased time that Senators and Representatives are spending in their constituencies. The House commonly schedules legislative business on a Tuesday to Thursday basis to allow Representatives to spend long weekends with their constituents. In a similar move, the Senate has adopted a 'three week/one week' schedule. The Senate is in session for three weeks and off for one week every month. In terms of workload the increased number of staff located in local offices has led to an increase in the amount of casework being undertaken. Many members now behave much like ombudsmen. They deal with requests from constituents to provide information about government benefits, to sort out problems with the bureaucracy, or just to give general advice.

In addition to structuring the work pattern and the workload of Congress, the concern that Representatives and Senators display towards their constituencies also affects their choice of policy. A common criticism is that members often neglect the interests of the country as a whole in order to look after the short-term interests of their constituents. The re-election imperative, in other words, encourages particularism (Mayhew, 1974, pp.127–31). David Stockman, a former director of the Office of Management and Budget, has suggested that: 'Two years and one Congressional District is the scope of [a Representative's] horizon' (Stockman, 1986, p.15). No solution to the budget deficit of the US has been found, for example, because members have remained committed to providing benefits for their constituents.

The possibility of congressional leadership is not only limited by the parochial instincts of Senators and Representatives. A lack of expertise and cumbersome procedures often frustrate congressional initiatives even when members might be willing to focus on national concerns. Many critics argue that members are generalists who lack the specialist knowledge that is necessary to craft solutions to the complex problems of modern society (Toffler, 1980). Other critics argue that the procedures of the Senate and House of Representatives contain so may veto points that the leadership necessary to enact legislation is impossible to sustain in the long term (Sundquist, 1981; Kingdon, 1984).

Aware of their lack of specialized knowledge, Senators and Representatives relied heavily upon the executive branch for policy initiatives until the early 1970s. The twin shocks of the Vietnam War and Watergate, however, destroyed the illusion that Congress could depend upon the President to provide information. The result was a series of reforms that were designed to enhance congressional expertise and lessen the reliance upon the President for information. The number of staff that members were able to employ rose dramatically. Between 1972 and 1980 the number of personal staff working for individual members rose from 7,706 to 11,117, and the number of staff working for congressional committees rose from 1,661 to 3,108. Funding and staffing for the General Accounting Office and the Congressional Research Service was increased, and an Office of Technology Assessment and a Congressional Budget Office were created. In total the number of staff working in the four congressional support agencies rose from 14,588 in 1972 to 20,637 in 1980.

The expansion of congressional resources since the early 1970s has certainly provided Senators and Representatives with the means of gathering information about specific issues. In many respects the information available to members is at least equal in quality to that available to the President. The economic forecasts of the Congressional Budget Office, for example, enjoy a better reputation than those provided by the President's Office of Management and Budget. Somewhat paradoxically, however, the increase in staff has meant that members have less time to consider and evaluate the information that is being provided (Malbin, 1979). In addition to their role as legislators, Senators and Representatives must also 'manage' their staff. As staff activities must be co-ordinated and personnel problems resolved, the time available for crafting policies is reduced.

A fragmented and arcane legislative process has often been regarded as a further impediment to congressional policy-making. Not only must legislation pass through various discrete stages in both the House of Representatives and the Senate, but differences in the versions produced by each chamber must be reconciled, presidential approval obtained, or a presidential veto overridden. The process tends to be slow at the best of times but often grinds to a halt if opposition to the legislation exists. A determined minority can obstruct the passage of legislation even when the majority favours enactment. Majorities must exist at each stage of the legislative process to ensure passage. Super majorities may even be required at certain stages. The support of three-fifths of the membership is required to end a filibuster in the Senate when opponents of a bill attempt to 'talk it to death' by refusing to end debate. Two-thirds majorities in both the House of Representatives and the Senate are required to override a presidential veto.

Congressional leadership on national issues only becomes possible if some control over the legislative process can be achieved. Weak political parties, however, mean that control is difficult to achieve in the first instance and almost impossible to sustain in the long term. The proportion of roll-call votes where a majority of Democrats have voted against a majority of Republicans has rarely risen above 50 per cent in either the House of Representatives or the Senate since the 1950s (see Table 2.2).

Table 2.2   Party unity votes in Congress[a]

Congress	House	Senate
83rd (1953–4)	45	n/a
84th (1955–6)	42	41.5
85th (1957–8)	49.5	40
86th (1959–60)	54	42.5
87th (1961–2)	48	51.5
88th (1963–4)	52	41.5
89th (1965–6)	46.5	46
90th (1967–8)	35.5	33.5
91st (1969–70)	29	35.5
92nd (1971–2)	33	39
93rd (1973–4)	36	42
94th (1975–6)	42	43
95th (1977–8)	38	43
96th (1979–80)	43	46
97th (1981–2)	36	45
98th (1983–4)	52	42
99th (1985–6)	59	51
100th (1987–8)	53	47
101st (1989–90)	52	44
102nd (1991–2)	60	51

[a] The table indicates the percentage of all votes on which a majority of voting Democrats opposed a majority of voting Republicans.
(Source: Congressional Quarterly Almanacs, various years)

A lack of homogeneity and an absence of means for enforcing party discipline explains the low levels of party unity in Congress. Both the Republican Party and the Democratic Party encompass such a wide variety of different interests that achieving a consensus that will unite the different elements of each party is difficult. Such difficulties are made worse by the lack of mechanisms to enforce party discipline. Party leaders in Congress have few means of punishing errant members. The party has little control over electoral success and only limited control over promotion within Congress.

The lack of cohesion within congressional parties makes sustained control of the legislative process impossible. Without the unity provided by strong parties, leaders must negotiate with members in order to construct winning coalitions at each stage of the legislative process. The winning coalitions constructed at each stage will be both temporary and issue specific. Committee, subcommittee, and individual prerogatives, in short, limit the potential for more permanent coalitions and undermine the possibility of congressional leadership. Congress can act quickly on national issues, but only if agreement on the best way to proceed exists. Where doubt and uncertainty exist, Congress will move slowly.

SUMMARY

Congress is a powerful and independent legislature and possesses the potential to legislate on national issues.

The role of Congress as a national legislator is undermined by the parochial focus of Senators and Representatives, and a fragmented power structure.

The need to construct winning coalitions at different stages of the legislative process and for different issues means that sustained congressional activism is unlikely.

5 CONCLUSION: A NEED FOR REFORM?

Few observers would dispute the claim that the constitutional arrangements of the United States make effective political leadership extremely difficult. Effective leadership can be exercised in the short term, but has proved unattainable in the long term. Power is diffused to such a degree that no institution or person can establish the domination of the political system that is required to reorder priorities and resources over a sustained period of time. The result is often stasis, with government apparently unable to respond to the problems facing twentieth-century America.

The solution in the view of some commentators is constitutional reform. If the constitutional arrangements promote deadlock, then those constitutional arrangements should be changed to facilitate effective leadership. Most advocates of constitutional reform in the US have sought to find mechanisms that would allow power to be exercised. Suggested reforms include requiring voters to choose among party slates of candidates for President, Vice-President, Senators, and Representatives; introducing some procedure for dissolving government followed by a new election; and giving cabinet members seats in Congress (Robinson, 1985; Sundquist, 1986; Hardin, 1989). The intention of all these proposed reforms is to inject an element of parliamentary government into the American political system.

Opponents of constitutional reform argue that the creation of parliamentary government in the US would be counter-productive on two grounds. First, constitutional reform would only work if deadlock has been caused by existing constitutional arrangements. If, on the other hand, deadlock has been caused by deep divisions within American society, then constitutional reform would prove to be a remedy for the wrong disease and would generate further problems. The articulation and protection of minority interests in government decision-making would be reduced to allow a majority to take programmatic action. Secondly, there is little evidence that parliamentary governments have been any more successful than American governments in dealing with the problems of the twentieth century. Parliamentary governments may be more efficient in producing coherent packages of legislation, but there is little evidence that such programmatic action has been any more effective in dealing with problems than the *ad hoc* legislation produced in the United States.

The weakness of American political parties supports the thesis that the primary cause of deadlock in the United States is not the constitutional system but the pluralism of American society. Conflict between the branches of government and within Congress should be viewed as the product of a heterogeneous society, and not as a consequence of structural defects within government. Periods of coherent, programmatic action are rare because the diversity of the US makes a consensus difficult to achieve. Government appears rudderless because of a lack of agreement as to the direction that the country should follow. Reforms designed to allow a majority to provide such direction would necessarily infringe upon the protection of minority rights. Given the diversity of America, however, the fact that regional, ethnic, economic and other interests can be represented and articulated, helps to ameliorate tensions that might otherwise tear the country apart. The experience of other heterogeneous societies suggests that instability and violence all too readily occur when minority ethnic groups perceive their interests to be ignored by majority ethnic groups.

In many respects deadlock should be viewed as a triumph of American democracy. A relatively open political system exists that allows a wide variety of interests to gain access to government decision-making and facilitates the protection of minority rights. The more closed political system that would be needed to overcome deadlock would necessarily limit democracy by restricting access to government decision-making. Government action would be determined, in the words of James Madison, 'not according to the rules of justice and the rights of the minor party, but by the superior force of an interested and overbearing majority' (*The Federalist Papers*, No.10). Given the poor record of parliamentary governments in dealing with the problems of the twentieth century, and the friction that would be generated by suppressing minority rights, efforts to limit American democracy in the manner suggested by most constitutional reformers are probably not warranted.

REFERENCES

American Political Science Association (1950) *Towards a More Responsible Two-Party System*, supplement to *American Political Science Review*, no.44, Committee on Political Parties.

Bowles, N. (1987) *The White House and Capitol Hill*, Oxford, Clarendon Press.

Burns, J.M. (1963) *The Deadlock of Democracy: Four-Party Politics in America*, Englewood Cliffs, Prentice-Hall.

Burns, J.M. (1984) *The Power to Lead*, New York, Simon & Schuster.

Cooper, J. and Brady, D. (1981) 'Toward a diachronic analysis of Congress', *American Political Science Review*, vol.75, pp.988–1006.

Cutler, L. (1988) 'Some reflections about divided government', *Presidential Studies Quarterly*, vol.18, pp.485–92.

Davidson, R.H. (1988) '"Invitation to struggle": an overview of legislative–executive relations', *The Annals*, vol.499, pp.9–21.

Davidson, R.H. (1991) 'The presidency and three eras of the modern Congress' in Thurber, J.A. (ed.) *Divided Democracy: Cooperation and Conflict Between the President and Congress*, Washington, DC, Congressional Quarterly Press.

Edwards, G.C. (1980) *Presidential Influence in Congress*, San Francisco, W.H. Freeman.

Edwards, G.C. (1989) *At the Margins*, New Haven, Yale University Press.

Ford, H.J. (1900) *The Rise and Growth of American Politics*, London, Macmillan.

Ginsberg, B. and Shefter, M. (1990) *Politics by Other Means*, New York, Basic Books.

Hardin, C.M. (1989) *Constitutional Reform in America*, Ames, Iowa State University Press.

Hart, J. (1987) *The Presidential Branch*, New York, Pergamon Press.

Jones, C.O. (1991) 'Presidents and agendas: who defines what for whom?' in Pfiffner, J.P. (ed.) *The Managerial Presidency*, Chicago, Dorsey.

Kellerman, B. (1984) *The Political Presidency*, New York, Oxford University Press.

Kingdon, J.W. (1984) *Agendas, Alternatives and Public Policies*, Boston, Little, Brown.

Koenig, L.W. (1981) *The Chief Executive*, New York, Harcourt Brace Jovanovich (4th edn).

Leuchtenburg, W.E. (1985) *In the Shadow of FDR*, Ithaca, Cornell University Press.

Lowi, T.J. (1985) *The Personal President*, Ithaca, Cornell University Press.

Malbin, M. (1979) *Unelected Representatives*, New York, Basic Books.

Mayhew, D. (1974) *Congress: the Electoral Connection*, New Haven, Yale University Press.

Mayhew, D. (1989) 'Does it make a difference whether party control of the American national government is unified or divided?', unpublished paper.

Mayhew, D. (1991) *Divided We Govern*, New Haven, Yale University Press.

Mezey, M.L. (1989) *Congress, the President and Public Policy*, Boulder, Westview Press.

Neustadt, R.E. (1980) *Presidential Power*, New York, John Wiley.

Pious, R.M. (1979) *The American Presidency*, New York, Basic Books.

Robinson, D.L. (1985) *Reforming American Government*, Boulder, Westview Press.

Robinson, D.L. (1986) 'The renewal of American constitutionalism' in Goldman, R. and Kaufman, A. (eds) *The Separation of Powers — Does It Still Work?*, Washington, DC, American Enterprise Institute.

Stockman, D. (1986) *The Triumph of Politics*, London, Coronet.

Sundquist, J.L. (1981) *The Decline and Resurgence of Congress*, Washington, DC, Brookings.

Sundquist, J.L. (1986) *Constitutional Reform*, Washington, DC, Brookings.

Sundquist, J.L. (1988) 'Needed: a political theory for the new era of coalition government in the United States', *Political Science Quarterly*, vol.103, pp.613–35.

Toffler, A. (1980) 'Congress in the year 2000', *GAO Review*, Fall, pp.38–48.

Welch, S., Gruhl, J., Steinman, M. and Comer, J. (1992) *American Government*, St. Paul, West Publishing Co. (4th edn).

FURTHER READING

See Mayhew (1991), Mezey (1989) and Sundquist (1986) in the references.

Cox, G. and Kernell, S. (eds) (1991) *The Politics of Divided Government*, Boulder, Westview Press.

Fiorina, M.P. (1992) 'An era of divided government' in Peele, G., Bailey, C.J. and Cain, B. (eds) *Developments in American Politics*, Basingstoke, Macmillan.

Thurber, J.A. (ed.) (1991) *Divided Democracy: Cooperation and Conflict Between the President and Congress*, Washington, DC, Congressional Quarterly Press.

OVERLOAD IN AMERICAN GOVERNMENT

Guy Peters ★

1   INTRODUCTION

> Today our image of government is ... more that of the sorcerer's apprentice. The waters rise. The apprentice rushes about with his bucket. The waters rise even faster. And none of us knows when, or whether, the magician will come home.
>
> (King, 1975, p.286)

The concept of 'overload' was coined to describe the difficulties encountered by governments during the early 1970s. Several post-Second World War decades of rapid and sustained economic growth had enabled governments to expand public programmes with little concern for their costs. In the 1970s, however, the economic concept of scarcity was reintroduced. The energy crises of the 1970s, and the subsequent economic slow-down in all industrialized democracies, forced some substantial and wide-spread rethinking of public expenditure and of the public sector more broadly. Even countries with enviable records of public sector performance were deemed to face problems of 'ungovernability' (Scheuch, 1976; *Schweizer Monatshefte*, 1975). This re-examination of the role of government in turn contributed politically to the election of a number of conservative politicians at the end of the 1970s and early 1980s. The United States never had as extensive a public sector as most other Western democracies, and government has rarely had a positive image among the American public (Free and Cantril, 1968; Page and Shapiro, 1992). Despite its relatively small size, however, there was a popular feeling by 1980 that American government had grown too large and that a committed conservative President like Ronald Reagan was needed to clean up the 'mess in Washington'.

Overload extends beyond simple economic questions of public expenditure and its relationship to the total productive resources in the society. In this chapter I will be conceptualizing overload as an imbalance between the decisional capacity of a government and the demands being placed upon it. Governance problems may arise because of too many demands, inadequate machinery for processing demands and making decisions, or both. Further, overload may arise because the nature of the demands being placed on the system are difficult or impossible for government to address successfully through its usual routines. This broader sense of overload is a more difficult concept to measure than the ratio of spending to Gross National Product (GNP), but it also strikes at the more fundamental problems for governance. The seeming inability to control public expenditure and the deficit discussed below may be merely reflections of the problem, rather than the problem itself. It is, therefore, essential to understand just how American government copes with the myriad of demands placed upon it, as well as the behavioural and structural characteristics that often limit government's capacity to respond effectively.

To some extent overload never really ended for American government after the 1970s. The 1980s were a decade of real and perceived difficulties in governance in the US, albeit masked by the 'feel good' politics and ideology of the Reagan Administration. As the enthusiasm surrounding the Reagan years waned, the 1990s have begun with even greater perceived problems in governing. Books critical of government, such as *Can the Government Govern?* (Chubb and Peterson, 1989), *Why Americans Hate Politics* (Dionne, 1991), *Who Will Tell the People?* (Greider, 1992) and *Still the Best Congress Money Can Buy* (Stern, 1992), have become popular again. The presidential election of 1992 was to a great extent fought over the issues of the massive federal deficit, the need for more effective government management of the economy, inadequate health care, and the negative image of American government. Whereas much of the earlier discussion of overload was concentrated directly on issues of public expenditure and taxation, the discussion in the 1990s is more general and goes to the fundamentals of politics and government in the United States. Therefore this chapter will look at the dimensions and manifestations of overload, examine the causes, and then look at some possible remedies for these problems.

2   MEASURES OF OVERLOAD

Are we certain that overload exists in American government? While there is good reason to believe that overload, or something like it does exist, it is also important to try to gain some better idea of the magnitude of the problem. Again we can examine some obvious economic indicators, but we will also attempt to examine the structural questions of both 'policy gridlock' (Sundquist, 1988; Levine, 1988) and 'divided government' (Fiorina, 1992; but see Mayhew, 1991) in Washington, as well as the 'hyper-pluralism' that appears to cause stagnation in the policy process. Further, we need to look at the increasing range of difficult issues that government is being asked to solve, and at its (perhaps) diminished capacity to do so effectively.

2.1   ECONOMIC INDICATORS

If Americans were asked to name a clear indicator of the failure of their government, for most it would almost certainly be the federal deficit. Few industrialized democracies have good records at making their expenditures match their revenue resources, but the record of the US federal government in the 1980s and early 1990s has been especially bad. The federal deficit increased dramatically after 1981 when President Reagan enacted his version of supply side economics with its massive tax cuts. Then it grew even more rapidly in current dollar terms during the Bush Administration (see Table 3.1). The estimate is that the deficit amassed during President Bush's last year of office is almost $330 billion, and the accumulated federal debt at the end of 1992 is well over $4 trillion.

Table 3.1   Federal debt, 1946–91 ($million)

	Current	Constant[a]	Percentage of GNP
1946	270,991	1,396,861	104.2
1950	256,853	1,074,699	93.3
1955	274,366	1,008,699	76.4
1960	290,862	941,301	47.1
1965	323,154	956,077	38.2
1970	382,603	911,024	38.6
1975	544,131	917,590	35.7
1978	780,425	1,080,921	34.1
1980	914,317	1,066,881	34.2
1981	1,003,941	1,068,022	33.6
1982	1,146,987	1,146,987	36.5
1983	1,381,886	1,330,015	41.6
1984	1,576,798	1,464,019	42.8
1985	1,827,234	1,643,196	46.3
1986	2,132,913	1,869,336	51.6
1987	2,372,429	2,015,658	53.7
1988	2,585,466	2,131,464	54.6
1989	2,866,188	2,269,349	55.6
1990	3,113,263	2,400,357	56.7
1991	3,319,161	2,514,515	56.3

[a] Constant prices based on 1982 = 100.

These numbers appear astronomical to the average citizen who worries about being a few thousand dollars in debt, but when they are related to the productivity of the American economy the numbers are not really so large. In the first place, when converted to real (constant purchasing power) terms the growth of the deficit and the accumulated federal debt are not so dramatic. This reduced magnitude is even clearer if the debt is related to Gross National Product. For most of the post-Second World War period federal debt has been declining as a percentage of GNP, but that ratio began to increase again in the 1980s. However, the ratio, in the early 1990s, is substantially lower than at the end of the Second World War when it exceeded 100 per cent of GNP (Table 3.1).

Most people would argue that public debt generated during wartime is justifiable in light of the demands then facing government, but that debts accumulated in peacetime simply because citizens are unwilling to pay sufficient taxes to cover their expenditure wants are much less justifiable. This inability to cover expenditures with revenues, therefore, can be seen as a failure of public decision makers to display sufficient courage to make the difficult choices needed in government. It might also be seen as a failure of the public to understand that there is a budget restraint in government, just as there is in the private sector (Brittan, 1975) and that government can not necessarily fulfil all of their wishes.

2.2   PUBLIC EXPENDITURE AND REVENUE

The deficit is the outcome of the separate decisions about levels of expenditure and revenue. For some citizens, however, the continuing increase of public revenues and expenditures are therefore indicators of the inadequate decisional capacity of government. After voting for several Presidents and numerous legislators who promised not to increase taxes and to cut the size of the federal government, the public has some right to be sceptical about the capacity of their leaders to deliver on such promises. During the 1992 presidential campaign a Republican President blamed the Democratic Congress for big spending programmes, and vice versa. It appears that no one has been willing, or able, to fulfil their promises about reducing the size of the federal government (or at least controlling its growth).

During the 1980s public expenditures at the federal level more than doubled in current dollar terms and increased by almost 14 per cent in constant dollars (Table 3.2). These expenditures are not likely to decrease in the near future, given that the Office of Management and Budget classifies almost 80 per cent of the budget as 'relatively uncontrollable', or impossible to control without direct legislative action. The growth in federal revenues during this period was not as great, and hence the deficit increased, but revenue growth was still substantial. Federal revenues doubled during the 1980s and increased by 11 per cent in constant (deflated) dollar terms during that period. For many Americans, there was a clear sense that public spending and revenue were out of control and that the federal government could not manage its own fiscal household.

Table 3.2 Federal revenue and expenditure, 1980–90 ($million)

	Revenue		Expenditure	
	current	constant[a]	current	constant[a]
1980	517,112	603,398	590,920	689,522
1981	599,272	637,523	678,209	721,499
1982	617,766	617,766	745,706	745,706
1983	600,562	578,019	808,327	777,986
1984	666,457	618,809	851,781	790,883
1985	734,057	661,909	946,316	853,306
1986	769,091	675,234	990,258	869,410
1987	854,413	725,924	1,003,830	852,872
1988	908,954	749,344	1,064,044	877,200
1989	990,691	784,395	1,142,643	904,705
1990	1,073,451	827,641	1,197,236	923,081

[a] Constant prices based on 1982 = 100.

These problems of taxing and spending are to some extent even more evident at the state and local levels of government than at the federal level (see Table 3.3). Part of the 'Reagan revolution' was shifting a substantial amount of responsibility for policy to lower levels of government (Nathan and Doolittle, 1987). With that responsibility went the necessity to tax and spend more. State and local expenditures increased in current terms by almost 120 per cent during this period and by almost 35 per cent in constant terms. Revenues did not increase quite so rapidly, so that toward the end of the period state and local debt was increasing along with federal debt. State and local debt increased by almost 150 per cent in current terms during the 1980s. Although most state constitutions forbid their governments from running a deficit on current accounts, they can accrue debt on capital expenditures. These debts tend to be funded by issuing bonds. During difficult budgetary times, state governments may attempt to classify ordinary expenditures as 'capital' so that they can borrow more money. While the perception of governing problems was concentrated at the federal level, much of the increase in public revenue and spending was occurring elsewhere, albeit prompted by decisions at the federal level.

Table 3.3 State and local government revenue and expenditure, 1980–8 ($million)

	Revenue		Expenditure	
	current	constant[a]	current	constant[a]
1980	451,537	526,881	434,073	506,503
1981	506,728	539,072	487,048	518,136
1982	547,719	547,719	524,817	524,817
1983	593,461	571,185	566,990	545,707
1984	652,114	605,491	600,576	557,638
1985	719,607	648,879	658,101	593,418
1986	783,193	687,615	718,316	630,655
1987	842,589	715,879	775,318	658,724
1988	884,500	729,184	827,164	681,916

[a] Constant prices based on 1982 = 100.

2.3 HEALTH CARE

The deficit and public expenditure are to some extent 'meta-problems', resulting from the cumulation of the policy choices made in a number of different areas. There is also a sense that within particular policy areas there have been failures because of difficulties of American government in making decisions that might adversely affect some powerful interests. In no policy area is the complexity and failure of policy-making as clear as in health care (Aaron, 1992). Americans spend more for health care as a proportion of GNP than does any other industrialized democracy but the health outcomes for the public, as measured by infant mortality, are worse than for almost any other developed country. The health status of the black and Hispanic population appears more like that found in many Third World countries (Peters, 1993).

Policy-making in health illustrates many of the problems that American government encounters in any policy arena. One is the large number of private interests involved — doctors, hospitals, nurses, insurers, etc. — each with a stake in the outcomes of policy formulation and each well organized to make its views known to Congress and the bureaucracy. Further, there are a number of public actors at all levels of government that have some role in health policy and who have to be consulted about any reforms. Another is the *a priori* claims of market solutions to most social and economic problems in the US, and the associated resistance to large-scale public interventions. President Clinton has certainly done his wife no favours by assigning her the task of producing meaningful reform in this policy area.

2.4 CONFIDENCE IN GOVERNMENT INSTITUTIONS

One of the products of the problems with taxing, spending, and the deficit, as well as of numerous other problems with government, is a declining confidence of citizens in their government. Table 3.4 shows citizens' confidence in American institutions and indicates that confidence is generally declining, but has been declining precipitously for political institutions — most notably the Congress. In the autumn of 1991, at the time of the check 'bouncing' scandal in which members of Congress were allowed to have free overdrafts at the House of Representatives Bank, and several other revelations concerning perceived congressional excesses, confidence in Congress was lower than it had ever been in this particular Gallup poll. It appears that citizens no longer have a great deal of trust in their governing institutions, and do not believe that those institutions have the capacity to govern.

Table 3.4 Citizens' confidence in American institutions (% saying 'great deal' or 'quite a lot')

	Military	Church	Presidency	Supreme Court	Congress	Organized labour (trade unions)
1975	58	68	n/a	49	40	38
1981	50	64	n/a	46	29	28
1985	61	66	n/a	56	39	28
1989	63	52	46	43	32	26
1990	68	56	n/a	47	24	27
1991	69	56	50	39	18	22

(Source: Gallup Monthly Poll, October 1991, p.37)

As well as indicating the perceived failures of government, this loss of confidence may contribute to even greater problems of governance in the future. Governments govern most easily when their actions are perceived as being authoritative and are accepted with little question by citizens. When public regard for these institutions is so low, it is difficult for them to legislate in a creative manner, for fear of further alienating the public. They are then thrown back onto the politics of constituency service and the 'pork barrel' (public spending spread among congressional districts) that arguably helped so much to get them into their already unenviable position (Bailey, 1992). Public reaction against Congress in the 1992 elections, and the replacement of almost one-quarter of its members, may help to return that institution to a more authoritative, and proper, position in the public mind.

This decline of confidence is most pronounced for the federal government, but there also has been some erosion of support for state and local governments. Most Americans still say that they receive better value for money from local governments than they do from the federal government and tend to find their state taxes fairer than federal taxes, but also express their doubts about the efficacy of those governments (Advisory Commission on Intergovernmental Relations, 1991). The advantage that citizens have at the local level is that there are more tools by which they can directly influence government, including the referendum, the initiative (propositions placed on the ballot for popular vote by petition, totally by-passing the legislature) and recall (removing an incumbent from office) (Cronin, 1989). Further, the outputs of this level of government are more readily observable by citizens than are those of the federal government. Citizens can therefore see what they are receiving for paying their tax money and are more likely to accept the necessary taxation.

2.5   CITIZENS' BEHAVIOUR

I have discussed a number of indicators of government failure, and there are also possible indicators of citizen reaction to those failures and to the problem of overload. One of these indicators is voting behaviour in the 1992 presidential election. Not only did the voters change Presidents and replace almost one-fourth of Congress (the biggest change in that institution since 1948) but they also voted in great numbers for Ross Perot. This can be seen as an indication of the voters' disgust with business-as-usual in Washington. The 19 per cent vote for Perot was the most for any third-party candidate since Theodore Roosevelt ran as a 'Bull Moose' (Progressive Party) in 1912. In addition, the voters approved term limitations in all fourteen states in which it appeared on the ballot by significant margins; on average term limits received 66 per cent support from the voters. The public has shown that it is willing to use the ballot box as a means of addressing the perceived failures of government. The good news, however, is that a larger percentage than usual of citizens turned out to vote, indicating that they still believed that voting could affect the conduct of their government.

Other reactions of the public to the 'mess in Washington' have been less overt. One of the most interesting of these is tax evasion, even in a society that has had low and declining tax rates (at least for the federal income tax). While tax evasion can be considered as strictly a rational economic action to maximize personal income, it can also be seen as a political protest (Listhaug and Miller, 1985; Peters, 1992a, pp.220–3). As Rose and Peters (1978) argued almost two decades ago, tax evasion can be seen as an indicator of 'political bankruptcy' as government lacks sufficient authority to have citizens pay their taxes. While measuring tax evasion is difficult, the indicators that are available appear to show increasing evasion in the United States.

2.6   AN EXCESS OF DEMANDS?

Overload as we will be using it here involves a general failure of the governing capacity of a political system. This is usually seen to be a function of an excess of demands being placed on the system, and possibly a function of the inadequate ability of the decision-making institutions to process the demands that are being placed upon them. We need to be sure to remember that the problems may not simply be too many demands, but that the system may not be able to process even a much lower level of demand.

Further, the seeming 'excess' of demand on American government may actually be beneficial to government rather than an impediment to effective governance. One source of failure of governments is inadequate contact with the society so that decisions are made based on faulty or incomplete information. A multiplicity of demands, if conceptualized as information, may provide government with an enhanced ability to make necessary decisions. This is especially the case if there are means to force the multiple and often conflicting demands to be brought together and to confront one another. There may not be too many demands, the problem is that they are not processed effectively through the policy-making system.

SUMMARY

One of the most important indicators of overload in American government is the continuing budget deficit. While the problems this presents may be exaggerated, it still represents the difficulties that government has in making some policy decisions. Budgetary deficit is a summary measure of the problems of revenue and spending of the federal government, but problems with expenditure control are encountered at all levels of government with demands for spending programmes increasing, usually more rapidly than the resources available.

One policy failure has been health care. American health care is more expensive and less widely available than in other industrialized democracies and illustrates the typical problems that the government faces in any policy arena.

Citizens' reactions to government in the US have reflected the real problems of governance. The perceived problems are especially evident for Congress, but extend across the entire spectrum of government. Responses by citizens to the failures of government have been through overt political activity, but also through covert action such as tax evasion.

3   CAUSES OF THE PROBLEM

In Section 2 I painted a somewhat dismal picture of governance in the US in the early 1990s: there are a number of important, interconnected, and seemingly intractable problems facing American government. These problems extend beyond the obvious question of the deficit and go to the very heart of questions of governance. What has produced these problems? Are they a problem of excessive demands being placed on the system by the American people, and especially by organized groups of those citizens? Are they rather a function of the supply side, with government institutions and the actors within them being unwilling or unable to make the difficult choices among competing purposes and interests? Is it both? It is difficult to provide any single definitive answer to the question of the cause of these problems, but in Sections 4 and 5 we can look at some of the evidence about the possible causes of overload.

4 THE DEMAND SIDE: HYPER-PLURALISM?

The most commonly cited cause for overload in American government is the number of demands being placed upon it, without an adequate means of integrating and choosing among priorities. Described as 'hyper-pluralism' (Lineberry, 1986) the basic idea is that the US is a society of joiners who have found that organizing and lobbying government can produce substantial private benefits for themselves and people like them. This pattern of decision making, rather similar to that described by Lowi (1979) as 'interest group liberalism', further argues that all groups in the society are equally entitled to have their demands fulfilled. Samuel Beer (1982) described a similar phenomenon in the UK as 'pluralistic stagnation'; likewise, Mancur Olson's (1982) arguments about the decline of nations as a result of interest groups and 'distributional coalitions' would also fit into this same intellectual camp. More recently this pattern has been referred to as 'demosclerosis' (Rauch, 1992). This unwillingness to make choices was perfectly acceptable so long as there was plenty of money and government could afford to buy social peace through public expenditures and programmes. Once the luxury of seemingly endless wealth was over, government has come face to face with living with a pattern of governance that has become excessively expensive.

In addition to pressure groups organized on economic or attitudinal bases, government in the US must contend with interest expressed on a geographical basis. There is a 'parochial imperative' in American government that is manifested through lobbying and other pressure activities as well as through the behaviour of members of Congress in support of their districts. Beer (1976), for example, once argued that the intergovernmental lobby was the most effective lobby in the US, and other analysts have since documented the power of state and local government in Washington (Levine and Thurber, 1986). The representatives of these governments have the particular advantages of representing official entities and that most of them hold official positions, so that it is difficult for federal officials to deny the legitimacy of the demands being expressed. Some of the pressures exerted by subnational governments are for the allocation of already authorized grants (e.g. President Clinton's plans for new programmes to aid cities have already sparked a round of lobbying for funds by mayors and congressional delegations), while other pressures are for specific new benefits. Further, many economic issues also have a pronounced regional impact so that it may be difficult to disaggregate these types of pressures, e.g. proposed cutbacks in defence spending may be popular in the country as a whole, but are far from popular in regions that depend heavily on defence spending for jobs (Schmitt, 1993). In short, the pluralism of American politics is based on geography as well as economics.

Although governors and mayors are effective lobbyists at the federal level for benefits to their subnational regions, the most effective lobbyists are often Congressmen and Congresswomen themselves. One persuasive characterization of the contemporary Congress is that it has ceased to be a deliberative body debating the important issues of public policy and has become a machine for the re-election of its members (Mayhew, 1974; Fiorina, 1989). One of the most important components of the re-election machinery is the ability of members of Congress to 'bring home the bacon' in the form of federal grants and contracts for their districts. No member of Congress likes anything better than to be able to announce a new federal highway project, or the preservation of a defence contract, or perhaps even money for a local institution of higher education. These activities will offend none of the constituents (except perhaps the few who understand the cumulative effects of *all* the members of Congress doing this), unlike taking strong stances on controversial legislation which is almost certain to cost some votes. Shepsle (1988) sees the changes in Congress more in terms of the representational role becoming more important than the governance role of the institution.

The United States is not alone in having such a plethora of interest groups. Most Western European countries have as many or more interest groups as the US. What may be different, however, is the dependence of decision-makers on those interests for funding and even for information in the US, and the absence of other legitimate mechanisms for accommodating the interests. The United States has not had even the limited sense of corporatism found in Britain (Jordan and Richardson, 1982) so that the demands of interest groups are injected into the decision process relatively unprocessed and without groups having been forced to bargain among themselves over priorities and possible policy trade-offs.

Nor can we argue that 'public interest groups' constitute much of a protection for the American public from hyper-pluralism. These groups, such as Common Cause (McFarland, 1984; Rothenberg, 1992), were developed originally as an attempt to supplant the bias in the interest-group population in favour of particularistic benefits to relatively small segments of the population. Although more successful than some conventional interest-group theory might have led us to expect (Olson, 1965), public interest groups are still largely outsiders in the halls of power. This was certainly true during the Reagan and Bush Administrations and will probably continue to be true during the Clinton Administration. Taxpayer groups have been very successful at the state and local levels, including the passage of the famous Proposition 13 in California that reduced property taxes, but the federal level has proven more resistant to these pressures. That is in part true because of the absence of instruments of direct democracy (initiative and referendum) at the federal level, as well as because of the greater difficulty of organizing on the national level.

4.1 ISSUES

American government, and indeed almost any government, can do well if the demands being placed upon it are familiar ones, and if the claims being placed are divisible and bargainable. The old conflicts between labour and management over the division of the economic pie, and between rural and urban interests over the division of other public spending pies, are relatively easy to manage. Those demands can be bargained over, with both sides often gaining enough from their conflicts that interest-group leaders can claim to their members that they won. Increasingly, however, the demands being placed on American government and many other governments are less bargainable and more absolute. Claims of rights and claims of status — often based on ethnicity — are much more difficult for a political system to process, given that one side or the other is a clear winner and the other is a clear loser. Likewise, perceived moral issues such as abortion, school prayer, and homosexuals in the military tend to be indigestible for a political system more comfortable with compromise and 'splitting the difference'. Even a limited number of demands of this sort create the appearance, and perhaps the reality, of overload in government.

As well as being faced with a number of rather indigestible problems, the old problems and issues of American government appear to have become more difficult. Presidents are often judged by how well they manage the economy — ask George Bush — but they may have a declining capacity to exert control over it. The internationalization of economies, including even that of the US which has been more autarkic than most, means that this issue will depend upon international as well as national actors. The reform of health care is also a pressing issue for American government and one about which President Clinton campaigned vigorously. American government has been involved in health (albeit often in rather minimal ways) but the magnitude of the contemporary problem and the multiplicity of interests involved makes reform a formidable challenge to his administration.

4.2 THE PARTY SYSTEM

The degree of pluralism in the US is exacerbated by the nature of American political parties. These political parties often are not real organizations but loose aggregations of individuals largely put together for electoral purposes. Party cohesion has been increasing in Congress during the 1980s and 1990s, but remains low by many European standards (Rohde, 1991). Further, with the election of a Congress in 1992 with one-quarter new members, many of whom gained office by pledging to be independent of usual congressional pressures, the party may become an even less significant factor in institutional politics. Without strong political parties to aggregate demands the demands being expressed by interest groups are able to enter politics more directly (Almond and Powell, 1967).

This basic individuality of American legislators is further increased by the manner in which members of Congress and other politicians in the society must raise campaign funds. Running for office in the US is an extremely expensive proposition. The average candidate running for the House of Representatives in the 1992 election spent over $275,000 on their campaign, with one spending over $5 million (*New York Times*, 1993). The candidates for President spent an average of over $45 million (Ross Perot spent over $60 million of his own money on his campaign). The need to raise all this money places members of Congress under some pressure to take funds from interest groups, largely through the conduit of Political Action Committees (PACs) (Conway, 1991). There is little evidence that the interest groups actually can 'buy' the votes of Congressmen or Congresswomen through contributions, especially given that almost all sides of every issue has its own PACs, and members of Congress tend to take campaign money from a huge variety of sources (Grentzke, 1989; but see Davis, 1992). Still, these financial structures do provide the interest groups access to decision-makers if not actually their votes.

Analysts often focus on the role that interest groups play in congressional elections and in lobbying Congress. The presidency, however, also is significantly influenced by interest groups and often appears to lack the autonomy seemingly inherent in the office. Presidential candidates must raise much more money than congressional candidates, and may be even more beholden to interest groups than are legislators. Running for President can be seen in part as assembling coalitions of groups to support the candidate, and subsequent policy proposals also may be tied to those interests (Waterman, 1989). Some Presidents are able to free themselves from the bonds of interest groups more readily than others, but all must be conscious of the potential damage that antagonistic groups can do to a presidency.

Further, Presidents must cater to social and economic interests in filling cabinet and sub-cabinet posts if they want to become successful in particular policy arenas. For example, President Clinton's cabinet reflects attempts not only to cater to gender and racial interests, but also to specific economic interests in the society as well: Lloyd Bentsen was selected as Secretary of the Treasury in large part because of his ability to pacify Wall Street, and Bruce Babbitt, as Secretary of the Interior, provided someone well-known to environmental groups. The role of interest groups will be even more apparent as lower echelon positions within the executive branch are filled. Presidents may think that they are autonomous giants in Washington but soon find that like Gulliver they are bound by countless thin threads.

It is difficult to say that there are too many interest groups in the US, given the absence of any clear standard of how many would be the correct number. Open democratic societies tend to spawn a large number of interest groups, and for democratic reasons it is generally considered to be better to have more rather than fewer. What can happen with a proliferation of interest groups, however, is that there is an imbalance between the broader public interest and the collection of private interests represented by the groups.

4.3 EVALUATION

We have documented the extent of pressure group organization and access in the United States. This appears to be a case of very strong pluralism, if not hyper-pluralism. The manner in which the interest-group politics game is played in the US appears substantially different from other industrialized democracies, and it tends to provide the groups more direct influence over decisions. There does appear to be a very high level of demand being placed on government, with few institutions that can mediate effectively between interests and decision-makers. This does not mean by itself, however, that the level of demand overloads the decision-making capacity of the system. We need to look at the nature of that decision-making system before attempting any such judgements.

SUMMARY

One of the principal causes of overload is the number of interest groups and their access to decision makers — hyper-pluralism. Further, unlike many European countries, there is no means of forcing these interest groups to bargain among themselves to reduce the level of total demand being placed on the political system.

The range of issues that American government must now process has expanded to include a number of moral and social issues that are difficult to reconcile through the usual bargaining mechanisms.

The US party system permits somewhat more influence by interest groups than would be true for most European party systems. This is in large part a function of campaign finance and the ability of groups, through their PACs, to purchase access if not influence.

5   THE SUPPLY SIDE: THE DECISION-MAKING SYSTEM

Even if a government were beset by a host of demands from a variety of sources if it has the capacity to make decisions effectively and efficiently it may have few significant problems. There is, however, little reason to believe that the government of the US is in such a fortunate position. There are a number of structural and behavioural factors in American government that appear to reduce its capacity to make difficult decisions or, at times, any decision at all. The decision-making institutions of American government are highly fragmented, and find it difficult to make redistributive decisions. The preferred style of decision making has been to provide benefits to all groups, but that luxury has been replaced by scarcity and government is faced with some apparent deficiencies in its style of coping with demands.

5.1   DIVIDED GOVERNMENT

One of the standard critiques of government in the United States is that it has become a 'divided government' (Fiorina, 1992). The Constitution of the United States established a presidential system in which the President and Congress are given co-ordinate powers over policy. This fundamental separation of powers has been accentuated by the increasing tendency of voters to elect a Congress and a President of different political parties. Since the end of the Second World War the President and both houses of Congress have been controlled by the same party for only eighteen years and in six of the remaining years just the Senate has been controlled by the same party as the presidency.

The Founding Fathers intended the separation of powers to restrain the activity of the federal government, but differences in partisan control have greatly accentuated a barrier to an active government. The election campaign in 1992 was filled with discussions of 'gridlock' in Washington and the negative consequences of the conflict between the President and Congress over policy. The Reagan and Bush years had a number of instances of the President vetoing legislation passed by Congress with the Congress trying (usually without success) to override the veto. The sense was that the two institutions were incapable of working together to govern the country.

No American President can be successful without good working relations with Congress. The President has several opportunities to influence Congress with speeches each year

The academic literature has also had its share of discussions (Sundquist, 1992; Fiorina, 1992) of the difficulties that divided government imposes on decision-makers. The sense of these discussions is that divided government is an almost inherent disqualification to effective governance. The election of Bill Clinton will end the partisan division between the executive and legislative institutions but the constitutional division between those institutions persists. Given the lack of integration in American parties and the need of individual Congressmen and Congresswomen to satisfy their own constituents, some division in practice may also remain. The Democratic controlled Congress may quickly tire of taking its cues from the President, especially if the President's programme will not reflect well in their constituencies. President Clinton promises a tighter federal budget with less in the way of 'pork barrel' programmes for members of Congress, and he has faced real difficulties with Congress. Those difficulties may be mitigated by the anti-incumbent, anti-business-as-usual stances of many of the newly elected members. Indeed in early March 1993 Congress was pressing the President for bigger expenditure cuts than he had proposed.

Likewise, there are also numerous new and continuing questions of institutional politics — such as proposals for a line item veto (the ability to eliminate one item from the budget without vetoing the entire budget) and continuing debates over the legislative veto — that may accentuate the political differences between the two branches. Even if the two branches are controlled by the same political party, they still have important institutional priorities and interests that will generate conflict, or at a minimum active politics. American government is almost inherently divided to some extent along these institutional lines and, along with the independence of the judiciary, there are continuing barriers to speedy governmental action.

However, the assumption that divided government is an inherent barrier to effective government is not supported by all analysts. David Mayhew (1991), for example, argues that for most of the post-Second World War period divided government was quite effective in running the US, and could pass needed legislation at almost the same rate as when the President and Congress were from the same party. In this analysis the real breakdown in governance has come in the 1980s and 1990s with a much stronger ideological division between the President and Congress. Especially during the Bush presidency there was strong partisanship and ideological 'warfare', with relatively little significant domestic legislation being passed. Even some of the bills that were passed, such as the Budget Enforcement Act of 1990, were so ridden with compromise that they have proven ineffective at their stated purposes.

During the Reagan and Bush presidencies Congress itself became a more partisan body, with party unity in voting on legislation becoming more like European parliamentary systems rather than their historical record would lead one to expect. Will this be an advantage to Clinton as an incoming Democratic President? It probably will be to some degree, except that with one-quarter of the Congress newly elected, and often elected as 'outsiders' who could act independently, party unity may again decrease as it did on the NAFTA (North American Free Trade Agreement) vote. The new members, and some old ones with marginal constituencies, may not be willing to accept so much direction from the party but will want, and have, to act more independently. Further, the unity of the Democratic Party may be a function of their opposition to relatively ideological Republican Presidents and may wane with a Democrat in the White House.

The apparent strength of the divided government argument can be minimized in several other ways. First, it is important to note the frequency of this pattern of division at the state level as well as at the federal level. Voters appear to choose to have a separation of partisan control in their governments, perhaps with the intention of limiting the ability of either party to implement too radical a set of programmes: this may be no more than a means of enforcing centripetal politics. Before the 1992 elections eighteen of the 50 state governments were divided, with both houses of the state legislature being controlled by a different party than the governor's. Another twelve states had one house of the legislature coming from a different party than the governor. Secondly, many other industrialized democracies have their own forms of division, and appear to be able to govern successfully (Pierce, 1991; Peters, 1992b). While the divided government critique is appealing, it must be seen as just one aspect of a complex set of institutional arrangements that may contribute to difficulties in governing a complex and increasingly divided society.

5.2   THE BUREAUCRACY

We have been looking at the executive branch of government as almost entirely consisting of the President: the manner in which the Constitution defined that branch. However, the modern reality is that the executive branch is composed of over 3 million civilian federal employees divided into a large and bewildering array of public organizations. The expansion of the public bureaucracy is characteristic of any contemporary government, but two factors tend to distinguish the American public bureaucracy from its counterparts elsewhere: first, there is recruitment of many senior officials from outside the public bureaucratic career structure and, secondly, its division into a number of relatively autonomous organizations. Both of these factors tend to accentuate the role of interest groups in the governing process.

The 'in' and 'outers'

First, unlike most industrialized democracies, the President and his or her department secretaries can appoint a number of political officials to leadership positions in the federal agencies. Whereas in most countries the internal career structure would fill all but a very few positions, a change in party in Washington means a change of some 3,000 officials (MacKenzie, 1987). Two or three tiers of positions in a department may be filled by 'outsiders' before one encounters career officials. These temporary public servants generally have strong political party connections, but they also frequently have interest-group connections as well. The practice increasingly appears to be that officials recruited from the outside will have strong connections with the 'policy community' surrounding the department or agency, meaning that he or she will have both substantive knowledge and some commitment to one side or the other of the policy disputes within that community.

The door to government employment is a revolving one, and many of the individuals who join an administration remain for only a limited time before returning to private sector employment. This pattern of recruitment gives government access to a pool of talent that would be unavailable to most other governments, but also means that government leaders are more closely linked to private sector interests. Again the increasing organization of all types of interests and all views on a policy makes the linkage to the private sector less one-sided than it might otherwise be, and a variety of views may be present in government. However, the degree of diversity varies from one administration to another: the Reagan Administration was particularly careful in appointing only individuals that agreed with its policy priorities. Generally the capacity to make autonomous and allocative decisions in the public sector is still diminished.

Autonomous organizations

Organizations in the American public bureaucracy generally have their own political connections to Congress and to pressure groups, rather than having those connections channelled through a minister and a few senior civil servants. For our purposes here, this political autonomy is important primarily because it makes the agencies more subject to interest-group pressures. They must make their own way in the world of institutional politics in Washington, and in so doing often must rely upon the support of organized interests in the society. These interest groups are the allies of the agencies, but they may also prevent them from making autonomous decisions that might harm the interests.

The pressure that interest groups can place on the bureaucracy come directly as well as through Congress, especially through congressional committees. The traditional means of describing this pattern of relationships among the three sets of actors — interest group, agency and congressional committees — is as an 'iron triangle' or a 'cozy little triangle' (Ripley and Franklin, 1987). The basic concept is that these three actors are linked in a symbiotic relationship and attempt to exclude other actors from involvement — even more than is true for other countries the US has a number of governments or sub-governments more than it has a government (Rose, 1980). This segmentation within government is a fundamental cause of many of the problems experienced in governing.

The dynamics of 'iron triangles' provide interest groups access to the agencies responsible for the programmes that directly benefit them. The commodity programmes within the US Department of Agriculture, for example, have numerous contacts with producers' groups and receive political support in exchange for access of those groups to decision-making. The interest groups also gain access to the congressional committees and subcommittees, in large part because these committees tend to be composed of representatives whose districts are directly affected by the programmes in question. For example, in the 102nd Congress (1990–2) the subcommittee in the House of Representatives responsible for the peanuts and tobacco crop support programme in the Department of Agriculture had members from the states of Texas (3), North Carolina (2), Kentucky, Georgia and Wisconsin, all but one being states that produce at least one of those two commodities. Likewise, the subcommittee of Banking, Finance and Urban Affairs — responsible for urban policy — had representatives from almost every major metropolitan district in the country. In each case, these Congressmen and Congresswomen on the committees must pay close attention to their constituents, whether as individual voters or when functioning as members of pressure groups.

Similarly, the administrative agency and the congressional subcommittee have a great deal to gain from their interactions. The agency has every incentive to co-operate with the congressional subcommittee(s) that oversee its programmes. That co-operation is essential for their receiving the financial and policy support they will require in the future. This support can be particularly important when the agency is likely to become involved in conflicts with others over bureaucratic 'turf'. The committee can gain information about policy from the agency. More importantly, its members want to be sure that the agency will continue to provide good service to their constituents.

The familiar 'iron triangle' description of American policy making is a good place to begin in understanding the process, but there are a number of caveats. The most important is that the exclusivity that once characterized these interactions has been broken down by the proliferation of interest groups described above. The conventional wisdom about how to describe the relation of interests to American government is now through 'issue networks' or 'policy communities' (Heclo, 1978; Walker, 1991); Jones (1982) refers to these emergent policy-making systems as 'big, sloppy hexagons'. These concepts imply that there are now a range of interest groups involved in each policy area, rather than just the producer groups that had tended to dominate decisions during the 'iron triangle' period. In particular, consumer groups have become better organized and have been able to gain greater access to decision making. For example, an issue like health care now evokes participation from organized groups of physicians, nurses, community health professionals, hospitals, insurance companies, state and local governments, and consumer groups. These groups certainly do not speak with a single voice on health care reform.

Whether the 'iron triangle' or 'issue network' approach is more accurate, both of them relate to an administrative structure that is highly decentralized by comparative standards. Rather than acting as if they were components of integrated departments, the ties with Congress and interest groups provide administrative agencies with sufficient autonomy to make many of their own decisions. This also results in overt conflict over policy by the agencies and their departments. For example, in late 1992 the Food Safety and Inspection Service of the Department of Agriculture became embroiled in a dispute over labelling packaged foods with the Food and Drug Administration (FDA) (Department of Health and Human Services). The Food Safety and Inspection Service, more responsive to agri-business interests (especially the meat and poultry industries), wanted minimal nutritional information on food labels, while the FDA wanted much more extensive labelling (Burros, 1992). The FDA was acting in response to the increasingly powerful consumer and health promotion groups, as well as to the professional values of its members. This internalization of interest-group conflict within government delayed new food labels by several months, although the FDA won in the end.

We must also remember that the structure of Congress is as decentralized as that of the federal bureaucracy. Despite numerous attempts to impose greater central control over committees, and to develop more responsible parties within Congress, the committees and subcommittees continue to exercise a great deal of autonomous control over policy (Smith and Deering, 1990). If the concept of hyper-pluralism at the demand stage states that every interest group is entitled to influence over policy, then the decentralization of Congress provides a number of receptive localities in which those numerous groups can exert that influence. Further, decentralization in Congress makes taking the difficult allocative decisions required to reduce some of the problems of overload all the more difficult.

The net result of the decentralization of Congress and the difficulty in making allocative decisions is that American government is prone to take inconsistent, and therefore inefficient, decisions about policy issues. The example most often cited is the continuing support for tobacco production through the Department of Agriculture whilst the Surgeon General (Department of Health and Human Services) and other health and consumer organizations spend a good deal of time and effort attempting to persuade Americans not to smoke. Even if these health groups were successful within the country, the Department of Agriculture and the Department of Commerce would probably continue to market US tobacco products overseas.

Procedures

Not only is the structure of decision making in the federal bureaucracy, and Congress, more subject to pressure-group influence than in other countries, the procedures they must follow in their work also permit a good deal of influence for interest groups. Most federal rule making is done through the process of writing regulations that ramify or specify the legislation passed by Congress and in so doing the agencies can exercise a good deal of discretion (Bryner, 1987). The Administrative Procedures Act of 1946, which governs the making of regulations (Freedman, 1980; Shapiro, 1988), specifies two forms of rule making. The simpler is informal or 'notice and comment' rule making in which the agency wishing to make a new regulation must publish notice of the intent to regulate, receive comments from affected citizens and/or interests, then publish a draft regulation and receive more comments before having the regulation go into effect. Interest groups monitor the *Federal Register*, in which all these notices are published, and are ready to respond with their own views on any regulation.

In some instances either the nature of the regulations or the specifications of the enabling legislation will require an agency to use a formal rule-making process. This procedure requires a formal hearing rather like a court room proceeding, with the participants represented by legal counsel and the rules of evidence in effect. Despite the appearance of a legalistic process, formal rule making also involves a large element of influence by the affected interests. The principal participants are usually affected industries or groups and the arguments, albeit couched in legal terms, are about the winners and losers. Thus, even this formalistic manner of making rules within the bureaucracy permits a substantial involvement of private interests.

The activities of the independent regulatory agencies are a special case of rule making by federal organizations. Beginning with the Interstate Commerce Commission in 1887 Congress has created a number of agencies that are independent of presidential control and have as their function the regulation of an important sector of the economy. In practice, many of these organizations have become dependent for political support upon the very economic interests they were designed to regulate (Noll, 1971; Bernstein, 1955). No one else could supply these 'independent' agencies with the expertise and the political support they required in order to do their jobs effectively.

Although simple 'capture' theories are now almost as *passé* as the 'iron triangle' characterizations of interest-group relations to Congress and agencies, these independent organizations still appear more subject to interest-group pressures than are the agencies that are clearly parts of the executive branch (McCubbins and Schwartz, 1989). What has changed, however, is that there is a larger variety of interest groups that are paying attention to the activities of these commissions and attempting to influence their decisions. In particular, consumer groups are now organized along similar lines than producer groups and are attempting to limit actions of the agencies that favour producers (Moe, 1989). In this instance hyper-pluralism may be beneficial for governance, given that it forces some direct confrontation of the conflicting interests of groups and also requires the agency to make a choice, or a compromise, between them.

5.3 THE COURTS

The courts might be thought of as the one area of government that would be immune to the influence of pressure groups, but this does not appear to be the case. There is an old adage in American politics that the 'courts follow the election returns', and indeed the power of appointment of federal judges enables the President to ensure that they do, albeit imperfectly given the life-time tenure of federal judges. Beyond the link to political parties, however, the courts are also responsive in many instances to organized interests. The influence that groups can have on judicial proceedings is exercised in two important ways.

First, there is the mechanism of the *amicus curiae* (friend of the court) brief. American courts, and especially the federal courts, permit groups who are not parties to a case but which have a view on it to file a brief stating their opinions on the issues at stake. These briefs may be legal arguments and originally were seen as legal advice to the court. More recently, these briefs have become expressions of the views of interest groups and the perceived effects that the decision may have on the interest writing the brief (Caldeira and Wright, 1990; O'Connor and Epstein, 1986). Perhaps the most famous *amicus curiae* brief was that filed by the National Association for the Advancement of Colored People in the *Brown v. Board of Education* case that led to the desegregation of public schools. The evidence in this brief was largely sociological and psychological, pointing to the impact that segregation had on the self-esteem and performance of black school students. This evidence went well beyond what might be expected from a conventional legal argument, and enabled this interest group to influence a case (in this instance seemingly in a significant manner) without actually being a part of the litigation.

The number of *amicus curiae* briefs indicates that interest groups must believe they have some impact: in one year the Supreme Court received almost 3,500 briefs from almost 1,000 organizations (Caldeira and Wright, 1990, p.793). If nothing else these briefs open the legal system to a variety of views that would be excluded under a more restrictive regimen of involvement of 'friends' in the legal process. They force the consideration of a range of issues concerning the potential impacts of the narrow decisions that courts must make. The courts may still decide a case on the narrow basis but, for better or worse, the full range of potential impacts is available to them.

Secondly, pressure groups may become involved in legal proceedings through class action suits. The conventional legal doctrine is that an individual or group must demonstrate some substantial and differential harm in order to have standing to sue. The courts have, however, also allowed groups of people, often organized interest groups, to bring a suit on behalf of themselves and all other similar people — the 'class' — who may be affected by a public decision or a private action. Suits of this manner have been especially important in the areas of environmental protection, consumer issues, and civil rights. They provide redress against harms that might be too vague or too generalized to receive any compensation under conventional rules of standing. Class action suits have been sufficiently successful that some conservative groups have sought to limit their use; for example, during the Reagan and Bush presidencies there were several attempts to limit their use in environmental regulations.

SUMMARY

The divided institutions of American government cause decision-making to be more difficult than in parliamentary regimes. The 'gridlock' that characterized the Bush Administration has already re-emerged in the first year of the Clinton Administration. Despite these problems there is some evidence that effective policies can still be made.

As well as being divided among the three major branches, the government is divided functionally. This division exists within the public bureaucracy and within Congress and makes the direct influence of pressure groups on government much easier. Furthermore, the recruitment of government executives from outside the civil service can also exaggerate those influences.

The court system of the US permits interest groups to have some influence over their decisions. Both the use of the *amicus curiae* brief and class action suits open the courts to the influence of groups other than the parties of the particular case in question.

6 CONCLUSION: IS THERE OVERLOAD AND IF SO WHOSE FAULT IS IT?

To be able to make a decision about whether overload exists in American government one must first decide what a properly functioning government would look like. We might look at some secondary evidence, such as the levels of deficit spending, to determine if government is coping with the demands being placed upon it. Likewise, we might want to look at the level of inconsistency of outputs of government in order to assess the response to all demands being placed upon it, rather than its making the difficult allocative decisions that it may need to make. Further, a well functioning government might have mechanisms for accommodating and aggregating these multiple demands, rather than finding it necessary to accede to most, if not all, of them.

Although seemingly very minimal, government in the United States may find it difficult to pass the above tests of competence. Certainly the level of federal deficit spending is substantial, especially given the American obsession with the question of deficits (Savage, 1988). Although constrained by their state constitutions, as mentioned above, the level of debt creation by state and local governments also has been increasing dramatically. American government appears incapable of getting its fiscal house in order, and the structural characteristics of the system may have a great deal to do with that difficulty. Similarly, government appears incapable of restraining the growth in spending, again after any number of politicians at federal, state and local levels have campaigned vigorously for restraint.

The potential culprits in this story have been identified, and all bear at least a part of the blame. There are numerous interest groups pounding on the doors of government agencies and Congress wanting benefits for their members. American political parties do not do a particularly good job of aggregating the numerous demands being expressed or at putting together coherent packages of ideas and programmes. The institutions of government are largely fragmented and are extremely susceptible to pressure group influences. These institutions often appear almost incapable of aggregating demands and making difficult choices. In short, the system of government in the US is well designed *not* to be able to make and implement tough decisions. There are contrary examples, e.g. tax reform in the late 1980s (Birnbaum and Murray, 1987), but the general pattern has not been one of effective resistance to interest group demands. This did not matter much when resources were plentiful, but that time has long since vanished.

Although we are not entirely certain where to affix the blame for any observed deficiencies in this system of government, there is no absence of proposed remedies for its shortcomings. Some of these are very simple, requiring 'only' the willingness to make the needed changes; Ross Perot received almost 20 million votes asking people whether they wanted to do it (fix the system) or only talk about it. The mere application of political will is seen by people like Perot's supporters to be sufficient to solve all the numerous and complex problems of policy making in American government.

If the simplistic remedy of political will is insufficient, there are a number of more 'tinkering' remedies that are available to decision makers. Again, these issues were raised frequently during the 1992 presidential campaign. For example, President Bush campaigned on behalf of a balanced budget amendment at the federal level such as that constraining most state governors (including Bill Clinton). He likewise argued on behalf of a line item veto so that a President could cut out particular items in a spending bill (presumably 'pork barrel' projects) while allowing most of the spending bill to go into effect. While both of these measures have their drawbacks, especially for a federal government more responsible for regulating economic conditions than subnational governments, they are often seen as means of addressing important policy problems in American government.

There is a wide selection of proposals for the reformer of American politics to choose among. All of these proposals have some merit, although in all probability none would really 'solve' the problem of overload. In part, many Americans rather like the complex and difficult process of governing enshrined in the Constitution and the developments since the adoption of the Constitution. These Americans believe that this complexity, and the associated difficulties in doing anything in government, help to make their government less likely to do things (like pass new tax legislation) that might harm them. Further, the ease of access in the system while sometimes producing 'gridlock' and minimal response to problems, also permits access to groups which might otherwise be excluded from the process altogether. These defenders of the system, combined with the monumental difficulties in producing significant change (especially of a constitutional sort) will mean that American government is likely to continue to struggle for the foreseeable future.

REFERENCES

Aaron, H.J. (1992) 'Health care financing' in Aaron, H.J. and Schultze, C.L. (eds) *Setting Domestic Priorities: What Can Government Do?*, Washington, DC, The Brookings Institution.

Advisory Commission on Intergovernmental Relations (1991) *Changing Public Attitudes on Government and Taxes*, Washington, DC.

Almond, G. and Powell, G.B. (1967) *Comparative Politics: a Developmental Approach*, Boston, Little, Brown.

Bailey, C.J. (1992) 'Congress and legislative activism' in Peele, G., Bailey, C.J. and Cain, B. (eds) *Developments in American Politics*, London, Macmillan.

Beer, S.H. (1976) 'The adoption of general revenue sharing: a case of public sector politics', *Public Policy*, vol.24, pp.127–95.

Beer, S.H. (1982) *Britain Against Itself*, New York, Norton.

Bernstein, M.H. (1955) *Regulating Business by Independent Commissions*, Princeton, Princeton University Press.

Birnbaum, J.H. and Murray, A.S. (1987) *Showdown at Gucci Gulch*, New York, Random House.

Brittan, S. (1975) 'The economic contradictions of democracy', *British Journal of Political Science*, vol.2, pp.1–23.

Bryner, G.C. (1987) *Bureaucratic Discretion: Law and Policy in Federal Regulatory Agencies*, New York, Pergamon Press.

Burros, M. (1992) 'Strict new rules on food labelling are being delayed', *New York Times*, 8 November.

Caldeira, G.A. and Wright, J.R. (1990) '*Amici curiae* before the Supreme Court: who participates, when, and how much?', *Journal of Politics*, vol.52, pp.782–806.

Chubb, J.E. and Peterson, P.E. (eds) (1989) *Can the Government Govern?*, Washington, DC, The Brookings Institution.

Cigler, A.J. and Loomis, B.A. (eds) (1989) *Interest Group Politics*, Washington, DC, CQ Press.

Conway, M.M. (1991) 'PACs in the political process' in Cigler, A.J. and Loomis, B.A. (eds).

Cronin, T. (1989) *Direct Democracy*, Cambridge, Mass., Harvard University Press.

Davis, F.L. (1992) 'Sophistication in corporate PAC contributions: demobilizing the opposition', *American Politics Quarterly*, vol.20, pp.388–410.

Dionne, E.J. (1991) *Why Americans Hate Politics*, New York, Simon & Schuster.

Fiorina, M.P. (1989) *Congress: the Keystone of the Washington Establishment*, New Haven, Yale University Press (2nd edn).

Fiorina, M.P. (1992) 'An era of divided government', *Political Science Quarterly*, vol.107, pp.387–410.

Free, L.A. and Cantril, H. (1968) *The Political Beliefs of Americans*, New Brunswick, Rutgers University Press.

Freedman, J.O. (1980) *Crisis and Legitimacy*, New York, Cambridge University Press.

Greider, W. (1992) *Who Will Tell the People?: the Betrayal of American Democracy*, New York, Simon & Schuster.

Grentzke, J.M. (1989) 'PACs and the congressional supermarket: the currency is complex', *American Journal of Political Science*, vol.33, pp.1–24.

Heclo, H. (1978) 'Issue networks and the executive establishment' in King, A. (ed.) *The New American Political System*, Washington, DC, American Enterprise Institute.

Jones, C.O. (1982) *The United States Congress*, Homewood, Dorsey.

Jordan, A.G. and Richardson, J.J. (1982) 'The British policy style, or the logic of negotiation' in Richardson, J.J. (ed.) *Policy Styles in Western Europe*, London, George Allen & Unwin.

King, A. (1975) 'Overload: problems of governing in the 1970s', *Political Studies*, vol.23, pp.284–96.

Levine, C.H. (1988) 'Human resource erosion and the uncertain future of the U.S. civil service', *Governance*, vol.1, pp.115–43.

Levine, C.H. and Thurber, J.A. (1986) 'The Reagan Administration and the intergovernmental lobby' in Cigler, A.J. and Loomis, B.A. (eds).

Lineberry, R.E. (1986) *Government in America*, Boston, Little, Brown (3rd edn).

Listhaug, O. and Miller, A.H. (1985) 'Public support for tax evasion: self-interest or symbolic politics?', *European Journal of Political Research*, vol.13, pp.265–82.

Lowi, T.J. (1979) *The End of Liberalism*, New York, Norton (2nd edn).

McCubbins, M.D. and Schwartz, T. (1989) 'Structure and process, politics and policy: administrative arrangements and the political control of agencies', *Virginia Law Review*, vol.75, pp.431–82.

McFarland, A.S. (1984) *Common Cause: Lobbying in the Public Interest*, Chatham, Chatham House.

MacKenzie, G.C. (1987) *The In and Outers*, Baltimore, Johns Hopkins University Press.

Mayhew, D. (1974) *Congress: the Electoral Connection*, New Haven, Yale University Press.

Mayhew, D. (1991) *Divided We Govern*, New Haven, Yale University Press.

Moe, T.M. (1989) 'The politics of bureaucratic structure' in Chubb, J.E. and Peterson, P.E. (eds).

Nathan, R.P. and Doolittle, J. (1987) *Reagan and the States*, Princeton, Princeton University Press.

New York Times (1993) 'Spending on races for U.S. House soars to a record $313.7 million', 2 January.

Noll, R.B. (1971) *Reforming Regulation: an Evaluation of the Ash Council Proposals*, Washington, DC, The Brookings Institution.

O'Connor, K. and Epstein, L. (1986) 'The role of interest groups in Supreme Court policy formation' in Eyestone, R. (ed.) *Annual Review of Public Policy*, New York, JAI Press.

Olson, M. (1965) *The Logic of Collective Action*, Cambridge, Mass., Harvard University Press.

Olson, M. (1982) *The Rise and Decline of Nations*, New Haven, Yale University Press.

Page, B.I. and Shapiro, R.Y. (1992) *The Rational Public*, Chicago, University of Chicago Press.

Peters, B.G. (1992a) *The Politics of Taxation: a Comparative Perspective*, Oxford, Basil Blackwell.

Peters, B.G. (1992b) 'Bureaucrats and political appointees in European democracies: who's who and does it make any difference?', paper presented at the annual meeting of the American Political Science Association, Chicago, September.

Peters, B.G. (1993) *American Public Policy*, Chatham, Chatham House (3rd edn).

Pierce, R. (1991) 'The executive divided against itself: cohabitation in France, 1986–1988', *Governance*, vol.4, pp.270–94.

Rauch, J. (1992) 'Demosclerosis', *National Journal*, 5 September, pp.1998–2003.

Ripley, R.B. and Franklin, G.A. (1987) *Congress, the Bureaucracy and Public Policy*, Chicago, Dorsey (4th edn).

Rohde, D.W. (1991) *Parties and Leaders in the Postreform House*, Chicago, University of Chicago Press.

Rose, R. (1980) 'Government against sub-governments: a European perspective on Washington' in Rose, R. and Suleiman, E.N. (eds) *Presidents and Prime Ministers*, Washington, DC, American Enterprise Institute.

Rose, R. and Peters, B.G. (1978) *Can Government Go Bankrupt?*, New York, Basic Books.

Rothenberg, L.S. (1992) *Linking Citizens to Government: Interest Group Politics at Common Cause*, New York, Cambridge University Press.

Savage, J.D. (1988) *Deficits and American Politics*, Ithaca, Cornell University Press.

Scheuch, E.K. (1976) *Wird Die Bundesrepublik Unregierbar? (Is the Federal Republic Ungovernable?)*, Köln, Arbeitgeberverband der Metallindustrie.

Schmitt, E. (1993) 'More aid for workers urged in military conversion plans', *New York Times*, 7 January.

Schweizer Monatshefte (1975) Wird Die Schweiz Unregierbar? (Is Switzerland ungovernable?), Symposium Issue, April.

Shapiro, M. (1988) *Who Guards the Guardians?*, Athens, University of Georgia Press.

Shepsle, K.A. (1988) 'Representation and governance: the great legislative trade-off', *Political Science Quarterly*, vol.103, pp.461–83.

Smith, S.S. and Deering, C. (1990) *Committees in Congress*, Washington, DC, CQ Press (2nd edn).

Stern, P.M. (1992) *Still the Best Congress Money Can Buy*, Washington, DC, Regnery Gateway.

Sundquist, J.L. (1988) 'Needed: a political theory for the new era of coalition government in the United States', *Political Science Quarterly*, vol.103, pp.613–35.

Sundquist, J.L. (1992) *Constitutional Reform and Effective Government*, Washington, DC, The Brookings Institution (rev. edn).

Walker, J.L. (1991) *Mobilizing Interest Groups in America*, Ann Arbor, University of Michigan Press.

Waterman, R.W. (1989) *Presidential Influence and the Administrative State*, Knoxville, University of Tennessee Press.

FURTHER READING

See Chubb and Peterson (1989), Mayhew (1991), Sundquist (1992) and Walker (1991) in the references.

A QUESTION OF PARTY

Alan Ware ★

1   INTRODUCTION

The role of political parties in the government of the United States seems paradoxical. On the one hand, the presidency and the Congress are occupied by people who are the nominees of political parties; most of the senior officials appointed to a President's administration have been active in, or supporters of, the President's party; Congress organizes its business around parties, especially in its committees, where influence is linked to length of service on a committee and that, in turn, is linked to being a member of a particular party caucus; and, despite the frequency with which members of Congress vote against the majority view in their congressional party, party is still the best predictor of how members will vote in the chamber. This suggests party power in the governing of America.

On the other hand, parties can be seen as relatively weak influences on public policy, at least by comparison with the role of parties in Europe; the President does select some non-party people, and even those associated with the opposing party, to the administration; often local and regional influences do override party influences in deciding how a member of Congress votes; and, most especially, one party may control the White House while another controls the Congress. Indeed, between 1952 and 1992 'divided government' was far more common than 'undivided government': only fourteen of those years were ones of 'undivided government'.

However, America's political parties are paradoxical in another way. In some respects they seem to be democratic — amongst the most democratic parties in the world; in other respects, though, they are highly undemocratic. It is these features which form the subject of this chapter which explores four aspects of the parties and the American party system:

1   The range of choice offered by the parties to voters at elections.

2   The barriers to individuals or groups becoming strong candidates for one of the parties.

3   The process of selecting candidates.

4   The process of policy formation and selection within the parties.

By examining these four aspects of relationships within the parties and between the parties a judgement may be made on how much control over government people can actually exercise through the parties. However, before turning to this, it is necessary to mention two key features of America's parties which are important in understanding these four aspects: the two-party character of politics in the United States and the long history of its two main parties.

1.1 TWO-PARTISM

The US has probably the most 'pure' two-party system in the world. This is evident in the various levels of elections: for the presidency, for the members of the Congress, and for the 50 state governments.

Presidential elections

Presidential elections are held every four years. Since the American Civil War (1861–5), every presidential election has been won by either the candidate of the Democratic Party or the candidate of the Republican Party. Indeed, on only one occasion since then (1912) has some other candidate even finished second in the ballot. (And that candidate in 1912 was the Progressive, Theodore Roosevelt, who had been President, as a Republican, from 1901 to 1909.) On no more than a few occasions have other candidates for the presidency received more than 1 or 2 per cent of the total vote — in the twentieth century this has happened only in 1912, 1924, 1948, 1968, 1980 and 1992. Apart from 1912, when the Democrats and Republicans received between them only 67 per cent of the vote, the lowest share of the vote they have obtained between them has been 81 per cent (in 1992).

In 1980 and 1992 the 'third' candidates did not bother even to form a new party; they ran as Independents against the candidates of the two main parties. It was not worth their while trying to do so, because third party candidacies have enjoyed even less success at other levels of office than at the presidential level.

Congressional elections

The 435 members of the House of Representatives are elected every two years. The members of the Senate (of whom there are 100) are elected for a six year term; one third of the chamber comes up for election every two years. Of the total votes cast in congressional elections, about 97 or 98 per cent are for the Democratic or Republican candidates. Success by third party candidates is rare. For example, in 1990 a Socialist candidate in the state of Vermont won a House seat, but this was the first time in more than 30 years that a third party candidate had won a seat in the chamber.

Elections for state governments

Each of the 50 states elects its own governor and its own state legislature. Here too we find a similar pattern to that evident in federal elections. Third party candidates hardly ever win elections, and usually receive little more than a small proportion of the votes. In recent years there have been one or two successful campaigns for state governorship by Independents, but these campaigns have not been matched by similar successes in the legislatures. One of the interesting features of the US party system is that it is the same parties which dominate state government elections — the Democrats and Republicans — as dominate federal elections. (This is not the case in all federal systems: in the Canadian provinces, for example, there are a number of parties which are powerful in provincial elections but which do not contest federal elections.) When strong third parties have emerged at the state level — and this has been rare — they have been absorbed a few years later into one of the two major parties. This happened in the 1940s to the Farmer-Labor Party in Minnesota which merged with the Democrats.

1.2   THE LONGEVITY OF THE PARTIES

The two American parties are survivors! The Democratic Party can trace its origins to the Democratic-Republican Party which emerged in the 1790s in opposition to the Federalist Party. That was the very first American party system. In the early 1800s the Federalists collapsed and America came to be governed by an élite who had been associated with the Democratic-Republicans. In the 1820s, though, a popular movement based in the expanding south and west of the country captured the Democratic Party presidential nomination for Andrew Jackson. This heralded the beginning of what is often referred to as the Second Party System. In opposition to the Democrats there developed a Whig Party which provided intense competition with the Democrats until the mid-1850s. In the growing crisis over the expansion of slavery during that decade the Whigs collapsed, and this permitted a new party — the Republicans — to become serious challengers to the Democrats. The victory of their presidential candidate, Abraham Lincoln, in the election of 1860, and the later victory for the Union Army in the Civil War cemented the Republican Party's position in the two party system.

Since the Civil War the Democrats and Republicans have resisted challenges from strong third parties: the Populists in the 1890s, the Socialists in the first two decades of the twentieth century and the Progressives in 1912 and 1924. Often the established parties incorporated some of their ideas and image, thereby reducing the distinctive appeal of the new party. Indeed, at no time since the Civil War has there been an intra-party crisis in either party that was so great as to make it appear as if the party system could be transformed radically. In no other country have the two largest parties enjoyed such dominance for so long. Even the party's symbols — the donkey of the Democrats and the Republican's elephant — date from the nineteenth century.

SUMMARY

At both state and federal levels of government the US has a two party system.

The Republican and Democratic Parties have been competing against each other since the mid-1850s. Third party challenges have been resisted.

2 THE RANGE OF CHOICE OFFERED BY PARTIES TO VOTERS

One of the most common criticisms made of American parties is that the policies they advocate are so alike that American voters are not offered a real choice at elections. Now there are two questions to be asked about this criticism. First, is it true that the parties are very similar? Secondly, if it is true, is it the case that most Americans would prefer to vote for a party which had very different kinds of policies? If the answers to both of these questions is 'yes', then we would be forced to conclude that the American party system was not very democratic. For a country to be described as a democracy it must surely be the case that voters have the opportunity to vote for the kinds of policies they would like to see their government pursue. Therefore, both of these questions should be examined.

2.1 HOW SIMILAR ARE THE PARTIES?

Those who claim that the American parties resemble Tweedledum and Tweedledee in being so alike often begin their argument by pointing to the absence of a large social democratic or a large Communist Party in the US. They claim that, unlike other liberal democracies, America does not have large parties of the left — parties that in the past have advocated state ownership of the means of production, social and economic equality, and extensive social welfare policies. This claim is largely, but not wholly, correct. Socialist and communist parties in the US have been insignificant electorally; they have so few resources that usually most voters do not even know that they have candidates contesting elections. But America is not quite so unusual as its critics sometimes suppose. There are other liberal democracies — notably, Ireland and Canada — where the parties of the left are relatively weak; the British, German and French models with their large and well-organized parties of the left, are not the only kinds of party system found in the liberal democratic world.

Nevertheless, America is unusual in having *such* a weak left wing. In Ireland the Labour Party usually obtains about 10 per cent of the vote, and has participated in coalition governments; in Canada the New Democratic Party usually wins about 15 per cent of the vote and on occasions holds the balance of power when neither of the two large parties has a parliamentary majority. Clearly, this represents much greater influence for parties of the social democratic left than they have in America.

However, even if the range of political beliefs espoused by the main political parties is narrower in the US than elsewhere, are the two parties really Tweedledum and Tweedledee in character? The answer to this question is actually slightly more complicated than one might suppose, and therefore I will answer it in two parts.

The first part of the answer is that, in general, there have been quite signifi-cant differences between Democrats and Republicans over a number of key issues. Since the New Deal in the 1930s Democrats have usually been far more sympathetic to federal government intervention in the economy. Again, from the 1930s onwards, most Democratic politicians have been more sympathetic than Republicans to the rights of trade unionists; this difference remains, although the salience of the issue has declined as trade unionism has declined. Furthermore, on a number of social issues since the 1960s — including abortion — the majority opinion among Democrats has been far more liberal than has been the view of most Republicans. Of course, there have been a number of issues on which the parties have not diverged mark-edly, notably on America's role in the world during the Cold War era. But it should be noted that the consensus in America on this issue parallels a simi-lar consensus in many European countries, such as the UK and West Ger-many, and on this matter the US was not the odd one out. Finally, if one tries to make an 'on-balance' judgement about how similar the Democrat and Republican Parties are, the striking point is that they are not the most obvious candidates for being the Tweedledum and Tweedledee of the politi-cal party world. That distinction probably belongs to the two main parties in Canada — the Liberals and Progressive Conservatives — whose policies have often displayed far greater similarity than those of the Democrats and Republicans.

Nevertheless, there is a complication in resolving the question of how alike the two parties are, and to understand this we must look at the second part of the question: how the parties developed after the end of the Civil War.

Amongst many white people in the defeated South, the Republicans were regarded as a Northern party who had made the war inevitable. Conse-quently, the Republican Party remained weak in the South, and this weak-ness was made even worse by the political upheavals of the early to mid-1890s. These upheavals produced a political system in which the South became overwhelmingly Democratic and much of the rest of the country heavily Republican; in only a few states was there genuine two-party com-petition. (In the South most black people became disenfranchised, so that from the 1890s onwards the Southern electorate became almost entirely a white electorate.) The result was that both parties contained large progress-ive wings and large conservative wings. Someone who was very conserva-tive in his views would likely be a Democrat if he came from the South but a Republican if he was from elsewhere in the country. This meant that in presidential elections both parties would be trying to appeal to a whole range of beliefs and traditions — and this helped to create the impression that the parties were really very similar.

The election of Franklin Roosevelt in 1932 and the advent of his New Deal legislation led to a partial change in this situation. The main wing of the Democratic Party was now based firmly in the North, with a fairly strong following among manual workers, and this was the wing of the party which supported, amongst other policies, government intervention in the economy and the rights of trade unionists. But the South remained a solid Democratic bastion, so that Democratic presidential candidates had to continue to try to appeal to very different kinds of voters in the two parts of the country. Democrats in Congress were also divided in this way; anything between one-third and one-half of the Democratic members would be Southerners who were usually far more conservative than their non-Southern counter-parts. The Republican Party was also split; it had a minority wing of moderate-liberal voters and politicians who came primarily from the north-eastern part of the country. The rest of the party was generally conservative in its views.

The result was that from about the 1930s to the 1960s the Democratic Party was primarily a moderate-liberal party with a strong conservative wing, while the Republican Party's conservatism was tempered by its moderate-liberal wing. As in the preceding era, therefore, presidential candidates had to try to woo a far wider cross-section of voters than parties in most other party systems had to. This contributed to the impression that there was really very little difference between the two parties.

One of the great changes in American politics over the last 25 years has been the ending of this 'sectional politics' dimension to the American party system. As this has occurred, the moderate-liberal wing of the Republican Party has been greatly diminished, as these kinds of voters have moved towards the Democrats; the result is a far more uniformly conservative party than in the past. In part, the collapse of its liberal wing was due to the influx of conservative activists into the party in the early 1960s; they sought to marginalize liberal influence. The transformation of the Democratic Party, though, is due to social, economic and political change in the South. The role of non-Southern Democrats in furthering civil rights in the South helped to end white Southern antagonism to the Republican Party. Newly enfranchised black people gave their support overwhelmingly to the Demo-crats, and this, together with economic modernization in the South, trans-formed the electoral geography of the region. The South is still far more conservative than most of the rest of the nation, but its most conservative voters and politicians now tend to be Republicans, while the moderates are more likely to be Democrats. The result is that nationally in the 1990s the Republican Party is more uniformly a conservative party than it was 30 years ago while the Democrat Party is more uniformly a moderate-to-liberal party.

(a) 1904–28 elections

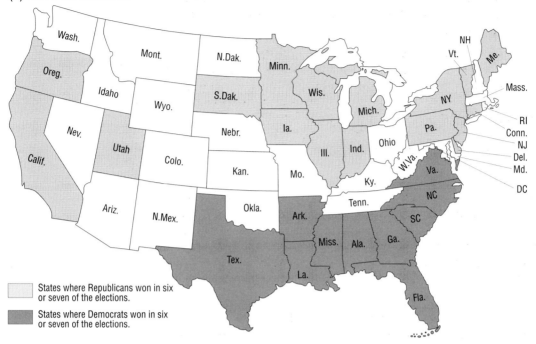

States where Republicans won in six or seven of the elections.

States where Democrats won in six or seven of the elections.

(b) 1968–92 elections

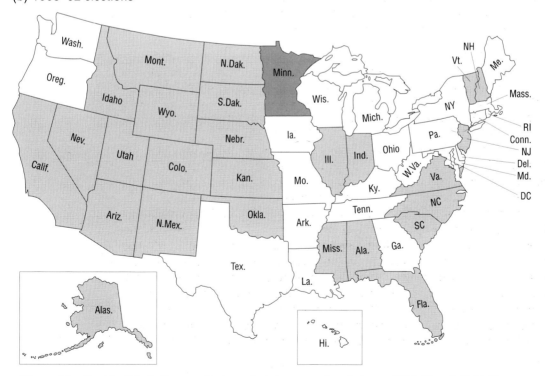

Figure 4.1 *Presidential election results in each state: comparison between 1904–28 and 1968–92*

An indication of how much the 'sectional' element in American politics has declined can be seen by comparing Figure 4.1(a) with (b). Figure 4.1(a) shows the results in each state of the seven presidential elections held between 1904 and 1928, two of which were won by Democrats and five by Republicans. Figure 4.1(b) shows the results in each state of the seven presidential elections held between 1968 and 1992. Once again, this was a period dominated by the Republicans: they won five of the seven presidential elections. Figure 4.1(a) shows the sectional element of American politics at the time. Despite losing most of the presidential elections, the Democrats still won ten of the eleven Southern states regularly, but nowhere else in the country did they enjoy such success. The states won regularly by the Republicans in the years 1904–28 were all in the north and west of the country. Electorally America used to be a country that was divided into two. This pattern disappears in the mid-twentieth century, and it is completely absent in Figure 4.1(b). There is only one state the Democrats won regularly, Minnesota. The states the Republicans won on six or seven occasions are to be found in all regions of America. From the map it would seem that Republican strength is concentrated in the far Midwest and in the Rocky Mountain states. But this stronghold is less significant than it might appear since none of the thirteen states is highly populated, between them they have a mere 12 per cent of the votes for electing a President.

Of course, the need to build up majorities in presidential elections still results in the parties moving towards the political centre and this creates an impression that they are alike. But the fact is that they are more distinct than they were in the past because now they are *national* parties competing for a national electorate. Moreover, the differences between the parties are quite clear in a number of areas — such as 'lifestyle' issues, including abortion — and these are areas on which voters are generally far more divided than they are in Europe.

2.2 WOULD AMERICAN VOTERS PREFER DIFFERENT PARTIES?

We have seen that American voters are faced by major parties which are probably more similar than those in Europe, although claims that they are identical ideologically are wrong. Given that the effective choice in the US seems to be rather limited, it is worth asking whether there is any evidence that Americans would vote for very different kinds of parties if these parties could obtain the resources to make themselves competitive.

One possible argument can be disposed of immediately. It is often argued, especially in the popular press, that evidence of American disillusionment with its parties is found in the very low, and falling, levels of voter turnout. Only about 50 per cent of Americans vote, compared with about 70 per cent of eligible voters in other countries. However, this comparison is misleading. If the electoral turnout of registered voters in the US is compared with turnout of registered voters elsewhere, America is *not* completely out of line with the rest of the liberal democratic world, although it does have one of the lower turnout rates. The problem in America lies in registering to vote.

This is often difficult and responsibility for doing so lies with the individual citizen — governments play a very limited role in registration. Moreover, in many states voters have to be registered to vote several months in advance of the November election. Given high residential mobility in the US, a rather large proportion of potential voters are not actually able to vote in November because they no longer live in the place where they are registered to vote. (Interestingly, just two weeks after the 1992 elections, in which electoral turnout increased for the first time since the early 1960s, it was reported that one effect of the economic depression of the early 1990s had been to reduce residential mobility in the US significantly; Nelson Polsby, personal communication.) Once these kinds of *structural* factors are taken into account, the US no longer seems so unusual. Of course, a good case can be made for saying that the difficulties associated with voter registration constitute a serious limitation in American democracy, but that is not a limitation emanating from the party system *per se*.

As for the fact that voter turnout has been falling since the 1960s, much of this too can be explained without reference to the unpopularity of the parties. In particular, the Voting Rights Act of 1965 enfranchised many of the poorest groups in American society; in most liberal democracies these are the groups least likely to vote because they are less likely to have the educational skills and so on with which they can engage the electoral process. Their turnout rates at elections are usually lower than those of other social groups, so that their inclusion in the electorate is always likely to be associated with a decline in electoral turnout; this, indeed, is what seems to have happened in the US.

Nevertheless, these factors do not entirely dispose of the point that American parties are not popular with the public. There is considerable evidence from opinion surveys that most voters do not trust the parties or believe that they are doing a good job, and public distrust in the parties has been evident since the mid-1960s, so it is not a short-term phenomenon. Yet very few of the respondents to these surveys indicate that they want parties with radically different policy agendas. Often they want politicians to behave differently, to be more honest, less self-seeking and so on; often they want them to be more effective, but without knowing how this might be achieved; and sometimes they want a different combination of policies than those seemingly offered by most Democrats and Republicans. (For example, part of the appeal of the Independent Ross Perot in his campaign for the presidency in 1992 was that he was thought to combine the social liberalism of the Democrats with the economic conservatism of the Republican Party.) But there is no evidence to support the view that a European-style social democratic party or Christian democratic party, or any other kind of party, would better represent the views of Americans than the Democrats and Republicans.

To use a phrase that is often heard in discussions of US politics, the very 'porousness' of American parties means that they try to respond to new movements by adapting their own stances. They try to offer the voters, by way of images and promises, what they think the voters want. New parties are not necessary because the existing parties are always trying to respond to what they think majority opinion is. But in making this point a problem with American parties is highlighted. They focus on responding to demands from within the electorate through the promises they make; they are ill-adapted to the need to make voters understand that governments must sometimes make unpopular choices in circumstances when there are no feasible popular choices. That is, the American party is responsive but it is not very responsible, and therein lies a weakness in its democratic nature.

SUMMARY

The two main parties in America do not differ as much as parties in European countries usually do, but there are still important differences between them.

The parties can respond to new issues, and there is no evidence that many voters would vote for very different kinds of party.

3   BARRIERS TO INDIVIDUALS OR GROUPS BECOMING STRONG PARTY CANDIDATES

In the United States it is usually easy for an individual to try to become a party's candidate for a public office. In many states that person has to obtain the signatures of a relatively small number of his or her fellow citizens. This enables the individual to enter the party's primary election, and the democratic character of primary elections is examined in Section 4. However, in this section we are concerned not with how easy are the *formal* procedures in becoming a candidate, but with the very different question of whether the whole process of contesting elections tends to favour some kinds of people and discriminate against others. To use an analogy: in theory, most people can try to gain selection for their country's Olympic games' team (by entering a large number of preliminary races and so on), but in practice selection is confined to a small number of full-time athletes. In some sports, such as show jumping, a person probably will not be a candidate for selection unless they have been riding horses from quite a young age. This means that few Olympic representatives in this sport will have grown up in poor households. By contrast, in track and field events the opportunities for competitors from these sorts of backgrounds are much greater. In the case of the American party system it is important to understand the barriers to someone becoming not merely a candidate, but a strong candidate of a party, that is, a candidate who stands a real chance of winning the election.

There are three factors to be considered here: the structure of political careers, the method of choosing candidates, and the resources required in running a campaign.

3.1   THE STRUCTURE OF POLITICAL CAREERS

Liberal democracies vary in the extent to which there is a political 'career ladder'. For example, it has been much more common in Canada than in the UK for someone to be elected as an MP having had very little experience of public office beforehand. Moreover, in Canada, the typical cabinet minister spends less time in parliament before becoming a minister than would his or her British counterpart. One feature of the US system is that there is quite a long political career ladder; on the other hand, there are probably more opportunities than in most countries for certain kinds of people to miss out on the lower 'rungs' of the ladder.

At the top of the ladder most serious contenders for the presidency would have held elected public office before running for the presidency. But even here there are three exceptions or qualifications to be noted to the general pattern. First, there is a strong tradition, dating back to the first President (George Washington) of important military leaders being nominated for the presidency or vice-presidency. Dwight Eisenhower became the Republican's candidate in 1952 — the first time he had run for public office — and he was re-elected President in 1956. In 1968 the strong third party candidate George Wallace had an ex-general as a vice-presidential running mate, and in 1992 Ross Perot had an ex-admiral as his running mate. Secondly, a candidate who has had only limited experience as an elected politician might have sufficient experience in appointive offices to make him or her an attractive candidate. George Bush falls into this category, before his nomination as vice-presidential candidate in 1980 his career in elective public office had been very brief. Thirdly, in periods when there is widespread dissatisfaction with politicians, some candidates with no experience of public office may be attractive to voters simply because they are not 'insiders'. This was part of the appeal of multi-millionaire Ross Perot in 1992.

The career ladder is long partly because there are so many different levels of office (local government, state government, a two-chamber legislature and so on) and partly because having a territorial political base is usually so important in developing a political career. Very often a US Senator will have served in the House of Representatives before gaining election to the Senate. The political profile and reputation he (and there is an important point attached to my use of the male pronoun here) has gained in the latter adds to his ability to be taken seriously as a Senate candidate. (Even after the 1992 elections in which women candidates did far better than ever before, more than 90 per cent of Senators were men.) He will have a core of previous financial backers and activists whom he can rely on in his campaign for the Senate. And, assuming he has been popular in his district, there is a solid group of voters who can be presumed to support him. Again, the typical member of the House will probably have had experience in the state legislature, and so on.

However, there are many politicians who have not had to build a career on a 'rung-by-rung' basis. At the level of state governor or the Senate there are more examples than there are at the presidential level. The very rich or the famous can sometimes run successfully for such offices: ex-actor Ronald Reagan is a good example. His first bid for public office was when he won the governorship of California in 1966. Similarly the famous basketball star Bill Bradley won a Senate seat without having held any elective public office previously. All the way down the ladder there are opportunities for this kind of 'leap-frogging', if one has the resources to do so.

Ronald Reagan's first election campaign for governorship of California, 1966

Today, because there is a career ladder of this kind, there are many types of potential candidate who are much less likely to embark on a political career or to carry on with one even after a successful start. Being a politician requires time and resources, and this makes it primarily a middle-class occupation. Certain careers are also more compatible with political activity, and lawyers are heavily represented amongst America's politicians, partly because the visibility of their political activity is often good for business. The continuity required in political careers has also been a major barrier to the participation of women. During child-rearing years many women have not been able to devote the time required to political activity, and afterwards they have, in effect, 'missed the boat'.

3.2 THE METHOD OF CHOOSING CANDIDATES

Section 4 examines in more detail the ways in which candidates for public office are chosen. For our purposes here there is one feature of the nominating system in America that is especially salient: there is no *co-ordinated* method of selecting candidates. A candidate for, say, a seat in the state legislature is selected in an entirely separate election from state legislature candidates in other districts or from the candidate for the House of

Representatives. This contrasts with the process used in many European countries, such as Norway, where a party-list electoral system means that members of the party are choosing a whole list of candidates at the same time. In these countries, if it is decided within a party that there are too few candidates from one social group — such as women — it is possible for the party to decide to have a quota for the number of women candidates. Indeed, this happened in the German Social Democratic Party a few years ago. But, for two reasons, it is not possible in America.

First, nearly all candidates in the US today are chosen in direct primary elections, so that it is the party voters, not the parties, who are selecting candidates. Quotas cannot easily be imposed on party voters. Secondly, candidates for the Congress or for the state legislatures are mostly chosen in single-member districts: that is, each member of the legislature represents a territorially-defined district (in other words, 'places') and each of them sits for a different 'place'. The people who are voting for a candidate in 'place' A are an entirely different set of people from those who vote in 'place' B. Even if most of the voters in both places agreed that there should be, for example, more women candidates, it is extremely difficult for them to co-ordinate their actions in the voting booths so as to ensure that at least one district will have a woman candidate. The result has been that the same groups which have always been over-represented in elected public office in America — white, middle-class, middle-aged men — continue to be over-represented. Whereas the political representation of women has increased dramatically in Scandinavia and Germany, for example, they are among the groups that continue to be heavily under-represented in the US. Despite the major advance made by women candidates in the 1992 elections, in 1993 only 6 per cent of Senators and 10 per cent of the members of the House were women.

The method of selecting candidates has not always been so decentralized. In the heyday of the urban political machines (the mid-nineteenth to the early twentieth century) county party organizations played a far greater role in party nominations. Then party bosses often did try to 'balance the ticket', selecting, say, an Irish-American for one area, an Italian-American for another area, and so on. The idea was to attract voters from a wide range of ethnic groups. But the idea of 'balance' was never extended to women, even after they obtained the franchise. Nor, usually, was it granted to new, or growing, ethnic groups until they had demonstrated that they were too big a force to ignore. The collapse of the party machines — and the critical period for this was the late 1930s and 1940s — ushered in an era of highly decentralized candidate selection. Paradoxically, this seemingly democratic move has made it more difficult for excluded groups to increase their share of 'strong' candidates.

3.3   RESOURCES REQUIRED FOR AN ELECTION CAMPAIGN

Election campaigning in the US is characterized by the expense of electioneering and by the fact that it is the individual candidates themselves who are largely responsible for raising the funds required. The major exception to this reliance on the candidates is the presidential election for which the cost of campaigning is borne largely by funds from federal taxes. A peculiarity of the American parties is that they raise a relatively small proportion of the money required for campaigning.

One of the main reasons for this is the absence of a fee-paying party membership: American parties do not have *members* in the way that most European parties do. The sheer expense of campaigning, combined with the centrality of the candidate in raising funds, once again tends to advantage those social groups who are already advantaged by the nomination process. Raising money from interest groups is best done by those with close connections to them, and the interest groups with the greatest resources are those connected to businesses, trades and professions.

Furthermore, interest groups themselves prefer to give money to those candidates they think are likely to win, and hence be influential. And, most often, these candidates are the incumbents. Consequently, incumbents find it much easier to raise funds than others, and this contributes to their continued incumbency. Change in the composition of any elected body in America, therefore, is likely to be rather slow; the domination of white, middle-class, middle-aged males is perpetuated.

In emphasizing the importance of money in American elections, however, we should not fall into the trap of assuming that the well-heeled always win elections or that politicians are always beholden to those who have contributed money to their campaigns. Political scandals can undermine the best-funded of campaigns; sometimes popular candidates with a large base of activists in a community can overcome much better-funded opponents; and not all candidates are personally wealthy, although US Senators, in particular, are drawn disproportionately from America's wealthiest section of the population. Interest groups can often secure no more from a successful candidate to whom they have given campaign funds than the right to be heard by the politician and his or her political staff. Campaign contributions do not usually buy votes directly in Congress (or elsewhere). The reason for this is that there are so many interest groups providing funds to candidates through Political Action Committees that no politicians, however unscrupulous they are, could end up by pleasing all the groups that have funded or supported them.

Nevertheless, it is clear that the reliance of American elections on money — relatively more than on campaign workers — further produces a bias in the process of electing political leaders. It is a bias in favour of a status quo in which a certain section of American society tends to be heavily over-represented amongst America's elected public officials. Of course, rather similar biases exist in other countries: politicians are more likely to be middle class, male, and fairly well-educated in most liberal democracies. The peculiarities of the American system are that the biases work more than elsewhere in favour of those with access to political money, so, for example, there are far more lawyers than teachers to be found in Congress and the state legislatures. Moreover, the importance of an 'early start' in electoral politics and the decentralization of candidate selection procedures both militate against rapid change in the political élite.

Where there has been significant change in the composition of America's political élite over the last 30 years has been in the growth of black and Hispanic representation. (In 1993 just under 9 per cent of members of the House of Representatives were black, while a further 4 per cent were Hispanics.) But, since these groups are disproportionately over-represented among the poorest sections of society, this raises the question of how such a breakthrough has been achieved. Two factors have been significant. First, the territorial concentration of these groups in particular neighbourhoods, combined with the use of single-member districts in legislative elections, has meant that concentrated minority ethnic groups have been increasingly able to elect their own people. Secondly, since the 1960s, federal and, increasingly, state courts have been vigilant in requiring that the boundaries of electoral districts are drawn in such a way that minority ethnic groups are not under-represented. But even in poor, inner-city districts the political leaders who emerge today are likely to be middle-class representatives of poor communities. Candidates' needs for electoral resources is present even here, so that the long-standing biases of the American process of leadership selection are perpetuated.

SUMMARY

Although not all politicians begin at the bottom rungs, there is a long career ladder in the US.

The process of selecting candidates is highly decentralized.

Individual candidates, and not the parties, are responsible for acquiring most of the resources for running an election campaign.

All these factors influence who is recruited to elective public office, with the result that white, middle-class, middle-aged men are over-represented.

4   THE PROCESS OF SELECTING CANDIDATES

Superficially, the processes for selecting the Democrat and Republican candidates for public offices seem highly democratic. In practice these procedures are rather less democratic than they appear at first sight. I will outline these processes, and in doing so it is necessary to distinguish those used for selecting the presidential candidates from the ones used for most other elected offices. The two procedures are different and some of the undemocratic features of the former are not present in the latter.

4.1 PRESIDENTIAL SELECTION

In theory, the Democratic and Republican Parties choose their presidential candidates at their National Conventions. The Conventions are held once every four years in the July or August preceding a general election (which is always held in early November). In practice, recently, the candidates have been chosen well in advance of the Conventions; the purpose of a Convention is solely to ratify the choice and to generate a great deal of publicity for the candidate and the party. Most of the delegates to the Convention are chosen in state primary elections held between February and June. About 30 or so of the states usually hold primary elections, while in the remaining states (many of them smaller states) delegates are chosen in a series of party meetings culminating in a state convention. Since most delegates are bound by the terms of their selection to vote for a particular candidate, it is public knowledge after each set of primary elections how many delegates each candidate has. Having a majority of delegates pledged to vote for him or her is sufficient for a candidate to be nominated, so that once a candidate has secured the appropriate number of delegates the nomination has thereby been secured.

"We Know It's Cockeyed, But It's The
Only Roulette Wheel In Town"

(Source: from Herblock *Herblock On All
Fronts*, New American Library, 1980)

At the very latest, it will be known by June of an election year who will be the party's candidate. But the dynamics of the selection process are such that the nomination is secured much earlier than this, often after only a few primaries have been held. At a very early stage in the selection one candidate always emerges as a 'front-runner', and the widespread belief that he or she is likely to secure the nomination makes it difficult for rivals to secure funds and maintain momentum for their campaigns. Many of them drop out after only a few primaries leaving the 'front-runner' with the easy task of beating the one or two candidates who remain.

Presidential selection has not always taken this form. Until 1968 most delegates were chosen in state caucuses and conventions. State delegations to the National Convention were often controlled by powerful political figures in the state parties. Although these party leaders might agree on whom the best candidate was, this did not always happen and it could be uncertain at the beginning of a Convention as to who would emerge eventually as the party's presidential candidate. Although most of the important decisions would be taken in private discussions — rather than on the floor of the Convention itself — the Convention was a major decision-making arena and not the stage-managed public-relations exercise that it is today.

The ultimate cause of the change in the presidential nomination process was the disastrous Democratic Convention in Chicago in 1968. That year President Johnson decided not to seek re-election because of the declining popularity of his policy on the Vietnam War. Johnson used his political influence to help secure the presidential nomination for his Vice-President, Hubert Humphrey. Humphrey did not win any of the primary elections that year, and his nomination was seen by anti-war Democrats as having been foisted on the party by county and state party leaders. The anti-Humphrey forces regarded the process as undemocratic because in several states the power of the party leaders prevented anti-war supporters from participating effectively in delegate selection. Partly as a sop to the defeated groups, it was

The controversial Democratic Convention in Chicago, 1968, and anti-Vietnam War demonstrators outside the Democratic Party's convention hotel

decided at the Convention to set up a Commission (the McGovern–Fraser Commission) to examine the process of delegate selection. The report of this Commission set in train a series of changes that were to transform the presidential nomination process.

Most members of the Commission did not envisage the consequences of their proposals, which were to establish binding rules on the process of selecting delegates. But administering these rules proved to be so complicated in those states which had previously used caucuses and conventions in delegate selection that many of them switched to the use of presidential primaries. Because of the publicity attached to primaries, most state Republican Parties had to follow this lead, and the result was a transformation of the nomination process. By 1976 that transformation was complete, with most delegates now being selected in primaries.

From the point of view of democracy this might seem to be a highly desirable way of selecting candidates. After all, a large number of people (the party's voters) can be involved in choosing a presidential candidate. Nevertheless, there are four reasons why there may be objections to these procedures:

1   Low voter turnout in presidential primary elections.

    Voter turnout can be quite low in presidential primaries; even in those elections with high turnout it is often no more than half the turnout in presidential elections. As a result, most Americans do not actually participate in the process of choosing the Democratic and Republican candidates.

2   Effective choice lies with a small minority of voters.

    Because of the 'band-wagon' effect in which the winner of the early primaries quickly becomes the party's candidate, many of the later primaries do little but ratify the choice made in the early primaries. Hence the effective choice over the presidential nomination lies with a relatively small number of voters who vote in the earlier primaries.

3   Many well-qualified candidates do not seek the nomination.

    In most election years many of the best-qualified candidates choose not to seek their party's nomination. In 1992, for example, several senior Democrats — including Governor Mario Cuomo and Senator Bill Bradley — stayed out of the presidential race. The main disincentive to running is that the process is long and expensive. Most bids for the presidency have to be planned over two years in advance of the presidential election itself. Not only does this place an enormous strain on candidates, but it can detract quite seriously from the work in the offices they hold currently. This is one reason why politicians who have left office are usually amongst the strongest candidates for the nomination: this was the case with Jimmy Carter in 1976 and Ronald Reagan in 1980. The point is that if the best candidates are not available to be selected, a supposedly democratic process is devalued.

4   The absence of a 'filter' to prevent poor candidates from being selected.

Any party politicians can put themselves forward as presidential candidates and, providing sufficient party voters vote for them, they will
become the party's presidential candidate. They may hold views, or
have an image, that makes them unelectable in the general election; they
may be ill-suited for the job they would have to do if they were elected
as President; and they may have little experience in government. But
despite these seeming disadvantages they can still become their party's
candidate. The previous system for nominating presidential candidates
'filtered out' such would-be candidates — the professional politicians
knew many of the weaknesses of presidential hopefuls. But party voters
cannot be expected to have such knowledge. Choice is not valuable
unless one has the skills to choose well (or at least not badly) and the
problem is that the present system of presidential primaries provides
few safeguards against bad choices by party voters.

There is nothing wrong with leaving the final choice of a presidential candidate to the party voters; indeed, from the viewpoint of democracy there is a
great deal to be said in favour of such a procedure. If, say, a party's members of Congress, Senators, state governors and party chairs met together to
draw up a list of three candidates for a national presidential primary, there
would be both a mechanism for 'filtering out' weak candidates and popular
participation in the selection process. However, this is not the process that is
used in the United States, and since 1972 the American system has yielded
candidates with the following fundamental weaknesses:

- George McGovern (too much on the liberal wing of the Democratic
  Party to be elected).

- Jimmy Carter (insufficient experience in government).

- Ronald Reagan (inability to grasp the details of policy issues).

- Walter Mondale (too much identified with a declining part of his party's
  electoral coalition).

- Michael Dukakis (lack of experience in national political institutions).

- George Bush (held many positions in government, but none of them for
  sufficiently long for the quality of his judgement to be known).

- Bill Clinton (lack of experience in national political institutions).[1]

A strong case can be made for claiming that their respective parties could
have found many better candidates in most, if not all, of these cases had the
selection process not depended so heavily on the self-recruitment of candidates.

[1]Richard Nixon (1972) and Gerald Ford (1976) are excluded from this list, as their nominations depended heavily on their status as presidential incumbents. For different reasons,
neither was really the product of the post-1968 nominating system.

4.2   SELECTION OF OTHER CANDIDATES

Candidates for most other offices in the US (including the House of Representatives, Senators and state governors) are chosen in *direct* primary elections. A direct primary differs from a presidential primary in that the winner of such a primary is automatically the party's candidate at the general election. (In a presidential primary in a state, the result of the primary is merely to select delegates to the National Convention; this is why it is said to be an *indirect* primary.) Party rules differ from one state to another. In most states virtually anyone who wants to can be a candidate for an elected public office; as with presidential candidates, therefore, they are largely self-recruited. In a few states, though, candidates must receive a certain proportion of the vote in party conventions to become a candidate. But here too the 'filtering power' of the party has been weakened greatly in recent decades. It is not that difficult for someone who is determined to run for public office to obtain the necessary support among the members of local party organizations and thereby gain a place on the primary ballot. Thus, even in these states, it is the candidates themselves — rather than the party organizations — who are the key actors in the selection process.

Some of the weaknesses of the presidential nomination process are not found in the procedures for selecting candidates for other offices. In particular, the period of planning a campaign is not as long, so there is not such a great risk that many of the best possible candidates will not run. Moreover, the decision period itself is much shorter. Usually there is just one primary election and the selection procedure is then concluded, although in some states there is provision for a 'run off' primary between the two leading candidates, should the candidate who receives the most votes fail to obtain 50 per cent of the total. However, the main limitation of presidential selection is evident here too: the lack of a 'filtering mechanism' (provided by those who are most active in the party) to ensure that candidates have the skills necessary for the position they are seeking. Voters can exercise judgement on the question of whether a candidate is attractive, 'plausible' or inspiring, but mass electorates cannot easily judge other skills required of elected politicians. Consequently, in a relatively open system of party selection like America's, it is always likely that wholly unsuitable candidates may emerge and be elected. Demagogues, like Senator Joseph McCarthy, have a somewhat easier route to institutional power in the US than they do in many other political systems.

SUMMARY

The choice of presidential candidate is ratified at their party's National Convention; most delegates to these Conventions are selected in (indirect) primary elections.

Voter turnout in primary elections is relatively low, and effective choice lies with a small number of voters in the earlier primaries.

Many well-qualified candidates do not seek their party's presidential nomination, whilst the candidates selected for the presidency often lack important political skills.

Candidates for other offices are chosen in direct primary elections.

5   THE PROCESS OF POLICY FORMATION AND SELECTION WITHIN PARTIES

In parliamentary democracies such as in the UK the question, 'What is the Conservative or Labour Party's policy on this matter or that matter?', is quite easy to resolve. There are party policy documents to which one can turn, especially party manifestos which are issued before a general election. A manifesto indicates what policies a party will pursue in government. In the UK there is a convention that a government should not pursue a radically new policy on a major matter if it had stated explicitly in its last manifesto that it would not do so. It can make such a change in direction only if wholly new circumstances, not foreseeable at the time of the previous election, justify it. Clearly, in these countries political scientists can examine the input that party activists, and organized groups within a party, have on the formation and selection of a particular policy agenda. Internally democratic parties would be ones which had a relatively high degree of responsiveness to their members.

In the United States, however, it is almost true to say that the *parties* as such have no policies at all — only individual party politicians have them. Certainly, at their National Conventions every four years a considerable amount of energy is put into constructing a document called the 'party programme'. But it is a document that is forgotten by nearly everyone soon after its publication! This is because no politician — not even the President — is committed to implementing that programme. The loose structure of American parties, and the central role of the individual politician himself or herself, makes it impossible to bind politicians to support particular programmes of the party. Individual candidates can support whatever policy programmes they choose to. Of course, given the conservatism of most Republican candidates and the moderate-liberal attitudes of most Democrats, there is some fit between the policies supported by the candidates and the party programmes. But the fit between the two is far from perfect, and party programmes are not used as a yardstick for judging performance in government in the way that a party manifesto in the UK is.

Given that it is only in a rather misleading way that we can speak of *party* policy in the US, the question of whether party policy is arrived at through democratic procedures becomes moot. Since elected politicians are left free to decide on their policy preferences, it may be concluded that the setting of policies is relatively undemocratic because it is left to party élites to do so. Naturally, party does constrain candidates in a variety of informal ways. Capturing a party's nomination requires the support of party activists to perform electoral tasks, raise money and so on. In most instances it would be difficult to capture a nomination — certainly for a major office — unless the candidate's views on policies found some resonance with at least some of these activists. Sometimes complete 'outsiders' do capture a party's nomination by mobilizing previously unmobilized sections of the public, but such campaigns are not typical. Usually, candidates will be seeking to mobilize sections of activists within the party, and this will constrain their choice of issues in a campaign and (indirectly) the policies they support once in office. But this kind of constraint does not amount to describing a policy-making process as democratic.

The lack of formal control by activists over elected politicians reflects the lack of a party membership in America. In early twentieth-century Europe bourgeois parties had to respond to the growing organizational challenge of social democratic parties. Social democrats created a large party organization based on individual members which enabled them to mobilize mass electorates. Membership involved a formal relationship with the party — rights for the members as well as duties. Among the rights was the right to participate in party decision-making. In theory, at least, formal control of a social democratic party rests with the membership. Bourgeois parties adapted (and modified) this form of organization to their circumstances, so that they could compete effectively with the social democrats. However, in the US the Democratic and Republican Parties were able to rebuff the challenge from the socialists far more easily, and they did not have to adapt. At that time many local party organizations in America were able to recruit activists to work in election campaigns through offering them material rewards, including jobs in local government. This enabled local party leaders to retain control over party strategy, a power which they shared with the party's candidates. When the political machines started to collapse, control over strategy passed almost entirely into the hands of the candidates.

SUMMARY

Individual politicians, and not the parties *per se*, have policy programmes. Party activists have relatively little direct control over the policy programmes adopted by politicians.

6 CONCLUSION

The discussion in this chapter suggests that an answer to the question, 'How democratic are American parties and the American party system?', is rather complex. Those who want to defend the democratic character of these institutions can point to a number of features in support of their case. There is little evidence that American voters would prefer radically different kinds of parties from the ones they have; in spite of the grip the Democrats and Republicans have had on the party system for nearly a century and a half, their ability to adapt to new movements in American society means that the party system is more responsive and less rigid than it might appear; and the selection of candidates in primary elections does facilitate much greater mass participation in party nominations for public offices than in virtually any other country.

However, against this must be offset several serious deficiencies in the democratic character of American parties:

1   Control over the policies pursued by parties is, at best, indirect. There is no party membership, and hence no formal control by members/ activists over public policy goals.

2   The dominance of the candidates themselves in the selection process means that part of the value of having mass participation in candidate selection is lost because of the absence of a 'filtering mechanism' to ensure that primary voters can choose between rival candidates of high quality. This problem is arguably even worse in the case of the presidency than for other offices.

3   The nomination process also provides for a strong bias in favour of certain kinds of candidate and for the influence of interest groups because of the importance of private money in campaigning.

On balance, this suggests that the American *party system* is fairly democratic: it is reasonably responsive to new demands emanating from within American society. It is much less clear that the *parties* themselves can be regarded as highly democratic institutions. While they permit considerable mass *participation* in their activities, the party structures mean that mass *control* of the parties is lacking; it is the individual politicians, pursuing their own aims and careers, who are the central actors in the process.

Moreover, it is far from clear that the most serious deficiencies of America's parties are likely to be corrected in the foreseeable future. The American political system is highly resistant to change until a political crisis forces the issue onto the agenda. The Watergate scandal of the early 1970s prompted reform of the election campaign finance laws but these reforms were incomplete, and in the case of congressional elections arguably made the problem of interest group influence even worse. After the mid-1970s, though, further proposed reforms failed to obtain significant political support. It remains to be seen whether the political upheavals of the early 1990s — including the defeat of an incumbent President, heavy support for an Independent presidential candidate, the increased electoral vulnerability of members of Congress in 1992 because of a series of political scandals, and the growth of support for term limits for members of Congress — will prompt new legislation in this area. Perhaps the most probable major reform is one to shorten the period of presidential selection so that it is more attractive to senior party politicians. Yet candidate-centred politics is likely to remain at the heart of the American political system for the foreseeable future. By comparison with most European parties, US parties will continue to be more like labels which politicians attach to themselves rather than structures for promoting collective action. And that constitutes one of the fundamental weaknesses in the American political system: dominance by the individual politician makes it difficult for effective participation by others in the process.

FURTHER READING

Chambers, W.N. and Burnham, W.D. (eds) (1967) *The American Party Systems*, Oxford, Oxford University Press.

Epstein, L.D. (1986) *Political Parties in the American Mold*, Madison, University of Wisconsin Press.

McSweeney, D. and Zvesper, J. (1991) *American Political Parties*, London, Routledge.

Ware, A. (1985) *The Breakdown of Democratic Party Organization, 1940–1980*, Oxford, Clarendon Press.

Wattenberg, M. (1991) *The Rise of Candidate-Centred Politics*, Cambridge, Mass., Harvard University Press.

Williams, S. and Lascher, E., Jr. (eds) (1993) *Ambition and Beyond: Career Paths of American Politicians*, Berkeley, Institute of Governmental Studies Press.

5

A JUDICIAL AUTOCRACY?

Robert McKeever ★

1 THE DEMOCRATIC PARADOX

The Supreme Court of the United States possesses the power of judicial review. This takes its most powerful form when the Court declares a federal or state law to be unconstitutional. This means that the nine judges, or Justices, who sit on the Court consider that a challenged statute is in conflict with the meaning of one or more clauses of the US Constitution. To take a concrete example, in 1989, in the case of *Texas v.* (versus) *Johnson*, the Court reviewed the constitutionality of a Texas law that banned the burning of the American flag as a political protest. It was alleged that the statute violated the First Amendment to the Constitution: this protects, among other things, the citizen's right to free speech. The case arose from demonstrations which took place during the Republican Party Convention in Dallas, in 1984. Gregory Lee Johnson and others had protested against the Reagan Administration's foreign policy by chanting slogans such as 'Reagan, Reagan, killer of the hour, Perfect symbol of US power'; and also 'America, the red, white and blue, we spit on you'. The demonstration had culminated in the burning of the American flag, the Stars and Stripes. Of course, burning the American flag is an action, not literally the speaking or writing of words, but a majority of the Justices interpreted the First Amendment to cover 'symbolic speech', such as burning the flag. Consequently, by a majority vote of five to four, they held that the Texas law was unconstitutional because it restricted Johnson's right to free speech.

Congress was outraged by the Court's decision. Within five months, both the House of Representatives and the Senate had passed the Flag Protection Act of 1989, by majorities of 380 to 38 and 91 to 9, respectively. The Act now made it a federal offence to burn the American flag in protest. It was immediately challenged in the courts and in 1990, in *US v. Eichman*, the Justices decided that it was unconstitutional for the same reasons as the Texas statute had been. The Flag Protection Act was therefore null and void.

The Court had thus carried out the *judicial* task of interpreting the Constitution; but the *political* result was that the elected representatives of both Texas and the United States had been rendered powerless to make policy on this issue. Paradoxically, then, the Supreme Court had strengthened one of the pillars of democratic government — free speech — but only by thwarting another — majority rule.

Gregory Johnson (left) protested against President Reagan's foreign policy by burning the American flag at a demonstration in Dallas, Texas. He was convicted, but the Supreme Court overturned that decision in 1989, arguing that his actions were protected by the First Amendment. The protests and arrests continued (right) when the Congress showed its disapproval of the Court's decision by passing the Flag Protection Act. However, the Court held firm and declared the Act unconstitutional

Some of you will no doubt agree that the Supreme Court's decisions on flag-burning were, as a matter of public policy, a good thing: civil liberties must be protected, even if that involves offending the patriotic pride of the mass of the American people. However, the Court has not confined its exercise of judicial review to the protection of civil liberties. In its history, it has also declared unconstitutional laws which were intended to restrict slavery to the states of the South; to require hotels and restaurants to treat people of all races equally; to introduce a national income-tax; and to establish minimum wages and maximum hours for factory workers. In fact, with the exception of the last 50 years, the main political effect of judicial review has been to buttress conservative policies.

Furthermore, the Supreme Court has not only employed judicial review in these various fields of public policy: it has also 'policed' the constitutional scheme of government by determining the limits of the authority of both the Congress and the President under the principle of separation of powers. For example, in the midst of the investigation by Congress into the Watergate scandal, the Court rejected President Nixon's claim that his power of 'executive privilege' entitled him to keep secret the tape-recordings of his conversations on the matter with his advisers (*US v. Nixon*, 1974). On the other hand, in 1983, the Court ruled unconstitutional the 'legislative veto', a device used by Congress since the 1930s. This procedure allowed the Congress to give the President a broad general authority, but then prevent any specific use of that authority of which it did not approve. Since hundreds of legislative acts contained some form of legislative veto, the decision (*INS v. Chadha*) was a major blow to the power of Congress and consequently a boon to presidential power.

The point to be considered here, then, is this: are Supreme Court decisions on questions of public policy or the separation of powers, either progressive or conservative, compatible with democracy? If an overwhelming majority of the democratically-elected legislature of a state or the nation vote for a certain policy, why should nine unelected judges, appointed for life, have the power to overrule them? Is this not a 'judicial autocracy'? Or rather, far from being a court of law at all, does it suggest that the Supreme Court of the United States in fact acts as a 'super-legislature' of a profoundly undemocratic kind?

To begin to answer these questions, and to discover why the United States is unique among democracies in granting its judiciary such great policy-making powers, it is necessary to examine the early history of the Republic.

2   THE ORIGINS OF THE SUPREME COURT AND JUDICIAL REVIEW

The Supreme Court was created by Article III of the Constitution of 1787. By endowing the Court with the national judicial power of the United States, Article III completed the constitutional framers' concept of 'the separation of powers'. However, unlike Articles I and II, which specified the powers of the Congress and the presidency, respectively, Article III was both brief and vague. As one historian of the Court pointed out, a simple word count reveals that whereas Article I contains 303 lines, and Article II has 127 lines, the judicial power takes up a mere 51 lines (Bates, 1963, p.30).

More importantly, Article III failed to specify exactly what the power or role of the Supreme Court was to be. It mentioned neither the power of judicial review nor the right of the Court to declare legislation unconstitutional. In short, the Constitution does not expressly give the Supreme Court the power to do what it did in the flag-burning cases described above. All it says in this respect is that, 'The judicial Power shall extend to all Cases, in Law and Equity, arising under this Constitution … ' (Article III, Section 2, i).

While this clearly establishes the Supreme Court as the highest judicial body in the land, it says nothing about its political power and role. As a leading American constitutional scholar, Archibald Cox, says: 'There is scarcely a hint in the text of the enormous power now exercised by the Supreme Court of the United States. Not a word indicates that the Court may review the constitutionality of Acts of Congress or of the President.' (Cox, 1987, p.38.)

The records of the Philadelphia Convention, which drew up the Constitution, reveal that the vagueness and brevity of Article III was partly due to the fact that little time was given over to the discussion of the judicial power. It was also due, however, to the Convention's inability to agree on the desirability of judicial review. Some delegates, including Benjamin Franklin, strenuously opposed it in any form, precisely because they thought it would make the judiciary more powerful than the legislature. Others, such as James Madison, disputed this conclusion and wanted some kind of judicial check on legislators to prevent them from enacting 'oppressive laws'. Even before the new Constitution came into operation, then, America's leaders were divided over how best to safeguard the rights of individuals and minorities, without simultaneously emasculating that cardinal principle of representative democracy, majority rule. The argument was not settled at Philadelphia, however, and the language of the Constitution was appropriately open-ended.

It was during the debates over the ratification of the Constitution that the first clear picture emerged of what role the supporters of judicial review intended the Supreme Court to play. Alexander Hamilton was a contributor to a series of newspaper articles, known collectively as *The Federalist Papers*, which urged states to ratify the new Constitution. In Number 78, Hamilton sought to explain and justify the power of judicial review. He argued that, by definition, the law of a written constitution must be deemed superior to a law passed by a legislature. Logically, Hamilton was quite right: there is no point in having a written constitution which establishes the permanent principles and powers of government, if it can be overruled or changed anytime a legislature feels like it. In the case of the US, the possibilities of a clash between the Constitution and legislation are multiple: not only might Congress pass a law which violates the Constitution, but there are today 50 state legislatures which may do the same.

Thus, in the event of an alleged clash between the Constitution and a legislative act, some institution or another must be empowered to decide whether there is indeed an incompatibility between the two. Hamilton argued that the Supreme Court should be that institution. He emphasized the fact that courts traditionally had performed the task of interpreting laws and that they were therefore best suited to decide if a statute conflicted with the Constitution. By contrast, he pointed out, it was hardly logical to allow a legislature which had passed a law to judge for itself whether it violated the Constitution.

Nevertheless, Hamilton acknowledged that judicial review did raise a potential problem for democracy:

> Some perplexity respecting the right of the courts to pronounce legislative acts void, because contrary to the constitution, has arisen from an imagination that the doctrine would imply a superiority of

the judiciary to the legislative power. It is urged that the authority which can declare the acts of another void, must necessarily be superior to the one whose acts may be declared void.

(Alexander Hamilton, The Federalist Papers, No.78)

In a famous passage, Hamilton rebutted this contention that judicial review would make the courts more powerful politically than legislatures or executives. He argued that the judiciary was *inherently* a weaker branch of the proposed Federal Government than either the Congress or the presidency. The passage is worth quoting at length, because it encapsulates many of the points that must be considered when evaluating the role of the Supreme Court today:

> Whoever attentively considers the different departments of power must perceive, that, in a government in which they are separated from each other, the judiciary, from the nature of its functions, will always be the least dangerous to the political rights of the constitution; because it will least be in a capacity to annoy or injure them. The executive not only dispenses the honours, but holds the sword of the community: The legislature not only commands the purse, but prescribes the rules by which the duties and rights of every citizen are to be regulated: The judiciary, on the contrary, has no influence over either the sword or the purse; no direction either of the strength or wealth of society; and can take no active resolution whatsoever. It may truly be said to have neither FORCE nor WILL, but merely judgement; and must ultimately depend upon the aid of the executive arm for the efficacious exercise even of this faculty.

(Alexander Hamilton, The Federalist Papers, No.78)

Hamilton was quite right in dismissing the fear that judicial review could lead to 'a government by judiciary'. Without taxing or spending powers ('the purse') or the means to enforce its judgements ('the sword'), the Supreme Court could never remotely hope to be a stronger political institution than the other two branches. Even in the modern period, as you will see later, the absence of financial and enforcement powers severely restricts the ability of the Court to ensure compliance with its judgements.

Nevertheless, Hamilton was wrong about the Court's powers in one very important respect. He assumed that when the Court exercised judicial review in a particular case, the Justices would employ not their 'will', but only their 'judgement'. In other words, the Justices would not allow their own political and ideological viewpoints and desires to influence them when deciding if a statute violated the Constitution; instead, they would be neutral and impartial as they made the technical judgement of whether, as a matter of law and logic, X (the statute) was compatible with Y (the Constitution). In the two centuries since Hamilton wrote his famous remarks, however, we have come to doubt whether any human being, even a judge acting conscientiously, can be as politically impartial as he thought. More importantly, the history of the Supreme Court since that time shows beyond all question that political considerations have often played a major part in the exercise of judicial review.

Hamilton's defence of judicial review in *The Federalist* did not mean a general agreement on the Supreme Court's power had been reached, even though, of course, the Constitution was duly ratified. This much became clear when Congress passed the Judiciary Act of 1789, which established the structure of the new national court system, but failed once again to spell out the power of the Court to declare an act of Congress unconstitutional. Judicial review was clearly too sensitive a political issue to resolve and the Supreme Court consequently began its life in a state of great uncertainty as to its powers and role. The more conservative of America's leaders had placed judicial review on their half-hidden political agenda, but their more democratic opponents were too powerful to be defeated outright.

It was not until 1803 that the question was resolved. Appropriately enough, that resolution emerged from a political crisis involving the conservatives, or Federalists, and the more democratic Jeffersonians. The Federalists had lost the election of 1800 but in the time before they were obliged to leave office, they attempted to make the federal judiciary a bastion of Federalist power. This included making John Marshall, the outgoing Secretary of State, Chief Justice of the Supreme Court. They also created dozens of new judgeships and then filled them with loyal Federalists. As it turned out, some of the written commissions for these new judges were not delivered before midnight on the day the Jeffersonians took control. The new Secretary of State, James Madison, decided not to complete delivery; one of the appointees, William Marbury, asked the Supreme Court to use its powers under Section 13 of the Judiciary Act of 1789 to order Madison to deliver his commission. Thus arose the most important single case in the history of the Supreme Court: *Marbury v. Madison* (1803).

The Supreme Court to which Marbury appealed was strongly Federalist and, of course, had Chief Justice John Marshall at its head. But the Court could not simply take the Federalist side, because the Jeffersonians had made it clear that they would simply ignore such a decision. This would expose the essential weakness of the Court and, by damaging its prestige, thwart the Federalist intention to use it as a power base. On the other hand, if the Court ruled for Madison, it would appear as if the Justices had buckled under Jeffersonian pressure and the political consequences would be the same: loss of power and prestige for both the Federalists and the Court.

With great ingenuity, Chief Justice Marshall stole a great victory from this apparent 'no-win' situation. By manipulating the legal technicalities of the case, he said the outcome depended on whether Section 13 of the Judiciary Act was constitutional and then declared that it was not. The Supreme Court, therefore, had no legitimate power to order Madison to give Marbury his commission.

A leading constitutional scholar described Marshall's legal argument as 'preposterous' (Pritchett, 1984, p.153). It was, however, politically astute. The Jeffersonians won the case, inasmuch as Marbury was not awarded his judgeship, and this made the decision acceptable to them. Much more important, though, was the fact that the decision was founded on Marshall's argument that the Supreme Court had the power to declare an act of Congress — the Judiciary Act of 1789 — unconstitutional. For the long term, this was much more significant than the question of William Marbury's commission. In effect, the Jeffersonians had won the battle over the judgeships, but the Federalists had won the war over judicial review.

SUMMARY

The question of whether the Supreme Court should possess the power of judicial review has always been controversial. Its early critics observed that it is anti-majoritarian and, therefore, anti-democratic. They feared that it would make appointed judges more politically powerful than democratically-elected legislators. Those who advocated judicial review believed that, under a written constitution which is the supreme law of the land, somebody must decide if a legislative act transgresses that constitution. They argued that the judiciary was best qualified to perform this task. They also believed, however, that unelected judges would act as a brake on what they considered to be 'the excesses' of democratic government.

3   THE SUPREME COURT AND DEMOCRACY, 1803–1937

Having established the legitimacy of judicial review in 1803, the Court proceeded to use it only sparingly. Between *Marbury v. Madison* and the outbreak of the Civil War (1861), the Court declared just one federal and 35 state laws unconstitutional (Gates, 1992, p.19). This does not mean that the Court's role was politically insignificant during this period. For example, the federal law struck down was the so-called Missouri Compromise of 1820. This involved a deal between the North and the South over whether new states entering the Union would permit slavery or not. However, in the case of *Dred Scott v. Sanford* (1857), the Court held that Congress had no power to regulate slavery in these new states and effectively ended any hope of a political compromise on this issue. The decision thus played a major role in precipitating the Civil War.

A second case of great significance from the *ante-bellum* period (pre-Civil War) is that of *McCulloch v. Maryland* (1819). This struck down a state tax on a federal bank, but its real importance is that it gave Chief Justice Marshall an opportunity to expand further the potential power of the Supreme Court. Marshall wanted to show that the Constitution had given the national government 'implied powers', that is, certain powers not explicitly laid down in the text of the Constitution. In order to achieve this, he had to argue that the Constitution was a document that the Justices must interpret flexibly and dynamically. In his written Opinion explaining the decision, Marshall said that the United States had devised,

> ... a constitution intended to endure for ages to come, and, conse-
> quently, to be adapted to the various crises of human affairs ... It
> would have been unwise to provide by immutable rules, for exigen-
> cies, which, if foreseen at all, must have been seen dimly, and which
> can best be provided for as they occur.

> (*McCulloch v. Maryland*, 1819)

In other words, if the Constitution is to stand the test of time, it must be
sufficiently flexible to meet the changing needs of American society. After
all, how could those who framed the Constitution in 1787 possibly have
imagined what the country would be like in 1887, never mind 1987? This
concept of adaptability is often referred to as 'the living Constitution',
because it suggests that the Constitution is like an organism, capable of
growth and development.

In terms of judicial power, 'the living Constitution' has significant implications. For if the Justices of the Supreme Court are charged with interpreting and applying the Constitution, then it is also they who will decide when
and how any 'updating' of its meaning occurs. It has been argued that this,
in effect, allows the Justices to amend the Constitution in the guise of interpreting it. These critics point out that the framers of the Constitution had
provided the means for amending it in Article V, which entrusts the power
of amendment to Congress and the state legislatures, not the Supreme
Court. But whether or not that criticism overstates the case, the fact remains
that flexibility of interpretation, or 'broad construction', of the Constitution
gives the Justices considerable scope for initiative and innovation in matters
of public policy. After all, as Chief Justice Charles Evan Hughes was to say
many years later, 'We are under a Constitution, but the Constitution is what
the judges say it is'.

One of the most important changes which took place in the United States in
the nineteenth-century was industrialization. Although some forms of
manufacturing were known in 1789, America at that time was essentially an
agrarian society. After the Civil War, however, the country was transformed
in a few decades into the world's greatest industrial power. Along with
industrialization came huge waves of immigration and rapid urbanization.
While these changes brought great benefits to many Americans, they also
brought the problems and conflicts typical of industrial society — urban
squalor, dangerous and unhealthy working conditions and ruthless exploi-
tation of the labour force, for example. Out of these circumstances arose new
social forces and new political and economic demands. Many Americans
now wanted government to intervene much more actively in economic and
social affairs. In short, the age of industrialization brought with it the inevitable impetus for the politics of reform. In many states, voters elected politicians who were responsive to their demands for reforming legislation.
They duly passed laws which offered new protection to industrial workers,
such as fixing minimum wages or maximum hours, or promoting the
growth of trade unionism. Furthermore, such measures were but part of a
growing conviction that government should take much greater responsibility
for the economic and social betterment of the country.

This trend was brought to a dramatic climax in the 1930s, when the Great Depression devastated the American economy. The banking system all but collapsed, at least 25 per cent of the workforce was unemployed and there was a pitifully inadequate provision of welfare for them and their families. In 1932, after three years of such economic crisis, the voters elected President Franklin D. Roosevelt, who had campaigned on a promise to experiment with new ways of stimulating the economy. He duly inaugurated his so-called New Deal, which, among other things, set out to plan and regulate both industrial and agricultural activity.

Here, then, was one of those crises about which Chief Justice Marshall had written in the *McCulloch* case in 1819. On the one hand, the Constitution had been written with the idea of providing a government of limited powers, with considerable protection for the property rights and economic liberties of individuals. On the other, over a century later, the people were demanding that the government take charge of the disastrous economic situation.

President Roosevelt's New Deal led to the greatest crisis in the history of the Supreme Court. It brought to a head a conflict between the Court and the elected branches of government that had been brewing for several decades. We saw above that before the Civil War, the Court had only rarely declared statutes unconstitutional. This began to change, however, in the last quarter of the nineteenth century. As the country industrialized and legislatures responded to new conditions and demands, the Supreme Court increasingly blocked reform legislation in the name of the Constitution. By the 1920s, this judicial resistance had reached alarming and unprecedented proportions: in that decade alone, the Court struck down fifteen federal laws and 140 state laws (Gates, 1992, p.19). When this trend continued into the Depression years of the 1930s and the Court declared key elements of the New Deal programme unconstitutional, President Roosevelt determined that the time had come to force the Justices to be more accommodating to the wishes of the voters and their elected representatives.

Roosevelt chose an indirect strategy for his attack on the Court's power. He proposed legislation that would allow him to appoint one new Justice for each current member of the Court over the age of 70. The claim was that the advancing years of the Justices was hindering their capacity to cope with their duties. No one took this seriously. It just so happened that six members of the Court were 70 or older and Roosevelt would be able to appoint six additional Justices, all of whom, it was assumed, would be chosen for their sympathy toward the New Deal. Rightly, then, the legislation was dubbed 'the Court-packing plan'.

Had the Court-packing plan been passed, it would have greatly enhanced the power of the presidency at the expense of the Court. For this reason, many members of Congress, despite their support for the New Deal, had grave reservations about it. What they feared was that the subordination of the Court to the presidency could one day be followed by an attempt to subordinate the Congress. Thus, the Supreme Court benefited from the desire to keep the power of the presidency broadly in check, even while it was being attacked for opposing the President's policy. Such is the subtlety of the operation of the concept of the separation of powers.

It was the Court itself which found a way out of this impasse. In 1937, a majority of the Justices effectively recognized that the Constitution would have to be interpreted to allow the national government a vastly increased freedom to determine socio-economic policy. In *West Coast Hotel v. Parrish* (1937), a five–four majority voted to uphold the constitutionality of a state minimum wage law for women, even though it had in the past repeatedly declared such laws to be a violation of the economic liberty of employers and employees. Although the Court did not say so explicitly, it had changed course for ever. After the *West Coast Hotel* decision, it upheld virtually every form of socio-economic legislation that it had declared unconstitutional in the previous 50 years and much more besides. The Supreme Court had bowed to the inevitable. In so doing, it seemed to reaffirm Hamilton's dictum that the Court was indeed 'the least dangerous branch' of the federal government. When firm judicial conviction on the meaning of the Constitution was countered by an equally intense political drive for change, it was the judges, rather than the politicians, who gave way.

SUMMARY

In the period from the end of the Civil War to 1937, the Court frustrated many of the attempts of state legislatures and the Congress to provide for the needs of a changing society. A majority of the Justices believed that the Constitution prohibited the new and vast powers being claimed by government. When they maintained this position even during the catastrophe of the Depression, the Court's critics charged that this judicial rigidity threatened the very right of the people to take the steps necessary for self-preservation. In the political struggle over control of socio-economic policy that ensued, the Court could not withstand the combined hostility of the President, the Congress and public opinion. Faced with a bill that would subordinate the judicial power permanently to that of the executive power, the Court retreated.

4 JUDICIAL ACTIVISM AND JUDICIAL RESTRAINT

The long struggle over the validity of socio-economic regulation by government did serious damage to the Court's prestige. Many Americans had come to believe that it was not the Constitution that was opposed to minimum wage laws or trade union rights, but simply the reactionary political views of the conservative Justices who formed a majority on the Court. In the eyes of liberals and progressives, these conservative Justices had practised 'judicial activism', the worst feature of which was to read their own political views into the general phrases of the Constitution. For example, they had taken the Fourteenth Amendment's ban on depriving a person 'of life, liberty, or property, without due process of law', and read into it a guarantee of liberty of contract that protected employers from most significant demands by their workers. Liberals therefore condemned judicial activism, arguing that it was undemocratic because it substituted the policy views of unelected judges for those of the electorate. In other words, judicial activism was bad, because it involved judicial legislation masquerading as constitutional interpretation.

Liberals argued that the proper approach for the Court was to practise judicial self-restraint. This meant, for example, deferring to the will of legislatures by presuming all laws to be valid unless there was overwhelming evidence to the contrary. Above all, it meant the Justices being careful not to allow their view of the desirability or wisdom of legislation to affect their judgement as to its constitutionality. Justice Felix Frankfurter, the great advocate of judicial restraint appointed by President Roosevelt in 1939, wrote:

> As a member of this Court I am not justified in writing my private notions of policy into the Constitution, no matter how deeply I may cherish them or how mischievous I may deem their disregard. The duty of a judge who must decide which of two claims before the Court shall prevail ... is not that of an ordinary person. It can never be emphasised too much that one's own opinion about the wisdom or evil of a law should be excluded altogether when doing one's duty on the bench.
>
> (*Board of Education v. Barnette*, 1943)

Or, as Justice Potter Stewart was to put it more succinctly some years later, 'Subjectivism is activism'.

After 1937, then, there was a renewed emphasis on the fact that judicial review was compatible with democratic government only if three basic conditions were satisfied:

1   The exercise of judicial review should only rarely lead to laws being declared unconstitutional.

2   When a law was declared unconstitutional, there must be a clear command from the Constitution to support the decision.

3   The Justices should be careful not to read their own policy preferences into their interpretation of the Constitution.

Together, these three conditions should ensure that legislatures, not courts, make public policy.

At first, judicial restraint indeed prevailed. As Table 5.1 shows, the number of laws declared unconstitutional dropped drastically in the 1940s and 1950s.

Table 5.1 Number of laws declared unconstitutional, 1920s–1970s

	Federal laws	State laws
1920s	15	140
1930s	13	91
1940s	2	58
1950s	4	69
1960s	18	140
1970s	16	177

(Source: Gates, 1992, p.19)

However, by the 1960s, the Court was striking down even more laws than in the previous peak decade of the 1920s, and the 1970s were worse still. Judicial activism was therefore back with a vengeance. Moreover, it was being practised by the very liberals who had so roundly condemned the activism of earlier years. By the end of the 1960s, the Supreme Court presented a mirror-image of the 1920s: liberal Justices practised judicial activism, while conservative politicians attacked them for usurping the powers of legislatures. In the remainder of this chapter, I shall analyse this contemporary form of judicial activism. And I shall ask whether it supports the view of many scholars that the function of the Supreme Court has changed permanently, so that it has become the main forum for resolving political conflicts over certain types of policy.

SUMMARY

In the period 1865–1937, the conflict over the constitutional legitimacy of socio-economic reforms reawakened the debate about the proper role of the Supreme Court in American politics. Liberals, who supported these reforms, wanted the Court to be essentially passive, to practise judicial restraint when confronted with innovative legislation. In this liberal view of the judicial role, activism was bad because it involved the denial of majority rule by unelected judges, who read their own minority views into the clauses of the Constitution. It is ironic, then, that when judicial activism resurfaced in the 1950s, it was advocated and defended by the very liberals who had so forcefully attacked it in the 1930s.

5 THE CONTEMPORARY SUPREME COURT

The return to judicial activism began with the arrival on the Supreme Court of Chief Justice Earl Warren. Warren was appointed by President Eisenhower in the belief that he would prove a cautious moderate — like the President himself. In fact, in the years during which Warren led the Court, 1953–69, there was a judicial revolution.

It began in 1954, when the Court decided in *Brown v. Board of Education* that racial segregation in state schools was unconstitutional. Such segregation was particularly prevalent in the states of the South, where a form of apartheid had been operated by white-controlled legislatures since the late nineteenth century. Not only schools but public transportation, parks, restaurants, hotels and even cemeteries were segregated. In a series of decisions that followed *Brown*, the Court declared all these forms of racial discrimination unconstitutional, because they violated the Fourteenth Amendment's guarantee of 'the equal protection of the laws' for all citizens. This ruling reversed the decision of the Court in *Plessy v. Ferguson* (1896), which had said that 'separate but equal' facilities for blacks and whites were compatible with the Fourteenth Amendment.

In *Brown*, the Court did much more than reverse a legal precedent. It mandated a social and political revolution in the South. Once again, then, the Court demonstrated its ability to make far-reaching contributions to public policy. *Brown*, however, also provided an opportunity to observe one of the principal weaknesses in the Court's power: its reliance upon other branches of government to enforce its decisions. Table 5.2 shows the rate of implementation of the *Brown* decision in the South.

Table 5.2 Percentage and number of black children in the South attending primary and secondary schools with white children

	%	Number
1954–5	0.001	23
1955–6	0.12	2,782
1956–7	0.14	3,514
1957–8	0.15	3,829
1958–9	0.13	3,456
1959–60	0.16	4,216
1960–1	0.16	4,308
1961–2	0.24	6,725
1962–3	0.45	12,868
1963–4	1.2	34,105
1964–5	2.3	66,135
1965–6	6.1	184,308
1966–7	16.9	489,900
1967–8	32.0	942,600

(Source: adapted from Rosenberg, 1991, p.50)

Despite the obvious moral justification for the *Brown* decision, many elected politicians were either indifferent or openly hostile to it. In the South, politicians shared or bowed to the racism of their constituents and launched a campaign of 'massive resistance' to desegregation. This included outright refusal to obey federal court orders, closing public facilities rather than integrate them, and terrorizing black people who tried to exercise their newly-won constitutional rights.

Many non-Southern politicians showed little enthusiasm for *Brown*. President Eisenhower refused to say publicly whether he approved of the decision or not. Many members of Congress, anxious not to upset traditional political alliances with Southern colleagues, declined to pass legislation that would have put the muscle of the federal government behind desegregation. The result was that ten years after *Brown*, the number of black children attending integrated schools in the South had barely changed. Rates of compliance did not begin to increase significantly until President Lyndon Johnson, supported by a liberal Congress, secured passage of the Civil Rights Act of 1964 and the Elementary and Secondary Education Act of 1965. In particular, both these acts offered large financial inducements — or punishments — to Southern states to secure compliance with *Brown*.

Gerald Rosenberg concluded from this and studies of other aspects of the desegregation campaign, that:

> ... before Congress and the executive branch acted, courts had virtually *no direct effect* on ending discrimination in the key fields of education, voting, transportation, accommodations and public places, and housing. Courageous and praiseworthy decisions were rendered, and nothing changed. Only when Congress and the executive branch acted in tandem with the courts did change occur in these fields.

> (Rosenberg, 1991, pp.70–1, original italics)

Nevertheless, the *Brown* decision was a landmark not only in the history of race relations in the United States, but also in the history of the Supreme Court as a policy-making institution. For it made clear that where reform movements failed to convince the Congress or President to act, the Supreme Court offered a third alternative. Moreover, precisely because the Justices were insulated from the electorate, they were less likely to be controlled by the prejudices of the majority. Thus groups which represented minority interests might well find it easier to persuade nine judges of the merits of their campaign, than to persuade elected politicians whose self-interest lay in listening to the majority. This is exactly what the National Association for the Advancement of Colored People had achieved in bringing the *Brown* case to the Supreme Court. After years of indifference and inaction by politicians, the Court had at least recognized the Constitutional legitimacy of the demands being made by the Civil Rights movement. Other reform groups quickly learned from *Brown*. In the words of Archibald Cox, they discovered the possibilities of 'constitutional decision as an instrument of reform' (Cox, 1968).

As well as encouraging reform groups to bring their causes to the federal judiciary, *Brown* also unleashed a new zeal on the Court for promoting the interests of minorities and individuals, often regardless of whether there was any clear language in the Constitution to support such action. In other words, the Justices developed a new rationale for the exercise of judicial review. This was that the Court had a special duty to protect what it regarded as the fundamental liberties of those whose rights were not adequately protected by the political process. As Justice Arthur Goldberg put it, ' ... it is just where, as a practical matter, the democratic political forum cannot adequately protect fundamental liberties that I have argued that the Court has a constitutional obligation to provide protection.' (Goldberg, 1971, p.52.) If you read this sentence again, you will see that, despite the inclusion of the word 'constitutional', Goldberg is not simply saying that the Court has a duty to uphold constitutional rights. Rather, he is saying that where the political process has failed in matters of fundamental liberties, the Court must step in. *Fundamental* liberties are not the same as *constitutional* liberties, as a quick reading of the Constitution makes clear. I am sure that there are many liberties which you consider to be fundamental, but which you will not find in the Constitution.

The new emphasis of the Court, then, was not upon simply interpreting the Constitution, but upon using judicial review as a means of advancing liberties that the Justices believed the other branches of government had neglected. A leading federal judge and judicial activist, J. Skelly Wright, effectively acknowledged that the Court was thereby exercising legislative, rather than judicial power: ' ... all too often, the practical choice has been between the Court doing the job as best it can and no-one doing it at all. Faced with these alternatives, *the Court must assume the legislature's responsibility.*' (Wright, 1968, pp.5–6, my italics.)

Of course, a major problem with this approach is that if the liberties to be protected by the Court are neither clearly present in the Constitution, nor deemed sufficiently fundamental by the legislature to require action, where do they come from? The answer is either from the Justices' own notions of what is good for society (their personal policy preferences); or their notions of what society will tolerate (consensus or compromise between opposing groups). Either way, the Court is playing a role normally associated with legislatures and exercising what Alexander Hamilton, you may remember, called 'will, not judgement'. Inevitably, therefore, the new activism inspired by the Warren Court reawakened the debate in American politics over whether judicial review was compatible with democracy.

The scale of the Warren Court reform initiatives was breathtaking. After desegregation came a ban on saying prayers in state schools; a considerable limitation of the right of legislatures to censor pornographic materials; a compulsory requirement that all states reapportion their legislative constituencies on the basis of exactly one person, one vote; a series of decisions that required the police and courts to observe strict procedures when arresting and prosecuting alleged criminals; and a declaration that the Constitution contained an unwritten 'right to privacy' that, among other things, included a new constitutional right to use contraceptives. Those of you of a more liberal persuasion are probably thinking 'a good thing, too'. But remember, if you concede to unelected judges the power to make policy judgements you support, you also give them the power to make policies you deplore.

Equally important, these decisions did not only 'liberalize' the Constitution. They also arrogated to the national government, in the form of the Supreme Court, powers which had previously been regarded as belonging to the state governments. For example, when the Warren Court ordered the reapportionment of state legislatures in 1962 (*Baker v. Carr*), it reversed its own 1946 decision in *Colegrove v. Green* which had said that the Supreme Court had no power to tell a state what to do on this matter. Similarly, school prayer, criminal procedures, and contraception had all, until now, been regarded as matters outside of the competence of the national government. Many scholars described this as 'the nationalization of the Bill of Rights' — the first ten Amendments to the Constitution which had previously been held applicable only to the federal government.

Of course, the Justices claimed that all they were doing was interpreting the Constitution as best they could. Many observers, however, whether on the political right or left, were not convinced. They argued that the Court was now practising what they called 'non-interpretive review': that is, deciding the validity of challenged laws not by finding and interpreting values contained in the Constitution, but by consulting some other source of values, including the Justices' personal values. On the liberal left, for example, Michael Perry wrote: ' ... The decisions in virtually all modern constitutional cases of consequence ... cannot plausibly be explained except in terms of non-interpretive review, because in virtually no such case can it plausibly be maintained that the framers constitutionalized the determinative value judgement.' (Perry, 1982, p.11.) On the right, Edwin Meese, US Attorney-General under President Reagan, also attacked this form of judicial review:

> In recent decades, many have come to view the Constitution ... as a charter for judicial activism on behalf of various constituencies. Those who hold this view often have lacked demonstrable textual or historical support for their conclusions. Instead they have 'grounded' their rulings in appeals to social theories, to moral philosophies or personal notions of human dignity ... The problem with this approach is not that it is bad constitutional law, but that it is not constitutional law in any meaningful sense at all.
>
> (address before the American Bar Association, Washington, DC,
> 9 July 1985)

As in previous periods of judicial activism, such controversial decisions eventually led to attempts by politicians to force the Court to retreat. In 1968, Richard Nixon campaigned for President with a platform that attacked the Warren Court and he promised, if given the opportunity, to appoint new members to the Court who would practise 'strict construction' of the Constitution. Yet despite making four appointments during his first term of office, Nixon failed to turn the Court around. In fact, under the new Chief Justice, Warren Burger, the Court's decisions caused even more intense controversy.

In 1971, in *Swann v. Charlotte-Mecklenburg Board of Education*, the Burger Court added a new string to the desegregation bow, by authorizing 'busing': this involved transporting white children to black neighbourhood schools and vice versa and proved to be very unpopular with parents. In the same year, in *Reed v. Reed*, the Supreme Court for the first time ever declared that the Constitution prohibited some forms of sex discrimination. In 1972, the Court broke more new constitutional ground by declaring that all existing capital punishment laws were invalid under the Eighth Amendment's ban on 'cruel and unusual punishments'.

Then, in 1973, came what was to prove the most politically controversial Supreme Court decision of the modern era. In *Roe v. Wade*, the Court declared that women had a constitutional right to choose to terminate a pregnancy by abortion. This decision led to a bitter war between 'pro-choice' and 'pro-life' activists that continues to the present day. Moreover, it also led to the most determined attempt by politicians since the Roosevelt 'court-packing' plan, to bend the Supreme Court to the wishes of the President. If we examine the history of abortion politics in some detail, we will see not only how the Supreme Court uses non-interpretive review to take legislative power out of the hands of elected politicians; but also, the strengths and weaknesses of the Court when it becomes engaged in serious political conflict.

SUMMARY

Beginning with the *Brown* decision in 1954, many liberals have come to see great virtues in judicial activism. This is because it allows the Supreme Court to act as an agency for liberal reforms, particularly those which improve the situation of minority or disadvantaged groups. Although such groups may lack the political power to persuade elected legislatures of the need for action, they can turn to the Supreme Court to vindicate their claims for 'fundamental rights'. Although these claims often have little or no support in the text and history of the Constitution, the Court may employ non-interpretive review to reach what they consider to be a just result. Such judicial activism on behalf of liberal causes inevitably produced a conservative backlash and a demand for a return to judicial restraint.

6   THE SUPREME COURT AND ABORTION RIGHTS

Prior to 1973, policy on abortion was determined by the individual states for themselves. This was in line with the framers' intention that the national government would exercise only a limited range of powers, with many policy areas being reserved to the competence of the states. Until the 1960s, all states placed strict controls on the termination of pregnancies by abortion: usually it was only permitted when allowing the pregnancy to continue would pose a serious threat to the mother's health or life. The medical profession began to take a different view, however, after an epidemic of German measles and the use of the drug thalidomide produced a spate of severely malformed babies.

Responding to the lead of doctors and other health care professionals, states such as California (1967) and New York (1970) passed new legislation which made abortion much more freely available.

Although the drive to liberalize abortion laws was led by the medical profession, other groups emerged about this time with significantly different motives for wanting change. In 1966, for example, a new era of feminism took off with the formation of the National Organization for Women (NOW). In 1967, NOW issued its Women's Bill of Rights, an agenda for change which, if implemented, would give women equality with men. One of these rights was 'reproductive freedom', which included easy access to abortion. NOW argued that until women had control over whether to have children and, if so, when and how many, they would never be able to compete in the workplace on equal terms with men. In 1969, a single-issue pressure group was formed to campaign for liberalized abortion rights: the National Association for the Repeal of Abortion Laws (NARAL). Groups such as NOW and NARAL certainly agreed with the medical case for abortion, but even more important for them was the *political* argument that the freedom to choose an abortion was a fundamental right for all women and a pre-condition of sex equality.

Unsurprisingly, the appearance of pressure groups dedicated to the reform of state abortion laws produced a political reaction and the creation of other groups to oppose liberalization. One of the first and most prominent of these was the National Right to Life Committee (NRLC), founded by John C. Willke. This anti-abortion movement achieved its first success in 1972, when Willke played a leading role in helping to defeat an abortion reform referendum in the state of Michigan. NRLC supporters believe that human life begins at conception and therefore they regard abortion as murder. For this reason, they identify their policy as 'pro-life'. NOW sympathizers, stressing the issue of women's freedom, refer to themselves as being 'pro-choice'.

By 1973, then, abortion policy was becoming a bitter and divisive political issue. Much to the relief of many national politicians, however, it was an issue on which they need not act, because it was seen as an issue to be decided by each state for itself. It was the pro-choice pressure groups who began the transformation of this national scene by deciding to take their cause to the Supreme Court. Choosing this judicial, as opposed to legislative path to reform offered several advantages for pro-choice activists. First, it would be financially cheaper than either a national or state-by-state campaign to enact liberal abortion legislation. Secondly, it would probably prove faster: although several years were normally required to prepare a lawsuit and take it through the lower courts to the Supreme Court, this was nothing compared with the prospect of campaigning state-by-state or persuading a majority of the members of the Senate and the House of Representatives to take action on such a controversial measure. Even then, such legislation might face the prospect of a presidential veto and a subsequent campaign to get a two-thirds majority of the House and Senate to override that veto. Thirdly, and above all, the judicial path simply offered a better chance of success. As noted above, since 1954, the Justices of the Supreme Court had shown themselves sympathetic to even controversial claims to constitutional protection by disadvantaged groups in American society. Because the Court tended to side with the liberal position on social issues, and because it was insulated from electoral pressures, the Justices might be willing to try to resolve the debate over abortion and to do so along the lines urged by the pro-choice forces.

Success was by no means guaranteed, of course. There were two obvious obstacles. First, as already mentioned, abortion policy had always been determined by the states, not the federal government. Secondly, if the Court wanted to announce a *constitutional* right to abortion, it would have to find a clause in the Constitution which supported such a decision. And that was highly problematic, because not only was abortion not mentioned in the text of the Constitution, but also no previous Supreme Court decision had suggested that it was implicitly contained in any broader phrase in the text.

Nevertheless, the risk was worth taking, if only because a Supreme Court decision on the constitutionality of abortion rights held out the prospect of the highest political victory possible in the American political system. For while an act of Congress or a state legislature can be reversed by a simple majority vote, a Supreme Court decision rooted in the Constitution can only be reversed either by a change of mind by the Justices themselves, or by the long and difficult process of constitutional amendment. If successful before the Supreme Court, then, the pro-choice forces would win not only a national right to abortion which nullified all contradictory state laws, but a 'constitutionalized' right to abortion that would be very difficult for the pro-life forces to overturn.

The gamble paid off. Pro-choice lawyers found a young, pregnant Texan who had tried unsuccessfully to obtain an abortion. The Texas abortion law was typical of the strict legislation still in operation in over half the states: enacted in 1854, it allowed abortion only when necessary to save the mother's life. Under the pseudonym of Jane Roe, the young woman filed a suit against the Attorney-General of Texas, Henry Wade, to prevent him from enforcing the state abortion law. Roe claimed that the law violated her constitutional right to privacy, which included the right to choose to have an abortion.

When, after three years, the case worked its way up to the Supreme Court, a seven–two majority of the Justices upheld her claim. Although the Constitution made no mention of privacy, the Court had decided in 1965 that several clauses of the Constitution, when taken together, added up to a right to privacy. And they now decided that the principle of privacy could be extended to cover abortion. Despite the clear majority, however, the Court failed to convince many observers, even some who supported abortion rights, either that the Constitution contained a right to abortion or that the Court possessed the power to settle the abortion issue. One of the two dissenting Justices, Byron White, expressed his reservations when he alleged that the Court had usurped the powers of the state legislatures and the democratic process. He said that abortion was a sensitive issue on which reasonable people disagree. And, since the Constitution said nothing about abortion, one way or the other, policy making ' … should be left with the people and to the political processes the people have devised to govern their affairs.' (Dissenting Opinion of Justice White, *Roe v. Wade*, 1973.)

At first glance, the *Roe* decision appeared to be a great victory for the cause of women's rights. Although it allowed some continued regulation of abortion by the states, it declared that they could not prohibit abortion under any circumstances during the first six months of pregnancy. The radical nature of the decision is shown by the fact that 49 of the 50 state abortion laws in existence were declared unconstitutional as a result.

However, if this demonstrates the capacity of the Court to make sweeping policy decisions through constitutional interpretation, the next 20 years revealed some severe limitations on the Court's powers. The decision in *Roe v. Wade* inspired a backlash by states, pressure groups and national politicians opposed to abortion rights. Between them, they gradually undermined the Court's decision and made it difficult for many American women to obtain abortions in practice.

This backlash took several forms. First, many states used the powers of regulation left to them by the *Roe* decision to try to deter women from choosing abortion. For example, some states passed laws which required any woman wanting an abortion to be given 'information' about her foetus which was thinly-disguised pro-life propaganda. Many states also refused to allow public hospitals and clinics to perform abortions, for while the Court had said that states could not ban abortions, it had not said that states had a duty to provide them. This tactic left women reliant upon private clinics willing to perform abortions, but these do not exist in many areas. For example, in the sixth most populous state, Illinois, abortion facilities exist in only twelve out of 102 counties. None exist in the state capital, Springfield, a city of 100,000 people. And in the state of Minnesota, abortions are only available in the cities of Minneapolis–St. Paul and Duluth (Rosenberg, 1991). The result is that many American women have to travel hundreds of miles, and even to other states, to find abortion facilities.

Both states and the Congress have made things even more difficult for poor women, by banning the use of public funds under the Medicare scheme to pay for their abortions, despite the fact that public funds are available to them for all other medical treatment, including those associated with childbirth. What we see here, then, is the inability of the Court to ensure the effective implementation of its abortion policy. It seems that the Supreme Court has the power to declare the existence of rights in the abstract, but lacks the political strength to make those rights a reality in practice. This is a major drawback to the strategy of securing reform through the judiciary, rather than the legislature.

A second method of undermining abortion rights has been the determined campaign by Presidents Reagan (1981–9) and Bush (1989–93) to appoint new Justices to the Court whom they believe will vote to reverse the *Roe* decision. Although this has not been wholly successful, it has ensured that many of the obstructive laws mentioned above are found acceptable when

Keeping up the political pressure on the Supreme Court. Pro-choice groups, including the National Abortion Rights Action League (formerly the National Association for the Repeal of Abortion Laws), demonstrate in Washington in 1989

Table 5.3   Changes in Justices, 1973–93

Justices in *Roe*, 1973		New Justices (with date of appointment and nominating President)
William O. Douglas	*replaced by*	John Paul Stevens (1975, Ford)
Potter Stewart		Sandra Day O'Connor (1981, Reagan)
Warren Burger		Antonin Scalia (1986, Reagan)
Lewis Powell		Anthony Kennedy (1987, Reagan)
William Brennan		David H. Souter (1990, Bush)
Thurgood Marshall		Clarence Thomas (1991, Bush)
Byron White		Ruth Bader Ginsburg (1993, Clinton)

sitting throughout this period

William Rehnquist
(promoted to Chief
Justice, 1986, Reagan)

Harry Blackmun

they are challenged in the Supreme Court. In the most recent abortion case, *Planned Parenthood v. Casey* (1992), the Court maintained the bare bones of *Roe*, but even that was only achieved by a five–four vote. However, the subsequent retirement of Justice White, a fierce critic of *Roe*, and his replacement by the pro-choice Ruth Bader Ginsburg, has made the basic abortion right safe for the moment. Table 5.3 shows the changes in Court personnel which have taken place since *Roe* (1973). As you can see, seven of the nine Justices have been replaced since *Roe*, five of them by Presidents who wanted it reversed.

Ironically, this judicial counter-attack has obliged the pro-choice forces to turn their attention to the very electoral and political processes that they shunned in the early 1970s when the Supreme Court appeared to offer a quicker and more complete victory. And contrary to most expectations, their campaign to win the votes of the American public and their elected representatives has met with considerable success. Most promising of all has been the drive to persuade Congress to pass the Freedom of Choice Act, which is under consideration at the time of writing. If passed, this would enshrine in federal law the same freedom to choose an abortion that was awarded to women in *Roe v. Wade*.

SUMMARY

The abortion decision in *Roe v. Wade* is seen by many as the epitome of modern judicial activism, a liberal policy imposed through non-interpretive review. Yet although at first glance it seems a great victory for women's rights, *Roe* also demonstrates the weaknesses inherent in judicial power. As with the *Brown* decision, the Court was able to declare a new policy, but it struggled to ensure compliance with it. Moreover, such was the outcry over *Roe*, that conservatives launched a powerful attack not merely upon abortion rights, but also upon liberal judicial activism in general. To some extent therefore, *Roe* and other activist decisions have been counter-productive.

7 CONCLUSION

I began this chapter by asking whether the Supreme Court had developed into a 'super-legislature', thereby endowing the United States with a 'judicial autocracy'. The history of abortion politics suggests that there is some evidence to support this contention. Although there was no clear mandate in the Constitution for it, the *Roe* decision took away much of the policy-making power over the issue from the Congress and state legislatures. However, when the pro-life forces inspired a legislative backlash, the Court was forced into a series of retreats which came perilously close to wholesale capitulation. Thus if the Court did aspire to act as a super-legislature on abortion, it has received a sharp reminder that, to a considerable extent, it does not possess the power to play such a role.

However, there is a still more important question which arises from this episode in the Court's history: even if the Court could play the role of super-legislature successfully, would this be desirable? For it is arguable that the activist use of judicial review is not merely anti-democratic in form and theory, but it has the practical effect of encouraging Americans to turn away from the democratic process. If those who seek to change American society for the better learn that it is easier to bring about reform by an appeal to nine unelected judges rather than to their fellow citizens, what incentive is there to cultivate democratic procedures? Likewise, if Americans expend effort and thought in participating in democratic politics, only to find that unelected judges make many of the most important policy decisions anyway, why should they bother? Moreover, not even those people who judicial legislation is intended to help may benefit in the long term. For example, the anger and surprise which greeted the *Roe* decision caused a backlash which saw poor women deprived of the financial means of obtaining an abortion. If pro-choice activists had done in the 1970s what they are doing now — fighting to win the hearts and minds of the public — it is quite possible that they would have won the rights they wanted by democratic persuasion, rather than by judicial command. The lesson of *Roe v. Wade* may be that rights are never truly won until the people have been convinced of their legitimacy.

In the final analysis, your view of the role of the Supreme Court in American society involves weighing up the advantages and disadvantages it brings. On the one hand, judicial review has produced results of which most people would approve: greater equality for black Americans and women, greater freedom of speech for unpopular dissenters and more fairly apportioned legislative districts, for example. All of these have greatly enhanced American democracy and social justice. And some of them would have taken much longer to come about, or might never have happened at all, if it had not been for the actions of the Supreme Court. On the other hand, there seems little point in the Supreme Court strengthening democracy if it frequently overrides the policies arrived at by the very democratic process it has enhanced. And as Chief Justice Burger once put it:

> When this Court rushes in to remedy what it perceives to be the failings of the political process, it deprives those processes of an opportunity to function. When the political institutions are not forced to exercise constitutionally allocated powers and responsibilities, those powers, like muscles not used, tend to atrophy.
>
> (*Plyler v. Doe*, 1982)

My own view is that the Court should not attempt to intervene too frequently in the policy-making process. The Justices must acknowledge the fact that there is a tension between the power of judicial review and democratic principles. They should only move to overturn the policies of the elected branches of government, therefore, when they have a clear constitutional mandate to do so. This does not mean that the Court must defer to Congress whenever the legislature feels strongly on a question. For example, to return to the flag-burning case which opened this chapter, there is no doubt in my mind that the Court's decision was quite correct: the First Amendment *was* designed to protect free speech against government suppression and Gregory Lee Johnson did no more than articulate his political views, offensive to many though his chosen means of expression were. Because the Court's decision was clearly rooted in the Constitution, it can claim political legitimacy from the very fount of American democracy and thus override the rival claim to legitimacy that arises from the fact that Congress was elected by the people.

However, where the Court, as in *Roe v. Wade*, seeks to introduce new principles into the Constitution, it loses all claim to democratic legitimacy. For here the Court is not interpreting a principle selected democratically by others: it is claiming the right to actually create the principle itself. As an inherently undemocratic body, the Supreme Court should not make that claim, even where the results are benign. After all, the Supreme Court is no exception to the general rule of political power that the ends do not justify the means.

REFERENCES

Bates, E.S. (1963) *The Story of the Supreme Court*, New York, Bobbs-Merrill.

Cox, A. (1968) *The Warren Court: Constitutional Decision as an Instrument of Reform*, Oxford, Oxford University Press.

Cox, A. (1987) *The Court and the Constitution*, Boston, Houghton Mifflin.

Gates, J.B. (1992) *The Supreme Court and Partisan Realignment*, Boulder, Westview.

Goldberg, A. (1971) *Equal Justice*, Evanston, Northwestern University Press.

Perry, M. (1982) *The Constitution, the Courts, and Human Rights*, New Haven, Yale University Press.

Pritchett, C.H. (1984) *Constitutional Law of the Federal System*, Englewood Cliffs, Prentice-Hall.

Rosenberg, G. (1991) *The Hollow Hope: Can Courts Bring About Social Change?*, Chicago, University of Chicago Press.

Wright, J.S. (1968) 'The role of the Supreme Court in a democratic society', *Cornell Law Review*, vol.54, pp.1–28.

FURTHER READING

See Cox (1968) in the references.

Lasser, W. (1988) *The Limits of Judicial Power: the Supreme Court in American Politics*, Chapel Hill, University of North Carolina Press.

McKeever, R. (1993) *Raw Judicial Power? The Supreme Court and American Society*, Manchester, Manchester University Press.

Wasby, S. (1988) *The Supreme Court in the Federal Judicial System*, Chicago, University of Chicago Press (3rd edn).

White, G. (1988) *The American Judicial Tradition*, Oxford, Oxford University Press (expanded edn).

THE POLITICS OF THE CITY

Desmond King ★

1 INTRODUCTION

Cities hold a pivotal position in the US federal political system. The United States' federal character devolves considerable power to state and city governments, and historically urban areas have held important powers of self-government. In the nineteenth century cities were institutions of integration for the millions of immigrants arriving in the US, an integration partially achieved through residence in areas populated by the new ethnic groups. In the twentieth century party machines developed in large urban areas structured around the residential segregation of ethnic neighbourhoods. Also in the twentieth century a large migrant movement of black Americans from the South to the northeast and Midwest transformed American cities consolidating the racial cleavage which is so powerful today.

The United States is undoubtedly an urban society and many of its characteristics are visibly concentrated in its cities (in strict terms cities are included by the official designation of municipalities: I use the terms interchangeably). Questions of race, power and inequality are all germane to urban politics. American social and political scientists have been intrigued by cities and urban phenomena for over a century and many have sought to elevate them to a special status in the American system. In his essay, 'Urbanism as a way of life', Louis Wirth made urban experience the defining one of modern life:

> the degree to which the contemporary world may be said to be 'urban' is not full or accurately measured by the proportion of the total population living in cities. The influences which cities exert upon the social life of man are greater than the ratio of the urban population would indicate, for the city is not only in ever larger degrees the dwelling-place and the workshop of modern man, but it is the initiating and controlling center of economic, political, and cultural life that has drawn the most remote parts of the world into its orbit and woven diverse areas, peoples, and activities into a cosmos.
>
> (Wirth, 1938, p.3)

Political scientists have identified cities as legitimate units in which to study power in the US polity in two senses. First, cities themselves, and local political conflicts, are deemed sufficiently important to justify a detailed study, and a distinguished tradition of community-power studies stretching from Floyd Hunter (1953) to Clarence Stone (1989) demonstrates the fruits of this approach. Secondly, the importance of urban political machines and of city politics to national politics has also encouraged political scientists to study them (see Banfield and Wilson, 1963; Dahl, 1961). Political scientists continue to study cities for their intrinsic interest and their illumination of general questions about American politics (see *inter alia* Katznelson, 1981; Peterson, 1981; Shefter, 1985; Mollenkopf, 1983, 1993; Elkin, 1987; Gurr and King, 1987; Fainstein and Fainstein, 1974; Logan and Molotch, 1987; Schneider, 1989).

Intellectually, scholars have expended much energy and effort in analysing the relationship between cities and capitalism, especially in the United States. As I suggest later there is a dichotomy in the urban studies literature between those theorists who view the city as self-contained and its politics as comprehensible in terms of events specific to each city; and those scholars who maintain that urban politics are, to a significant extent, the outcome of processes external to cities — particularly national economic patterns and national politics. Illustrative of this second approach is David Gordon's (1976) categorization of US cities' growth into three stages, each corresponding to a distinct level of capitalist development: commercial accumulation, industrial accumulation, and advanced corporate or monopoly accumulation. Gordon argues that 'within each stage of urban development ... the process of capital accumulation itself was the most important factor structuring the growth of cities. Capitalist development in the United States has bred, according to my historical argument, the capitalist city' (Gordon, 1976, p.86). In the commercial stage of accumulation cities perform four main political and economic functions. They serve as a political capital, a commercial metropolis, as central transport nodes and a location for artisans specializing in luxury goods. In the second, industrial accumulation, stage, cities become the basis for factory production. Factories were concentrated in urban areas because of the density of workers there and the proximity to markets and to critical resources and transportation systems. Gordon emphasizes the class basis of residence in large cities, a feature enabling employers 'more easily [to] achieve labor control' (ibid., p.97). In the third stage of accumulation the emphasis shifts to corporate or monopoly accumulation, in which cities assume a leading role in financial and other services. The stage at which a city reaches its population peak indelibly colours its character, physically and sociologically.

Gordon's generalized conceptual work is complemented, and to some extent confirmed, by Warner's (1968) detailed history of Philadelphia. Warner also distinguishes three stages of development. First between 1770 and 1780 when the city was really a small town with an economy based on one-man artisans and shops. Mildly resembling a medieval European city in residential patterns, there was also evidence of latent commercial development:

> the settlement pattern of the town combined two opposing social
> tendencies. The clustering of marine trades and merchants next to

the Delaware suggested the beginnings of the specialized industrial quarters then characteristic of European cities. On the other hand, the rummage of classes and occupations found in many Philadelphia blocks continued the old tradition of mixed work and residence characteristic of American and English country towns.

(Warner, 1968, p.11)

In the second stage of development, 1830–60, Philadelphia experienced substantial growth, the population rising from 161,400 to 565,500 and industrialization which 'manifested itself as an increase in the reach of the city and its business' (ibid., p.62). Warner documents the not inconsiderable rioting and social unrest which accompanied these changes as immigrants and economic change intruded themselves upon the prevailing community. These elements were exacerbated by the persistence of racially mixed patterns of settlement: separate residential patterns were not consolidated until the third stage of urban growth, when 'during the seventy years from 1860–1930 the residential areas of Philadelphia shifted from mild to pronounced segregation by income and ethnicity' (ibid., p.169). The history of Philadelphia illustrates nicely Gordon's thesis; furthermore, by the middle of this century Philadelphia had a settlement and residential pattern common to many older US cities: 'a core city of poverty, low skills and low status surrounded by a ring of working class and middle class homes' (ibid.).

Immigration and migration were fundamental to the urbanization of the United States and the tensions resulting from clashes between different religious and racial groups have been profoundly important to urban politics in the nineteenth and twentieth centuries. Class conflict has certainly not been absent from US urban politics but it has been tempered by religious and racial cleavages in a way quite dissimilar from European experience. One powerful analysis of this comparatively distinct pattern is provided by Ira Katznelson in his important book *City Trenches* (1981). He maintains that the way in which community was organized in a highly decentralized federal system resulted in a schism between the experience and politics of work, and the experience and politics of community. American workers were not any different to their European peers seeking improved conditions and pay, but unlike European workers these issues of production politics were never linked with issues of consumption politics as experienced in cities and the community. Katznelson writes:

> American urban politics has been governed by boundaries and rules that stress ethnicity, race, and territoriality, rather than class, and that emphasize the distribution of goods and services, while excluding questions of production or workplace relations. *The centrepiece of these rules has been the radical separation in people's consciousness, speech, and activity of the politics of work from the politics of community.*

(Katznelson, 1981, p.6, original italics)

This pattern of 'city trenches' rests on three aspects of the US polity: 'trade unions at the workplace; a quite separate decentralized party system; and an array of new government services that were delivered to citizens in their residential communities' (ibid., p.55). These commonplace features of American politics combined to maintain the distinction between work and community, a dichotomy fundamental to urban politics. In a decentralized federal policy with weak national political parties, city politicians and their party machines thrived from the closing decades of the nineteenth century in the tough urban environment created by a seemingly inexhaustible stream of immigrants constructing and defending new identities there — depicted in Upton Sinclair's eponymously titled novel *The Jungle* (1906).

SUMMARY

Urban studies are divided between those scholars who see the city as self-contained and those who maintain that urban politics are significantly influenced by external processes such as national economic patterns.

Warner's historical study of Philadelphia distinguishes three stages of development and emphasizes the importance of immigration and migration to urbanization. Katznelson advances the distinction between work and community as fundamental to urban politics. These factors reflect in part the decentralized nature of the federal system and the weakness of American political parties at the national level.

2   CITIES IN THE FEDERAL POLITICAL SYSTEM

2.1   CITIES AND STATE GOVERNMENTS

The relationship between cities and the federal government has historically been mediated by the importance of states' rights in the US polity. States have sought jealously to guard activities within their jurisdictions and to limit the role of federal government. The constitutional position of cities was stated unequivocally in Dillon's Rule, pronounced in 1868:

> it is a general and undisputed proposition of law that a municipal corporation possesses and can exercise the following powers, and no others: first, those granted in express words; second, those necessarily or fairly implied in or incident to the powers expressly granted; third, those essential to the accomplishment of the declared objects and purposes of the corporation — not simply convenient, but indispensable. Any fair, reasonable, substantial doubt concerning the existence of power is resolved by the courts against a corporation, and the power is denied.

> (Dillon, 1911, vol.1, section 237, p.448)

On a subsequent occasion Dillon added that 'cities are the creatures, mere political subdivisions, of the state for the purpose of exercising a part of its powers' (*Atkins v. Kansas*, 1903, see Gurr and King, 1987, p.64).

These restrictions are less severe than they appear: cities and local governments hold discretionary powers including powers of revenue raising (King, 1988). Many states have enacted laws delegating parts of the state's sovereignty to city governments for responsibilities such as police powers, eminent domain, and taxation. The extent of this constitutional home rule arrangement differs by state. In most it is limited to issues of a 'local' character and certain issues are excluded from the home rule provision.

Constitutionally, until recently, the power of states over cities, relative to that of federal government power, was unquestioned. In a ruling in 1907 the Supreme Court declared that

> municipal corporations are political subdivisions of the State created as convenient agencies for exercising such of the governmental powers of the State as may be entrusted to them. In all these respects the State is supreme, and its legislative body, conforming its actions to the State constitution, may do as it will.
>
> (*Hunter v. Pittsburgh*, 1907)

2.2   CITIES AND FEDERAL GOVERNMENT

Between the New Deal of the 1930s and Reagan's New Federalism of the 1980s the dominant trend in city–federal relations was the forging of closer links. The catastrophe of the Great Depression exposed the inability of state and local governments to address the pressing fiscal and welfare needs located within their jurisdiction. Consequently Roosevelt's temporary public works and permanent welfare programmes were all responses to the demands for a greater federal role in the nation's domestic affairs (Gurr and King, 1987, ch.3; Weir and Skocpol, 1985). During the 1950s highway and urban renewal programmes resulted in additional funds for cities. This pattern was given a powerful push by the Johnson presidency. The President inaugurated an ambitious War on Poverty programme including an expansion of funds granted directly to city governments. The trend continued under Nixon and Carter peaking in 1978 (see Table 6.1). From 1981 and the beginning of the Reagan Administration federal grants in aid to cities declined and the power of states relative to cities was enhanced (King, 1992).

Table 6.1   Aggregate federal aid to cities of 200,000 plus population size ($million)

	Current	Constant
1965	401.7	425.8
1970	1,367.0	1,175.6
1975	4,530.5	2,808.9
1978	6,290.6	3,208.2
1980	6,677.8	2,737.9

(Source: derived from Gurr and King, 1987, p.122)

Although the federal government's commitment to cities and to urban needs varies within the ideology of each administration, there are certain enduring or primary interests which must be satisfied (Gurr and King, 1987, ch.1). The national government must maintain its legitimacy and ensure a revenue supply; and it must respond to short-term crises such as that resultant upon the riots in Los Angeles in May 1992. However, federal and city government officials are unlikely to overlap in their respective assessments of an individual city's needs since the national officials must take a broader picture, as Gurr and King observe:

> it follows from the spatial and political location of local officials ... that they are more concerned with the maintenance of essential urban services, and the economic wellbeing of their *city* than are national officials, who are interested more in the aggregate wellbeing of the urban city than of individual cities.
>
> (Gurr and King, 1987, p.42)

Not all cities will benefit all of the time from federal attention and that indeed there will be competition for federal resources.

The relationship between the federal government and cities is a dynamic one: there is no fixed pattern, and historically cities rise and decline in national salience. The territorial division of authority and power in a federal system is contested (often in the courts) and there are few binding principles (though some are set out in the Constitution) about this division. Madison's characterization of the Constitution in *The Federalist* No.10 as a 'happy combination' in which the 'great and aggregate interests [are] referred to the national, the local and particular to the State legislatures' leaves the detailed division of powers unspecified (Madison *et al.*, 1987, p.127). Recent decisions taken by the Supreme Court illustrate this process. In 1976 the Court ruled (in *National League of Cities v. Usery*) that federal minimum age laws set under the Fair Labor Standards Act were not binding upon local governments when they made payments to their employees. This ruling provided city governments with some protection from federal intervention. However, in 1985 *Garcia v. San Antonio Metropolitan Transit Authority* overruled the *Usery* decision with the Supreme Court now ruling that local governments were bound by federal minimum wage laws when paying their employees. This judgement incensed many conservative Republicans since it violated the principle of states' rights and limited local discretion.

2.3   CITY GOVERNMENT

There are three forms of government in American municipalities.

- First, the *mayor–council* system consists of a mayor elected at a city-wide election and a council elected from wards throughout the city. The mayor acts as a chief executive and the council as a policy-making body, a distinction paralleling that at the national level. It is common to distinguish between weak-mayor systems defined by restrictions upon the mayor's power; and strong-mayor systems, more common as the size of the city increases, in which mayors have important executive and leadership powers. Strong mayors appoint and sack heads of city government departments independently of the council and also control budget preparation.

- Secondly, the *commission* system is distinguished by the integration of mayoral and council functions into a single body. The system originated in Galveston, Texas in 1900 after the town was devastated by a tidal wave, the consequences of which the existing mayor–council administration proved incapable of alleviating. Five commissioners are elected directly on a city-wide basis and each commissioner takes responsibility for a substantial area of city government. The political and electoral imperatives of becoming a commissioner constitute serious fetters upon their administrative roles.

- Thirdly, the *council–manager* system is intended to bring a business style to the administration of services. This system originated in Staunton, Virginia in 1908 when the city created the new position of city manager. The elected council appoints a professionally trained administrator to act as city manager. Appointees must be accepted by the International City Management Association.

Historically urban politics have been dominated by party machines controlled by leaders known as party bosses with colourful appellations including 'Honest John Kelly' in New York, and 'Big Bill Thompson' and 'Bathhouse John Couglin' in Chicago (Erie, 1988). Jones defines a machine thus:

> a machine is a form of party organization that induces its members to participate primarily through the use of material benefits. Party workers are marshalled by the promise of jobs; voters are induced to support the party because they believe that they will be favored with government services if their party holds power; leaders contribute because they can advance to better positions if their party is electorally successful. A machine ... will be staffed primarily by professionals.
>
> (Jones, 1983, p.128)

Party machines were based upon a high voter turnout delivered by ward and precinct officers in return for favours and patronage, principally city jobs and contracts for business (Gosnell, 1968). During the reign of the Daley machine in Chicago from 1955 to December 1976, the party machine controlled over 30,000 jobs. These organizations developed for several reasons. First, the highly decentralized nature of the US polity's federal system advantaged grass-roots organization. Secondly, the organization of urban populations into precincts and wards based on ethnic lines ensured that an area would support a candidate uniformly. The maxim 'vote early and vote often' was a favourite exhortation employed by party workers. Machines were based in neighbourhoods and guaranteed the delivery of votes at election time in exchange for a range of material incentives.

Urban machines were enhanced by the strong-mayor–council system of government and precluded by the other systems. Consequently, urban machines were a feature of large cities. They were often criticized for breed-

Mayor of Chicago Richard Daley, the epitome of the political machine, at the 1968 Democratic Convention

ing and perpetuating corruption, constraining the successful absorption of immigrants into the American polity by reinforcing traditional ethnic divisions, and encouraging an individualistic response to problems rather than a collective approach. It was often argued that those ethnic groups excluded from party machines fared better economically in the long run than those groups integrated through machines (for a discussion see Jencks, 1992, ch.1).

Such complaints and others prompted the funding of reform movements focused upon improving city government. A powerful reform movement developed during the beginning of this century (Holt, 1974; Griffiths, 1974; Haber, 1964). One important force for change was the National Municipal League founded in 1894. Another force was the press publishing stories about municipal corruption, a style pioneered by Lincoln Steffens writing in *McClure's Magazine*. The reform movement's aims included introducing competitive and merit based entry requirements for municipal civil service appointments, non-partisan election ballots, and replacing ward-based elections with ones conducted over the whole city. The reform achieved many successes especially in small and medium sized cities. Some larger cities such as Boston and Detroit adopted non-partisan city-wide elections too. According to some scholars reformed cities respond better to political needs than do unreformed cities (Lineberry and Fowler, 1967).

Municipal reforms were intended to weaken the role of urban party machines. By placing controls upon the powers of patronage available to party bosses it was intended to limit their influence. While party machines and party bosses have not disappeared, especially in large cities, they have fewer resources to distribute and they operate under constraints (Gottdiener and Pickvance, 1991; Savitch and Thomas, 1991). Furthermore, local parties have lost their crucial roles within national politics as they have been marginalized from the presidential nomination process (Ware, 1985). Parties remain important organizational resources in urban politics, particularly for new groups such as black politicians entering city government (Browning *et al.*, 1990). Such politicians seek to redirect municipal power toward their interests but not fundamentally to alter existing institutional arrangements (Mladenka, 1989).

SUMMARY

State restrictions on cities are less severe than they appear; some states have delegated sovereignty to city governments and cities have discretionary powers including those of revenue raising. Cities' relationship with federal government has always been a dynamic one, and was enhanced between the 1930s and the 1980s. Typically federal government responds to particular short-term needs of a city.

Three forms of city government have been identified. The strong-mayor–council form enhanced urban party machines which became a feature of large cities and were often criticized as reinforcing ethnic divisions and perpetuating corruption.

3   RACIAL AND CITY–SUBURB DIVISIONS

The powers granted to cities by their state has interacted with a series of federal measures to produce the modern city. There are two salient characteristics, which are discussed in this section: a significant pattern of segregation along racial lines and a significant division between central cities and their surrounding suburbs.

American cities have been historically, and continue to be, characterized by profound patterns of residential segregation based initially around ethnic groups (which often coincided with class and religion) and now around race. Cities are organized in neighbourhoods whose dominant group is clearly evident. Neighbourhoods change over time and once this change reaches a certain threshold the metamorphosis is rapid. Theoretically the housing market is a free one with no restrictions on grounds of race permitted. In practice, city governments have used zoning and other laws to ensure that these powerful residential patterns reifying segregation remain little modified.

Research by John Landis suggests the degree of residential segregation. Landis constructed an index of racial segregation to compare the ratio of a racial group in a central city with the larger metropolitan area: if the index is 1.0 this indicates parity between the proportion of a racial group concentrated in a central city compared with the metropolitan area. As the index raises so the degree of segregation is greater. Table 6.2 reports the results. These results are startling, as Landis observes: 'of the cities in the fifty largest metropolitan areas, the percentage of Blacks in the central city population exceeded the percentage of Blacks in the metropolitan area by a 2-to-1 margin in thirty-one of them' (Landis, 1987, p.237). The index for the Hispanic population also follows a similar pattern.

Table 6.2   Racial segregation in American central cities (selected)

City/metropolitan area	Segregation index	
	Black population	Hispanic population
Oakland (San Francisco)	5.38	0.78
Hartford	4.91	4.86
Boston	4.77	2.56
Providence	4.21	2.76
Minneapolis	3.35	1.18
Rochester	3.23	2.70
Detroit	3.16	1.13
Pittsburgh	3.12	1.47
Dayton	2.93	1.26
Albany–Schenectady–Troy	2.84	1.40
Cincinnati	2.73	1.39
Atlanta	2.71	1.27
Newark	2.68	2.84
St. Louis	2.65	1.28
Philadelphia	2.01	1.52
Chicago	1.78	1.33
Richmond	1.76	1.08
Salt Lake City	1.70	0.88

(Source: derived from Landis, 1987, p.236)

A significant division between central cities and their surrounding suburbs has developed in the decades since 1945, partly stimulated by federal funding of housing (through mortgage subsidies) and of transportation. In 1980 74.8 per cent of Americans lived in metropolitan areas compared with 47.8

146

per cent in 1940; of that 74.8 per cent, 30 per cent lived in central cities and 44.8 per cent in suburbs, compared with 32.5 per cent and 15.3 per cent respectively in 1940 (Fox, 1985, p.51).

This cleavage is now of cardinal importance because it coincides with a racial one: black Americans dominate in central cities, while the suburbs are the preserve of white Americans (though some predominantly black suburbs are developing). While white Americans were migrating to the suburbs, black Americans were still leaving the rural South for northern and Mid-western cities (Lemann, 1991). As cities' black populations have grown so the propensity toward white movement to the suburbs has increased (Peterson, 1985). Furthermore, this racial cleavage is overlapped by a class one. Suburbanization has been facilitated by local government laws (Mills, 1987; Danielson, 1976; Clark and Dear, 1984), as zoning restrictions and land regulations have been used to enforce illegal racial patterns of residential segregation. Finally, the black middle class, frustrated in their efforts to find accommodation in white suburbs, has reinforced these divisions by creating separate black suburbs (Logan and Schneider, 1984).

Federal subsidization of housing has been concentrated in inner cities, and shunned by the suburbs, because of its usage by low income households. With data from the 1980 US census Caraley calculates that the highest median income of any city was San Jose with $25,598 and the lowest Newark at $11,989; however, suburbs are far richer:

> when suburban rings are also included in the comparison with large cities, eleven suburban rings — those of Washington DC, San Jose, Chicago, New York City, Detroit, Houston, Newark, Milwaukee, San Francisco–Oakland, Minneapolis–St. Paul and Seattle — had median incomes higher than the city of San Jose. At the other end of the scale, of the twenty-five places with the lowest median income, twenty-two were central cities and only three were suburban rings — those of El Paso, Tampa, and Albuquerque.
>
> (Caraley, 1992, p.4)

Poverty is disproportionately concentrated in American central cities while wealth is enjoyed predominantly by those living in suburbs.

SUMMARY

Two crucial characteristics of American cities have been identified. First, there is a division between ethnic and racial groups crystallized in distinct residential patterns; these patterns are more powerful in the older eastern and Midwestern cities than in some of the western and southern ones. Early industrialization and urbanization was accompanied by segregation on a racial basis which also overlapped with class distinctions. Secondly, there is an increasingly significant division between poor and economically disadvantaged central cities and their affluent suburbs. Both divisions underpin many aspects of contemporary American urban politics.

4 PROBLEMS OF THE CITIES

Although cities have historically occupied a key position in the US polity both as centres of population and as political actors, modern cities no longer bask in these roles. Rather they labour under a series of difficulties partly of their own making but principally the result of the dominance of conservative Republicans in Washington during the last two decades.

4.1 FISCAL PROBLEMS

The foremost problem confronting most American cities is a shortage of sufficient funds to meet their expenditure commitments (Fuchs, 1992; Shefter, 1985). The combined revenues of taxes and of federal grants are insufficient given city needs. Federal grants to cities grew from the 1930s, expanding rapidly from the mid-1970s, and peaking in 1978. From 1980 the Reagan Administration systematically reduced federal grants-in-aid to city governments and placed restrictions upon their revenue raising powers. By the end of that decade cities were receiving 25 per cent less in real terms from Washington.

Cities have important revenue-raising powers but if they exercise them too vigorously they run the danger of losing citizens. This principle is explained by Paul Peterson in his book *City Limits* (1981); he argues that in a federal system local politicians must heed the interests of their taxpayers or risk losing them to other areas with lower rates. Throughout the 1980s city governments were under pressure to raise taxes — and many did — as federal grants were reduced in real terms (see Table 6.1, Section 2.2). However, most have now reached the limits of their local taxation levels and still face formidable policy responsibilities for education, welfare, health and transportation. The Reagan presidency not only reduced federal assistance but increased the responsibilities of state and local governments in many areas (King, 1992; Wolman, 1990).

4.2 WELFARE AND SOCIO-ECONOMIC PROBLEMS

Cities play a key role in administering welfare, education and health programmes in the US polity. The cuts in federal assistance and the diffusion of the AIDS epidemic have made these responsibilities demanding ones. At present most cities have insufficient funds — from federal and state grants or local taxation revenues — effectively to discharge their responsibilities in these areas.

At the root of urban problems is the devastation of the US manufacturing base. Large urban areas located in the Midwest and northeast have suffered disproportionately from the decline of industry with resultant effects for their corporate taxation base and level of employment (see Table 6.3).

Table 6.3   Employment in selected cities

	Employment (000s)		Change (%)	Unemployment (%)	
	1960	1986	1960–80	1960	1986
Atlanta	197	210	6.6	3.6	7.5
Boston	288	278	−3.5	5.0	4.4
Chicago	1,502	1,264	−15.9	5.4	9.3
Detroit	612	407	−33.5	9.9	11.8
Philadelphia	789	679	−13.9	6.5	6.9
St. Louis	294	179	−39.1	5.4	9.4

(Source: derived from Savitch and Thomas, 1991, p.241)

These trends were compounded by the Reagan philosophy of 'trickle-down' economics whose advocates placed national economic activity at the centre of its strategy, maintaining that the benefits would percolate to all levels of the economy. This view was articulated by US Department of Housing and Urban Development official June Koch to Congress in 1984: the Administration sought 'to create the right economic climate for stable urban growth, strengthen state and local governments, and stimulate public and private co-operation to improve social and physical conditions'. The 1982 National Urban Policy offered critical assessments of most existing urban programmes and urged giving 'maximum feasible responsibility for urban matters to states and through them to their local governments' (US Department of Housing and Urban Development, 1982, p.46). The results of this injunction for city governments have been less federal funding and greater responsibilities. Federal funding for urban development, health and housing all fell during the 1980s, and the structural federal budget deficit is of such magnitude as to limit national initiatives to assist cities. In the 1970s the federal government funded the construction of an annual average of 200,000 units of public housing; by 1986 the number had plummeted to 27,000 units.

SUMMARY

American cities lack the resources effectively to address the serious social and economic problems over which they preside. Many of these problems have been exacerbated by the withdrawal of federal assistance during the Reagan and Bush Administrations and by the constraint imposed on domestic policy effected by the federal deficit.

5   THE STUDY OF URBAN POLITICS

The study of urban politics has occupied a distinct place in the work of American social and political scientists. In this section some of the dominant approaches are reviewed. Table 6.4 suggests how these can be categorized in terms of unit of analysis and how the city is related to economic and political phenomena beyond its immediate control.

Table 6.4 Categorization of the study of urban politics

Unit of analysis	Politics dominant	Market dominant
City is self-contained	Pluralism (Dahl) Regime theory (Stone)	Neo-élitism (Crenson) Growth machine theory (Logan and Molotch) Public choice theory (Peterson, Schneider)
City is part of a larger system	State-centred theory (Gurr and King, Mollenkopf)	Marxist theory (Harvey, Katznelson)

The two organizing criteria used in Table 6.4 reveal the two issues which have characterized the epistemology of urban studies. First, can the city and associated politics be studied meaningfully as a unit independent of external economic and political events? In other words, are urban politics self-contained and given meaning exclusively from events and personalities within each city? Secondly, can urban politics be dissociated from economic forces, be these located within the city or beyond its jurisdiction? As Table 6.4 suggests scholars have answered these questions in a variety of ways using a range of theories. Over time the dominant intellectual trend has been a movement from viewing cities as autonomous self-contained units to conceiving of them as constrained regimes fuelled significantly by economic dynamics and needs.

Pluralists, of whom the most famous is Robert Dahl for his study of New Haven in *Who Governs?* (1961), believe urban politics to be confined to observable political behaviour within an institutionally defined metropolis (though the study did include a socio-economic profile of New Haven). Dahl analysed three decisions taken by the city government in New Haven to assess where power lay. This approach encouraged a view of city politics as self-contained to the urban area; it also encouraged a methodological individualism which acknowledged that individuals may act as members of groups but did not base group membership and mobilization on economic relations or interests. Under regime theory, pioneered especially by Clarence Stone (1989) in his study of Atlanta, the leading politicians required, for the economic needs of the city, to develop an electoral coalition which included the dominant business interests in Atlanta; however, initiative lies with politicians and not just economic actors.

In contrast élitist, public choice and growth machine theorists all contended, in different ways, that urban politics was intimately related to economic interests. Neo-élitists, such as Crenson (1971), maintained that within a city the most powerful individuals are able effectively to exclude issues from the political agenda which may prove harmful to them. This power to control the agenda implies that studying observable decisions held in public, the pluralists' strategy, will fail to elicit an accurate picture of politics. Decision-making rules and institutions themselves embody the 'mobilization of bias' and their biases need therefore to be integral to analysis. In his study of policies to control air pollution, Crenson demonstrated the importance of local business élites. This latter group also featured in Logan and Molotch's (1987) analysis of urban growth machines. Maintaining that in each city there is a 'growth coalition' composed of politicians, developers and other business leaders devoted to increasing the use value of land. Urban development rests in the hands of this coalition, dominated by developers, including some located outside the city, and the role of local politicians is necessarily limited. For public choice influenced theorists, notably Peterson (1981), the balance of taxes levied and programmes funded provides the framework within which urban politics occurs. However, within this matrix these theorists believe the power of taxpayers is superior to that of other citizens and a significant constraint upon policy-making: without tax revenues there can be no local government or policy, and hence redistributive policies claim a lower priority to growth initiatives.

Both state-centred and neo-Marxist theorists emphasize the extent to which urban politics are the outcome of processes external to the city and that to study city politics without attention to these external processes is inadequate. However, they differ in their focus with state-centred theorists such as Mollenkopf (1983) and Gurr and King (1987) stressing the role of national politics and neo-Marxists such as Harvey (1973) or Katznelson (1981) emphasizing national (and international) economic forces as powerful influences upon urban politics. State-centred theorists based their arguments on the growth of the federal government from the Roosevelt Administration through initiatives such as President Johnson's Great Society, developments which increased federal grants to cities and the role of national government in city politics. For neo-Marxists the crucial determinant of urban politics is economic: understanding and analysing national economic and employment trends is judged critical to patterns of urban employment and unemployment, with secondary effects upon other issues such as race relations and education. The flavour of this approach is conveyed by Katznelson in his study of Manhattan:

> no urban community exists in isolation, even if from within residents find it difficult to discern how changes in the larger society alter the context which their community is embedded. In assessing the ways northern Manhattan changed after 1940, we would be derelict if we did not make these connections. Both the place of northern Manhattan in the larger social order and the content of its daily life and political conflicts were shaped in the first instance by the loss of traditional economic functions that affected all the large older Eastern and Midwestern cities of this period.

(Katznelson, 1981, p.90)

Table 6.5 presents a summary of the major American urban studies with some details about their methodology and conclusions.

Table 6.5   From Hunter to Stone: studying community power

	City	Method	Approach	Findings
Hunter (1953)	Atlanta	Reputational	Elitist	Concentration of power
Dahl (1961)	New Haven	Observation of decisions	Pluralist	Power dispersed
Crenson (1971)	Gary and Chicago	Non-decision making	Neo-élitist	Power concentrated in élite who control the political agenda
Stone (1989)	Atlanta	Historical sociology	Elite regime	Power shared between political and business élite, former pre-eminent

SUMMARY

Students of urban politics have divided between those scholars who believe urban politics are self-contained and those who maintain that the role of external economic and political factors is of crucial import-ance. Furthermore, many have emphasized the importance of treating political and economic factors concurrently, an approach best represented in notions of an 'urban regime'.

6   CONCLUSION: FUTURE PROSPECTS

This chapter has provided an overview of the problems facing cities in the United States. In this conclusion key themes in their future development are highlighted.

6.1   RACE AND CONFLICT

The division between central cities and surrounding suburbs overlaps with racial and class dichotomies. The multiplicity of cleavages renders the city–suburb division a potent one. For many Americans living in cities or sub-urbs results in different experiences racially, economically and politically. The central cities are disproportionately black, burdened by high unemploy-ment and Democratic; the suburbs are disproportionately white, economi-cally prosperous and Republican.

Residents of the inner cities are thus amongst the least advantaged of American society (Jencks and Peterson, 1991) and this position provides an hospitable environment for riotous behaviour and underground activities such as drug dealing. The potential for the former was epitomized by the riots in Los Angeles in April and May 1992 which resulted in 44 dead and were in many ways reminiscent of the 1960s (*New York Times*, 1–3 May 1992; Gurr and King, 1987, chs 3, 4; Button, 1978) (see Table 6.6). However, such parallels should not be overdrawn. It is significant that the widespread rioting of the mid-1960s was not repeated in 1992, and that in some cities the causes of violence have changed. In the 1960s anger at the police was common and indeed this factor was germane to Los Angeles in 1992; but in many other American cities police forces are racially integrated and a much less potent source of tension. Riots are not a new phenomenon to American cities historically: religious riots were common throughout the nineteenth century and hundreds of people were killed in draft riots in New York during the Civil War. It is unlikely that there will not be further riots in American central cities but their extent and location are unpredictable.

Table 6.6 Major urban riots in American cities (selected)

July–August 1964	Riots in Harlem and Bedford-Stuyvesant in New York and in Rochester, NY; Jersey City, Paterson and Elizabeth, NJ; and Philadelphia
11–17 August 1965	Watts riot in Los Angeles: 34 dead; 1,032 injured; 3,775 arrests; National Guard deployed
30 January and 15 March 1966	Further riots in Watts: 2 dead; 20 injured; 49 arrests
Summer 1966	43 cities suffer violence including Chicago, Omaha, Cleveland, Dayton, OH; San Francisco and Atlanta: 11 killed; over 400 injured
12–17 July 1967	Newark, NJ: 26 dead; 1,500 injured. Other cities in New Jersey affected
23–28 July 1967	Riots in Detroit: 43 dead; over 2,000 injured; 7,000 arrested. Violence also in Cairo, Ill.; Durham, NC; Memphis, Tenn.; and Cambridge, Mass.
4–11 April 1968	Violence in 125 cities after news of Martin Luther King's assassination: 46 dead; 2,600 injured
18–20 May 1980	Violence in Liberty City, Miami: 18 dead; 400 injured
28–30 December 1982	Violence in Overtown, Miami: 2 dead
16–18 January 1989	Violence in Overtown, Miami: 6 injured
30 April–3 May 1992	Los Angeles riots: 44 dead; 1,765 injured; 6,345 arrests

Inner city residents are also disproportionate victims of crime (see Table 6.7). Not only do the residents suffer from poor economic opportunity, poor health and education services and inadequate housing but they are exposed to strikingly high crime rates.

Table 6.7   Crimes against the person in selected cities in 1989 (per 10,000 of population)

	Murder +	Rape +	Robbery +	Assault =	Total	1960–89 increase, %
Atlanta	.58	1.62	15.94	21.38	39.52	2,079
Boston	.17	.83	10.11	11.16	22.27	1,005
Chicago	.25	.00	10.57	12.59	23.41	279
Detroit	.60	1.37	11.45	10.59	24.01	323
Houston	.27	.67	5.73	4.73	11.40	326
Miami	.35	.75	19.12	16.75	36.97	475
St. Louis	.39	.81	10.42	19.59	31.21	407

(Source: derived from Savitch and Thomas, 1991, p.242)

In the worst cases cities resemble what Gurr and King termed 'welfare cities', defined by a stagnant economic base and an inactive federal government (Gurr and King, 1987, p.193). In these cities unemployment is over 50 per cent, at least a third of the citizens depend upon public assistance and homelessness is high. The New Right conservatism which dominated the Reagan and Bush Administrations (1981–92) implied an abandoning of the cities: electorally city voters are peripheral to Republican interests and materially urban areas constituted a host of problems all requiring that scarce resource, money.

6.2   CITY POLITICS

The politics of large American cities has altered to reflect the racial and class composition of their residents. Politics in many, though far from all, large cities have been entered into by black and to a lesser extent Hispanic politicians seeking to redistribute municipal resources for their electoral populations. Cities such as Atlanta, Los Angeles, Cleveland, Detroit, Chicago, New York, and Philadelphia have all had black mayors: Harold Washington, Wilson Goode, Andrew Young, Tom Bradley, Coleman Young, Sidney Barthelemy and Norman Rice among them, and Hispanic mayors include Maurice Ferre, Zavier Suarez and Frederico Pena. In Chicago this control was brief (Grimshaw, 1992; Guterbock, 1980); in others black dominance has become the norm. In some cities, notably Los Angeles and Seattle, black mayors have been elected although whites are the most numerous groups in the electorate.

While this trend is set to continue there is no easier panacea for black than for white politicians in large American cities faced with mounting fiscal, welfare, health, education, transport and infrastructure problems. Each problem requires a commitment of federal, state and local money and political will if it is to be addressed effectively. Neither funding nor will was available during the Republican control of the White House. It remains to be seen whether they will be forthcoming under the Clinton Administration. If they are not then the crisis of cities and the problems of America's most disadvantaged citizens will continue and intensify.

SUMMARY

American cities confront major problems arising from their disproportionately poor citizens and from racial divisions apparent throughout US politics and society. These problems have influenced the character of urban politics and will continue to do so as the disadvantaged struggle to ameliorate their circumstances.

REFERENCES

Banfield, E.C. and Wilson, J.Q. (1963) *City Politics*, New York, Vintage.

Browning, R.P., Marshall, D.R. and Tabb, D.H. (eds) (1990) *Racial Politics in American Cities*, New York, Longman.

Button, J. (1978) *Black Violence*, Princeton, Princeton University Press.

Caraley, D. (1992) 'Washington abandons the cities', *Political Science Quarterly*, vol.107, no.1, pp.1–30.

Clark, G.L. and Dear, M. (1984) *State Apparatus*, London, George Allen & Unwin.

Crenson, M. (1971) *The Unpolitics of Air Pollution*, Baltimore, John Hopkins University Press.

Dahl, R.A. (1961) *Who Governs?*, New Haven, Yale University Press.

Danielson, M.N. (1976) *The Politics of Exclusion*, New York, Columbia University Press.

Dillon, J. (1911) *Commentaries on the Law of Municipal Corporations*, Boston, Little, Brown (5th edn).

Elkin, S.L. (1987) *City and Regime in the American Republic*, Chicago, University of Chicago Press.

Erie, S.P. (1988) *Rainbow's End*, Berkeley, University of California Press.

Fainstein, N.I. and Fainstein, S.S. (1974) *Urban Political Movements*, Englewood Cliffs, Prentice-Hall.

Fox, K. (1985) *Metropolitan America: Urban Life and Urban Policy in the United States*, London, Macmillan.

Fuchs, E. (1992) *Mayors and Money*, Chicago, University of Chicago Press.

Gordon, D. (1976) 'Capitalism and the roots of urban crisis' in Alcahy, R. and Mermelstein, D. (eds) *The Fiscal Crisis of American Cities*, New York, Vintage.

Gosnell, H. (1968) *Machine Politics, Chicago Models*, Chicago, University of Chicago Press.

Gottdiener, M. and Pickvance, C.G. (eds) (1991) *Urban Life in Transition*, Newbury Park, Sage.

Griffiths, E.S. (1974) *A History of American City Government*, New York, Praeger.

Grimshaw, W. (1992) *Bitter Fruit: Black Politics and the Chicago Machine*, Chicago, University of Chicago Press.

Gurr, T.R. and King, D. (1987) *The State and the City*, Chicago, University of Chicago Press.

Guterbock, T. (1980) *Machine Politics in Transition: Party and Community*, Chicago, University of Chicago Press.

Haber, S. (1964) *Efficiency and Uplift: Scientific Management in the Progressive Era 1890–1920*, Chicago, University of Chicago Press.

Harvey, D. (1973) *Social Justice and the City*, Baltimore, Johns Hopkins University Press.

Holt, M.G. (1974) 'Urban reform in the progressive era' in Gould, L.L. (ed.) *The Progressive Era*, Syracuse, Syracuse University Press.

Hunter, F. (1953) *Community Power Structure*, Chapel Hill, University of North Carolina.

Jencks, C. (1992) *Rethinking Social Policy*, Cambridge, Mass., Harvard University Press.

Jencks, C. and Peterson, P. (eds) (1991) *The Urban Underclass*, Washington, DC, Brookings.

Jones, B.D. (1983) *Governing Urban America*, Boston, Little, Brown.

Katznelson, I. (1981) *City Trenches*, New York, Pantheon Books.

King, D. (1988) 'Local finance in the United States' in Paddison, R. and Bailey, S. (eds) *Local Government Finance*, London, Routledge.

King, D. (1992) 'The changing federal balance' in Peele, G., Bailey, C. and Cain, B. (eds) *Developments in American Politics*, London, Macmillan.

Landis, J.D. (1987) 'The future of America's central cities', *Built Environment*, vol.13, no.2, pp.228–45.

Lemann, N. (1991) *The Promised Land*, New York, Knopf.

Lineberry, R.L. and Fowler, E.P. (1967) 'Reformism and public policies in American cities', *American Political Science Review*, vol.61, no.3, pp.701–16.

Logan, J.R. and Molotch, H.L. (1987) *Urban Fortunes*, Berkeley, University of California Press.

Logan, J.R. and Schneider, M. (1984) 'Racial segregation and racial change in American suburbs 1970–1980', *American Journal of Sociology*, vol.89, no.4, pp.874–88.

Madison, J., Hamilton, A. and Jay, J. (1987) *The Federalist Papers*, Harmondsworth, Penguin Books.

Mills, E.S. (1987) 'Non-urban policies as urban policies', *Urban Studies*, vol.24, no.2, pp.41–68.

Mladenka, K.R. (1989) 'Blacks and Hispanics in urban politics', *American Political Science Review*, vol.83, pp.165–92.

Mollenkopf, J.H. (1983) *The Contested City*, Princeton, Princeton University Press.

Mollenkopf, J.H. (1993) *A Phoenix in the Ashes*, Princeton, Princeton University Press.

Peterson, P. (1981) *City Limits*, Chicago, University of Chicago Press.

Peterson, P. (ed.) (1985) *The Urban Reality*, Washington, DC, Brookings.

Savitch, H.V. and Thomas, J.C. (eds) (1991) *Big City Politics in Transition*, Newbury Park, Sage.

Schneider, M. (1989) *The Competitive City*, Pittsburgh, University of Pittsburgh Press.

Shefter, M. (1985) *Political Crisis/Fiscal Crisis*, New York, Basic Books.

Stone, C. (1989) *Regime Politics*, Lawrence, University Press of Kansas.

US Department of Housing and Urban Development (1982) *The President's National Urban Policy Report 1982*, Washington, DC, US Government Printing Office.

Ware, A. (1985) *The Breakdown of Democratic Party Organisation 1940–1980*, Oxford, Oxford University Press.

Warner, S.B. (1968) *The Private City: Philadelphia in Three Periods of its Growth*, Philadelphia, University of Pennsylvania Press.

Weir, M. and Skocpol, T. (1985) 'State structures and the possibilities for Keynesian responses to the Great Depression in Sweden, Britain and the United States' in Evans, P., Rueschmeyer, D. and Skocpol, T. (eds) *Bringing the State Back In*, Cambridge, Cambridge University Press.

Wirth, L. (1938) 'Urbanism as a way of life', *American Journal of Sociology*, vol.44, no.1, pp.3–24.

Wolman, H. (1990) 'The Reagan urban policy and its impacts' in King, D.S. and Pierre, J. (eds) *Challenges to Local Government*, London, Sage.

FURTHER READING

See Erie (1988), Grimshaw (1992), Katznelson (1981), Peterson (1981) and Stone (1989) in the references.

ETHNICITY AND 'RACE' IN AMERICAN POLITICS

John Zvesper ★

1 INTRODUCTION

Perceptions of ethnic and racial difference have posed perhaps the severest test of liberal democratic politics in the United States. Beginning to investigate how well or how badly the political system has passed this test is the purpose of this chapter. It can only be a beginning of such an investigation because anything approaching a full investigation, even if that is possible, would surely require several volumes. What we can reasonably aim to achieve in this chapter is (in Section 2) a clear picture of the two basic strategies that have been pursued by Americans in this area of policy, and (in Section 3) a sense of how these alternative strategies have helped to produce contradictory policy results.

2 CONTENDING POLICY GOALS

One of the clearest lessons of the history of twentieth-century American policies directed toward the management or improvement of ethnic and racial relations is that the strategic vision of those policies is deeply controversial. Among participants and observers there have been, and continue to be, profound differences about the appropriate ends of these policies. What is the most desirable and possible future shape of relations among ethnic and racial groups in America? What is the proper role of ethnicity and race in a liberal democracy? What, if anything, can and should American citizenship demand of members of ethnic and racial groups? The difficulty of answering these questions is one of the reasons why it is not surprising to find that there are very different judgements about the results of policies in this area, and about the health of the policy process that produces them, as well as about the wisdom of the policies themselves.

2.1 THE TENSION BETWEEN JUSTICE AND CONSENT IN LIBERAL DEMOCRATIC POLITICS

The US polity illustrates in numerous ways the basic tension inherent in the main principle of modern democratic politics. This tension is between the demands for justice and the demands for consent. This is not just a tension between liberty and equality. It is a tension within the idea of equality itself. On the one hand, the idea of political equality demands equal treatment, or justice. In other words, it demands government that respects and secures the equal rights of all citizens. On the other hand, the idea of equality also demands that government be based on consent, because it denies that there are any human beings who are so superior to others that they justly rule them without consent. Basing government on consent means paying attention to majority opinion, however irrational, prejudiced and unjust that opinion might be. Thus the demands for just government and for government by consent — both of them demands of the principle of human equality — can pull in opposite directions. One of the most important questions to ask about liberal democracy is whether and how this tension can and should be resolved. Is the tension within the idea of equality a debilitating contradiction? Is democratic politics fatally flawed? Or does the tension simply provide liberal democracy with a vitality and liveliness inseparable from political life?

Especially in an area like ethnicity and race, where opinions frequently include unjust prejudices, this inner tension of the basic principle of liberal democracy often produces serious political problems. Liberal democratic citizens and policy makers sometimes find it tempting to absolutize one or the other of the conflicting demands of equality: justice or consent. But if you pursue either of these demands without regard for the other, then you undermine the justification of the demand that you pursue. If a democratic government were to insist on immediate, pure, abstract justice, with no attention to powerful contrary opinions, it would not only risk being ignored or resisted, more fundamentally it would contradict and undermine its own democratic authority by denying one of the basic demands of equality, government by consent. Perhaps more common in American politics is the opposite error, when a government gives so much attention to the demands of consent that it ignores the demands of justice; this also is a self-contradictory position. Many commentators on the US polity have criticized it for showing far too much concern for deferring to powerful, entrenched opinions — that is, for the process of consent — and far too little to pursuing justice with policies that secure equal rights. But both demands must be met in order to satisfy the ideals of liberal democracy.

What this means in practice is that those concerned with pursuing just policies sooner or later have to be concerned to persuade public opinion to embrace those policies. Educating public opinion has to be a central task of democratic statecraft. Pessimists in the field of ethnic and race relations sometimes conclude that there are not only limits to this process of educating consent in any given circumstances, but also absolute limits to the extent to which ethnic and racial prejudices and related injustices can be expelled from democratic politics in any circumstances. Perhaps the accuracy of the pessimistic view can be assessed, if ever, only after the history of modern liberal democracies comes to an end. What is clear at this point is that pursuers of justice within liberal democracies have to operate on some level as optimists, trying to spot and to build upon the sound elements of public

opinion. (If there were no sound elements to build upon, they could conclude — as John Stuart Mill, a good liberal democratic theorist, concluded
about such dire, barbarian circumstances — that despotic government was
more appropriate than liberal democratic government.)

What this means for studying the success or failure of the American polity
in ethnic and racial matters is that we have to bear in mind two questions.
First, we must ask how well public opinion has been educated, or how supportive of justice in these matters American political culture is (and can be).
Secondly, we must ask how well the political system has succeeded in cultivating and representing the most enlightened elements of public opinion.
The American Constitution was originally justified by James Madison, in *The
Federalist* No.51, on the grounds that within the enlarged republic, with its
greater variety of groups than any one state contained, 'a coalition of a
majority of the whole society could seldom take place on any other principles than those of justice and the general good'. The severest test of that
theory is the continuing history of ethnic and racial politics in Madison's
republic.

2.2 CONTRADICTORY AMERICAN VISIONS OF LIBERAL ETHNIC AND RACIAL RELATIONS

The American motto, *e pluribus unum* — many made into one — referred
originally to federalism, the unity of several independent states. Today it is
also taken to refer to the ethnic diversity of the US. As with federalism,
there are questions about how unity and plurality can peacefully coexist. To
what extent can ethnic groups pursue their own aims, and what are the
overriding demands of American citizenship? Two extreme responses to
these questions have been developed in American political history, one
extreme pursuing pluralism, the other pursuing unity, each extreme denying
the claims of the other. There have also been visions that combine these
claims, but the extreme responses have often influenced policy making, and
the extremes are by no means absent from American politics in the last
quarter of the twentieth century. Even when the extreme responses have not
been dominant, tendencies towards them have been evident in policy thinking, legislation and adjudication, so it is worth starting by focusing on those
extreme responses, in which the frequently murky logic of ethnic and racial
politics is somewhat clearer.

The extreme pursuit of ethnic unity was a dominant strand of American
immigration policy in the early twentieth century. From the early days of
the republic to 1924, American immigration policy had been, historically
speaking, amazingly liberal, as far as 'free white persons' were concerned
(black Africans and, after 1882, Asians, were excluded); even the racial
exclusions — difficult for immigration officials and courts to define — were
often ignored in practice. 'The United States was the first country to decide,
as a matter of national policy, that it would be an immigrant-receiving country.' (Mann, 1979, ch.4.) However, in the latter half of the nineteenth century,
the composition of the immigrant population shifted away from northern

and western European natives towards natives of southern and eastern Europe. This change prompted a long debate on the proper policy towards this 'new immigration', a debate full of ethnic and racial stereotypes that suggested the 'new immigrants' were less assimilable than the older ones. This debate culminated in the restrictive legislation of the 1920s — not repealed until 1965 — which imposed quotas favouring those entering from the older immigrant-sending countries of northern and western Europe. Supporting this legislation was the argument of Anglo-Saxon supremacism, the argument that Americanism required conformity to an Anglo-Saxon ethnic model. 'Americanization' programmes were put into place, in order to cultivate this conformity and to suppress the new immigrant cultures (Hartmann, 1948, ch.10).

'Americanization' had always been thought of as an essential function of political culture in the United States, but the more traditional model of Americanization had emphasized the ideas associated with the American polity, rather than the ethnic or racial composition of the country. Understanding and acceptance of these ideas had been expected of immigrants (as of 'native' citizens) from the earliest days of the republic. (Of course, the real natives — the 'Indians' — had been constantly pushed westward, and occasionally subjected to genocide.) This super-ethnic 'creed' of political ideas, rather than any particular set of ethnic practices or beliefs, had been thought of as the source of political unity. Abraham Lincoln's reflections in 1858 on the American celebration of the anniversary of the Declaration of Independence (the Fourth of July) beautifully capture the genius of this non-ethnic kind of Americanization:

> We are now a mighty nation, we are thirty — or about thirty millions of people, and we own and inhabit about one-fifteenth part of the dry land of the whole earth. We run our memory back over the pages of history for about eighty-two years and we discover that we were then a very small people in point of numbers, vastly inferior to what we are now, with a vastly less extent of country, — with vastly less of everything we deem desirable among men, — we look upon the change as exceedingly advantageous to us and to our posterity, and we fix upon something that happened away back, as in some way or other being connected with this rise of prosperity. We find a race of men living in that day whom we claim as our fathers and grandfathers; they were iron men, they fought for the principle that they were contending for; and we understand that by what they then did it has followed that the degree of prosperity that we now enjoy has come to us. We hold this annual celebration to remind ourselves of all the good done in this process of time of how it was done and who did it, and how we are historically connected with it; and we go from these meetings in better humor with ourselves — we feel more attached the one to the other, and more firmly bound to the country we inhabit. In every way we are better men in the age, and race, and country in which we live for these celebrations. But after we have done all this we have not yet reached the whole. There is something else connected with it. We have besides these

men — descended by blood from our ancestors — among us perhaps half our people who are not descendants at all of these men, they are men who have come from Europe — German, Irish, French and Scandinavian — men that have come from Europe themselves, or whose ancestors have come hither and settled here, finding themselves our equals in all things. If they look back through this history to trace their connection with those days by blood, they find they have none, they cannot carry themselves back into that glorious epoch and make themselves feel that they are part of us, but when they look through that old Declaration of Independence they find that those old men say that 'We hold these truths to be self-evident, that all men are created equal', and then they feel that that moral sentiment taught in that day evidences their relation to those men, that it is the father of all moral principle in them, and that they have a right to claim it as though they were blood of the blood, and flesh of the flesh of the men who wrote that Declaration, and so they are. That is the electric cord in that Declaration that links the hearts of patriotic and liberty-loving men together, that will link those patriotic hearts as long as the love of freedom exists in the minds of men throughout the world.

(Abraham Lincoln, 1858, reproduced in Basler, 1953–5, vol.2, pp.499ff.)

' … and so they are': that is, immigrants who have no ethnic ties to the Founding Fathers can nevertheless be and feel themselves to be on a par with those who do, because they share a common humanity, and a recognition of human equality that is the source of a common morality. Ethical Founding Fathers, teaching a liberal political creed, take the place of ethnic patriarchs in this classical formulation of the demands of American citizenship. Ethnic loyalties and ethnic diversity are assumed to be compatible with the degree of unity required by the larger liberal community.

In this vision of ideological Americanization, the emphasis is on unity, but not to the exclusion of plurality. Lincoln's formulation is in this sense similar to Justice Harlan's famous Dissenting Opinion in *Plessy v. Ferguson* (discussed in Section 3.1), which described the US Constitution as 'color blind', while at the same time suggesting that 'pride of race' can have a legitimate place in the country, if it is expressed 'under appropriate circumstances, when the rights of others … are not to be affected' (163 US 556f., 1896). The combination of liberal democratic citizenship and ethnic solidarities may seem very promising, but it can be quite demanding on the ethnicities involved. In his argument that liberal democracy stands at the 'end of history', Francis Fukuyama notes that nationalism has to be 'defanged' — as it has been, he argues, in western Europe (in contrast to central Europe) — in order for national identities to be acceptable as political forces (Fukuyama, 1992, ch.25); in American politics, moderation if not complete extinction of ethnic loyalties has been a price demanded by Americanism. American experience suggests that it is difficult for this taming moderation of ethnicity to occur unless a strong sense of liberal community and citizenship is cultivated, by means of a liberal creed.

The 'assimilationist' ideal of Anglo-Saxon supremacism was challenged by this more traditional, ideological understanding of Americanism, but it was also challenged by two other schools of thought, both more fascinated by ethnicity and less concerned with political ideas as the necessary basis of political unity. First is the pursuit of the 'melting pot' image, or the argument that not Anglo-Saxonism but some new amalgamation of genes and cultures will produce a race of Americans, essentially an entirely new ethnic group. Secondly, and opposed to all three of the unity-oriented visions of ethnicity and politics — opposed, that is, to the assimilationist, ideological, and amalgamationist visions — is the notion of ethnic pluralism. This set of ideas, developed by certain intellectuals opposed to assimilationism and amalgamationism in the early twentieth century, has enjoyed a rebirth in the latter half of the twentieth century. Many of the most controversial ethnic policies of the current period — for example, bilingualism and multiculturalism — reflect this kind of thinking. A clear if rather extreme version of this policy vision can be found in the writings of Horace Kallen, who championed what he called 'a commonwealth of national cultures' (first published in 1924, see Kallen, 1970, p.116), and upheld 'the deep-lying cultural diversities of the ethnic groups' as 'the strongest shield' against the monotony and regimentation of those powerful modern (and American) forces, science and industry (ibid., p.229). Similar concerns were voiced by some of the supporters of the ethnic revival of the 1970s; for example, Michael Novak's defence of ethnicity saw it being challenged by American 'mass culture', an 'ersatz culture, a sort of false consciousness' arising 'from no particular culture' (Novak, 1980, pp.772–81). The emphasis in this policy school is all on the necessity of defending ethnic diversity and plurality, to the neglect of unity; thus it tends to attack Americanization, whether ethnic or ideological, as an unnecessarily alienating, uprooting process, that replaces the warmth of ethnic life with the cold modern state. The logical political strategy of ethnic pluralism is to move towards what the political scientist Arend Lijphart has called 'consociational democracy', a regime (such as Belgium or Switzerland) that incorporates citizens as members of groups rather than as individuals (Lijphart, 1977). In the second half of the twentieth century, that strategy has been explored not so much by or for American ethnic groups in general as by and for groups that have been perceived as being particularly beleaguered, such as certain Native Americans (Amerindians), black Americans, and Hispanic Americans.

2.3 WHITE RACISM AND BLACK AMERICANS

Up to this point, we have treated ethnicity and race as similar phenomena, but this is misleading if not wholly inaccurate. Ethnicity is a murky enough concept, but there is doubt that 'race' can be satisfactorily defined at all — partly because those who use the concept imply that it is rather precise. Racial prejudice is real enough, but assuming that there is something real to which such prejudices (however inaccurately) refer is unwarranted. Ethnicity, on the other hand, can be tolerably well-defined, whether as a greatly extended family (in terms of gene pools) or as an identifiable set of cultural practices and beliefs. Racism, or racial prejudice, then, would seem to consist in the mistaking of visible but unreliable ethnic markers (such as height or skin colour) as sure signs of ethnic difference, plus the view that the ethnic difference in question (such as — let us be a little fanciful here — a capacity to write sonnets) is shared by all members of the ethnic group, plus the mistaken judgement that this difference (itself quite possibly mistaken) is an important moral and political characteristic of the person and group judged to embody it, overshadowing any human moral and intellectual virtues that they might display. It is generally accompanied by the judgement that the person and group to whom the characteristics are being attributed are morally and politically inferior, if not indeed a lower species — a different 'race'. Racism, then, is a confused, mistaken, and invidious perception of ethnic difference.

In spite of the questionable reality of 'race', as everyone knows, racial prejudice and associated injustices have been rife in American politics. Although or because racism may be an extreme and irrational form of ethnic consciousness, the politics of 'race' in the United States has followed some of the same lines of development as the politics of ethnicity in general that we have just looked at. The group whose experience has been most massively and clearly involved in the politics of 'race' in America has been 'black' Americans. The strategies that they have used to come to terms with, to change or to escape from their situation (strategies to be discussed in Section 2.4) can be understood with reference to the ethnic strategies or visions surveyed in Section 2.2. Like those strategies, they divide roughly into unity-oriented and plurality-oriented strategies. The political problems facing black Americans have made them come up with some stark and therefore clearly stated versions of these strategies.

However, in drawing these parallels, the differences between ethnic politics and 'racial' politics must not be forgotten. To take black Americans as the epitome of the American ethnic group would be a very dubious step. In the first place, no other group has been subjected to slavery and then systematic, legally-sanctioned segregation. In the second place, one thing that has often characterized and troubled black Americans is precisely their *lack* of ethnicity. The traditional ethnic backgrounds of many African-Americans were quite consciously and thoroughly destroyed when they were first brought to America as slaves. It is deeply ironic, therefore, that they should have become the objects of a prejudice allegedly based on neutral or even scientific observations about their ethnic and 'racial' character. It would seem more logical to think of them — in the words of one of the most profound black American political thinkers, W.E. Burghardt Du Bois — as the truest 'exponents of the pure *human* spirit of the Declaration of Independence' (Du Bois, 1903, reproduced in Storing, 1970, p.91, my italics). Black Americans themselves have had trouble defining their ethnic or racial culture.

In essays published in 1953, James Baldwin remarked that African slaves in America, unlike slaves in past epochs, had no means of maintaining their identity; this fact was related to the fact that, also unlike some former slaves, they could never suppose that they 'would ever be able to wrest the power' from their masters' hands (Baldwin, 1953, reproduced in Storing, 1970, p.221).

> ... the American Negro slave is unique among the black men of the world in that his past was taken from him, almost literally, at one blow. One wonders what on earth the first slave found to say to the first dark child he bore. I am told that there are Haitians able to trace their ancestry back to African kings, but any American Negro wishing to go back so far will find his journey through time abruptly arrested by the signature on the bill of sale which served as the entrance paper for his ancestor. At the time — to say nothing of the circumstances — of the enslavement of the captive black man who was to become the American Negro, there was not the remotest possibility that he would ever take power from his master's hands. There was no reason to suppose that his situation would ever change, nor was there, shortly, anything to indicate that his situation had ever been different. It was his necessity, in the words of E. Franklin Frazier, to find a 'motive for living under American culture or die'. The identity of the American Negro comes out of this extreme situation, and the evolution of this identity was a source of the most intolerable anxiety in the minds and the lives of his masters.
>
> (James Baldwin, 1953, reproduced in Storing, 1970, p.221)

This extreme situation of blacks in America, Baldwin noted, inevitably affected whites in America. It provides one explanation for whites' prejudices that try to dehumanize blacks:

> ... the white man prefers to keep the black man at a certain human remove because it is easier for him thus to preserve his simplicity and avoid being called to account for crimes committed by his forefathers, or his neighbors. He is inescapably aware, nevertheless, that he is in a better position in the world than black men are, nor can he quite put to death the suspicion that he is hated by black men therefore. He does not wish to be hated, neither does he wish to change places, and at this point in his uneasiness he can scarcely avoid having recourse to those legends which white men have created about black men, the most usual effect of which is that the white man finds himself enmeshed, so to speak, in his own language which describes hell, as well as the attributes which lead one to hell, as being as black as night.
>
> (James Baldwin, 1953, reproduced in Storing, 1970, p.219)

Thus, feeling complicity in the crimes against blacks, whites are psychologically propelled to justify and to perpetuate those crimes.

Baldwin also noticed another important effect that the extreme situation of blacks had on the situation of whites: 'the interracial drama acted out on the American continent has not only created a new black man, it has created a new white man, too' (ibid., p.224).

For the history of the American Negro is unique also in this: that the question of his humanity, and of his rights therefore as a human being, became a burning one for several generations of Americans, so burning a question that it ultimately became one of those used to divide the nation.

(James Baldwin, 1953, reproduced in Storing, 1970, p.221)

And while 'the strain of denying the overwhelmingly undeniable' — the human reality of the black — forced some whites into 'rationalizations so fantastic that they approached the pathological', there were also white Americans who 'rose to be greater than themselves by virtue of the fact that the challenge he represented was inescapable' (ibid., p.223). Baldwin thus observed that the close confrontation between blacks and prejudiced whites in America held some potential for breaking down the prejudices, as well as for strengthening them. Optimistically, one could reasonably hope that, although racial prejudice might never die, political and social life could be elevated because of the greater awareness of humanity that could arise out of the relationships between black and white Americans.

2.4 BLACK POLITICAL STRATEGIES

During the four decades that have passed since Baldwin published these reflections, both the optimistic and the pessimistic possibilities that he felt have been witnessed in American political history. It is a debateable question whether the optimistic or the pessimistic potential has proved greater. It is clear, however, that responses to that question have been closely linked to the divergent political strategies of black Americans. The more optimistic have chosen strategies aimed at accepting America as a country in which they can live as citizens, and be treated as individuals; the more pessimistic have developed strategies aimed at cultivating their rights and entitlements as members of a group, and have raised doubts about whether they can ever truly regard America as their country. Many of the most thoughtful black Americans have voiced both strategies, and combinations of them all the way along the spectrum from one to the other; sometimes they have also tried to find a basis for their strategy in such diverse sources as Islam, Marxism, and pan-Africanism. This is a sign of their desperation, but it has also been a sign of their recognition of the desirability of synthesizing both strategies, rather as some broader ethnic strategies (for example, Lincoln's and Harlan's, noted in Section 2.2) try to combine the advantages, or at least the necessity, of ethnic consciousness with the advantages of liberal citizenship.

An integrationist strategy has characterized the mainstreams of black American political thinking, although especially in the 1960s and 1970s there developed alongside the mainstreams — and within them — more serious consideration of a separatist approach. Integrationism was clearly the strategy of the Civil Rights movement that has pushed for desegregation, equal employment opportunities and voting rights, with notable judicial and legislative successes (which we shall look at in the following section). The emphasis of this strategy is on individual rights rather than group rights, and on holding Americans to their basic political creed, claiming the blessings of that creed for every citizen, regardless of any ethnic or 'racial' characteristics. James Weldon Johnson compactly stated the core of this strategy:

> From early times there have been sincere thinkers among us who were brought to the conclusion that our only salvation lies in the making of the race into a self-contained economic, social, and cultural unit; in a word, in the building of an *imperium in imperio* [dominion within a dominion].
>
> All along, however, majority opinion has held that the only salvation worth achieving lies in the making of the race into a component part of the nation, with all the common rights and privileges, as well as duties, of citizenship. ... the outcome of voluntary isolation would be a permanent secondary status ... We should gather all the strength and experience we can from imposed segregation. But any good we are able to derive from the system we should consider as a means, not an end. The strength and experience we gain from it should be applied to the objective of *entering into*, not *staying out of* the body politic.
>
> (James Weldon Johnson, 1934, reproduced in Storing, 1970, pp.106–9)

One of the most moving and famous statements of this strategy was surely the speech by Martin Luther King, Jr., during the August 1963 Civil Rights march on Washington:

> There will be neither rest nor tranquillity in America until the Negro is granted his citizenship rights. The whirlwinds of revolt will continue to shake the foundations of our nation until the bright day of justice emerges ... I have a dream that my four little children will one day live in a nation where they will not be judged by the color of their skin but by the content of their character.
>
> (Martin Luther King, Jr., Lincoln Memorial, 28 August 1963, reproduced in Williams, 1987, pp.204–5)

To some blacks in America who heard King talking about his 'dream', this strategy seemed flawed. Malcolm X, a leader of the Black Muslim movement (which temporally coincided with and played a forceful role within the officially integrationist Civil Rights movement), spoke about the American system in terms not of a dream but of 'an American nightmare'. His case for a separatist, black nationalist strategy was based on rejection of the idea that blacks in America could or should consider themselves as Americans: 'If I could consider myself an American, we wouldn't even have any problem' (Malcolm X, 1964, reproduced in Epps, 1969, pp.134–5):

> Being born here in America doesn't make you an American. Why, if birth made you American, you wouldn't need any legislation, you wouldn't need any amendments to the Constitution, you wouldn't be faced with civil-rights filibustering in Washington, DC, right now.

Malcolm X in 1961 at a Black Muslim rally in Washington, DC. Malcolm X (who aban-doned his last name as a relic of slavery) was the son of a Baptist minister. He converted to Islam during his imprisonment for burglary (1946–53), and became one of the chief proponents of black nationalism, sharply critical of the integrationist ideals of the main-stream Civil Rights movement

The Reverend Doctor Martin Luther King, Jr., in 1963, at the 17th Street Baptist Church in Birmingham, Alabama (a church that was later bombed, injuring several children). Churches played an important part in the Civil Rights movement in the North as well as in the South

They don't have to pass civil-rights legislation to make a Polack an American.

No, I'm not an American. I'm one of the 22 million black people who are the victims of Americanism.

(Malcolm X, 1965, reproduced in Storing, 1970, pp.148–9)

In their purest form, separatist strategies have called for separation of blacks and whites, either by black emigration to Africa or some other land, or by carving out from US territory a new country for blacks. According to this argument, only by physical and political separation can blacks (and whites) escape from America's racist culture and political structure. Moreover, and more positively, only by ex-American blacks engaging in the founding of their own country can they fulfil some of their noblest human potential, the potential to construct and to manage a political community. Until black Americans get their promised land, their Israel, they have to live as (in Eldridge Cleaver's words) a 'black colony dispersed throughout the continent', preparing to free itself from 'their enemies ... the white mother country of America' (Eldridge Cleaver, 1968, reproduced in Storing, 1970, p.189). In this analysis, integration is a delusive strategy, a form of false consciousness that prevents blacks from seeing their true situation and acting accordingly:

> Integration embodies the dream of the mother country which sees America as a huge melting pot. ... The mother country's euphemism of 'second class citizenship' is a smokescreen that seeks to obscure the colonial status of black people in America. ... Integration represents an attempt by the white mother country to forestall the drive for national liberation by its colonial subjects in precisely the same manner as France sought to hold onto its colonial spoils by defining its holdings as 'overseas provinces', or as Britain tried to do with its Commonwealth, or as Portugal tried to do with its 'overseas provinces'.

(Eldridge Cleaver, 1968, reproduced in Storing, 1970, pp.186f.)

In the 1960s and 1970s, some blacks who turned away from integrationism developed the idea of 'Black Power'. The Black Power movement has drawn much of its inspiration from separatist strategies. It is 'a call for black people in this country to unite, to recognize their heritage, to build a sense of community. It is a call for black people to begin to define their own goals, to lead their own organizations and to support those organizations.' (Carmichael and Hamilton, 1967, reproduced in Storing, 1970, p.173.) It emphasizes that 'while color blindness *may* be a sound goal ultimately, we must realize that race is an overwhelming fact of life in this historical period.' However, the Black Power movement also presents itself as a means of accomplishing true integration — integration not by assimilation to the existing political community, but by becoming an active and respected part of an enlarged and more complex political community, just as other groups have done in the United States in the past and present. Stokely Carmichael and Charles V. Hamilton, two of the leading voices in the early days of the

Black Power movement, were thus able to articulate the movement's strategy in terms that compared this movement to previous ethnic group politics in America:

> The concept of Black Power rests on a fundamental premise: *Before a group can enter the open society, it must first close ranks.* By this we mean that group solidarity is necessary before a group can operate effectively from a bargaining position of strength in a pluralistic society. Traditionally, each new ethnic group in this society has found the route to social and political viability through the organization of its own institutions with which to represent its needs within the larger society …
>
> It does not mean *merely* putting black faces into office. Black visibility is not Black Power. Most of the black politicians around the country today are not examples of Black Power. The power must be that of a community, and emanate from there.
>
> (Carmichael and Hamilton, 1967, reproduced in Storing, 1970, pp.173, 175, original italics)

In the Black Power strategy, collective black efforts are needed, not only in order successfully to play the pluralist game of American politics, but also in order to play a proud rather than a submissive and therefore permanently subordinate part in American politics and society:

> The racial and cultural personality of the black community must be preserved and that community must win its freedom while preserving its cultural integrity. Integrity includes a pride — in the sense of self-acceptance, not chauvinism — in being black, in the historical attainments and contributions of black people. No person can be healthy, complete and mature if he must deny a part of himself; this is what 'integration' has required thus far. This is the essential difference between integration as it is currently practiced and the concept of Black Power.
>
> (Carmichael and Hamilton, 1967, reproduced in Storing, 1970, p.181)

Black Power advocates share a suspicion that integration without the necessary preparation of building black consciousness means acceptance of the demeaning and false idea that 'there is nothing of value in the black community and that little of value could be created among black people', and has the effect of siphoning off 'the "acceptable" black people into the surrounding middle-class white community', sapping the black community 'of leadership potential and know-how', and 'draining skills and energies from the black ghetto into white neighborhoods'. This kind of '"integration" is a subterfuge for the maintenance of white supremacy', for it 'reinforces, among both black and white, the idea that "white" is automatically superior and "black" is by definition inferior' (ibid., pp.179f.).

The Black Power strategy thus offers a promising mixture of the themes of unity and plurality. However, it raises again the problem of defining 'black culture', and makes a response to that question more urgent.

SUMMARY

Liberal democracy requires attention to consent and public opinion as well as to considerations of equal justice. This poses difficult problems for ethnic and racial politics, because public opinion includes prejudiced opinion.

Moreover, in liberal democracies, ethnic policies can be — as in the US they have been — steered towards two often conflicting goals: greater unity (whether through genetic assimilation or amalgamation, or by means of a liberal political creed), or deepened plurality (through the maintenance of ethnic group identities).

The 'racial' divide between white and black Americans has driven blacks to develop these conflicting policy goals rather clearly, with separatist strategies developing alongside — sometimes conflicting with, and sometimes complementing — a more dominant integrationist strategy.

3　AMBIGUOUS POLICY RESULTS OF A CHANGING POLICY PROCESS

The ambiguity of the achievements of the American Civil Rights movements during the last four decades is understandable, against the background of this mixture of motives, strategies, hopes and fears about the relations of black Americans to the American polity. Different judgements on the extent and significance of the achievements of the civil rights struggles can be understood partly as a reflection of the very different expectations associated with different participants in and observers of those struggles. The ambiguity of the policy results is increased by changes in the policy process, changes which have been one of the major themes of this book. In this section, then, we look at the first and second phases of the 'Civil Rights era', in order to see something of these connections between policy strategies and results, and between policy processes and results.

3.1　INTEGRATIONIST LEGAL AND POLITICAL ACHIEVEMENTS IN THE 1950s AND 1960s

There are many reasons why the Civil Rights movement came to the centre of the public stage in the 1950s and 1960s: the black population had changed from being largely based on southern farming communities to being based in cities and less restricted to the South (by 1960 40 per cent of the black population lived in the north), and they were registering to vote in larger (though not massive) numbers; the fight against racist Nazis in the Second World War had highlighted America's legally-entrenched racism; and the Cold War continued this pressure on public opinion, with communist leaders ridiculing America's faithlessness to the country's professed ideals. Given the astonishing degree of legal discrimination and segregation that confronted black Americans in the early twentieth century, perhaps it was natural that the more integrationist strands of political strategy should have been the ones that eventually came to dominate public attention and to effect so many changes in public policy in the Civil Rights era. There was obviously so much that could and should be done simply in eliminating racist laws, that this integration-oriented project seemed more compelling, both to blacks and to their white allies, than the more local and longer-term project of building black consciousness and black communities. Those less integrationist strategies continued to be cultivated, and would have a greater impact on policy in the second phase of the Civil Rights era, from the late 1960s into the 1970s and beyond.

Legally speaking, the 'Second Reconstruction' of the Civil Rights era largely consisted of steps to put into effect the Amendments to the Constitution that had been enacted during the 'First Reconstruction', the period immediately following the Civil War. These Amendments outlaw slavery (Amendment XIII, 1865); define as citizens 'All persons born or naturalized in the United States' and forbid any state to 'deprive any person of life, liberty, or property, without due process of law' or 'deny to any person within its jurisdiction the equal protection of the laws' (Amendment XIV, 1868); and state that the right to vote 'shall not be denied or abridged … on account of race, color, or previous condition of servitude' (Amendment XV, 1870). In the decade following the Civil War, Civil Rights Acts following through these Amendments had been passed by a radical Republican-controlled Congress; these laws made it a federal crime to interfere with the right to vote or with other rights secured by the Constitution or by federal law, and penalized violators of the right to full and equal enjoyment of public accommodations. However, these post-Civil War measures had been passed before the defeated southerners returned to playing a full role in national politics; and when many of the measures were declared unconstitutional by the Supreme Court in the *Civil Rights Cases* (109 US 3) in 1883, on the ground that they were too broad to be warranted by the post-Civil War Amendments, there was no great public outcry against the Court. Nor was there a few years later, when the Court, in *Plessy v. Ferguson*, declared that various states' statutes providing for separate public accommodations for blacks did not violate the Fourteenth Amendment's provision for 'equal protection of the laws': 'separate but equal' accommodations were deemed to be legal, so Homer Plessy's exclusion from a railway carriage restricted to whites, and the whole set of such 'Jim Crow' (segregation) laws set up in this period, were given the Court's sanction.

In the middle of the twentieth century, American public opinion was more receptive to decisions and laws protecting civil rights. Nevertheless there were hard battles to get the decisions made and respected, and to get the laws enacted and implemented. Many of these battles were carried on at the state and local level long before they were fought out in the national arena. When they reached the national arena, the slow, deliberate, non-parliamentarian, non-party government character of the American political system was exemplified even when such important legislation as the Civil Rights Act of 1964 was actually passed.

The first great successes of the Civil Rights movement were achieved in the courts, where civil rights lawyers attacked racially restrictive covenants in housing, segregation in interstate transportation, discrimination in publicly owned recreational facilities, and, most triumphantly, in the *Brown v. Board of Education* decisions of 1954 and 1955 (347 US 483 and 349 US 294), segregation in public schools. The *Brown* decisions illustrated many of the strengths and the weaknesses of the position of the judicial branch in the American polity (discussed in Chapter 5). On the one hand, the judiciary, especially the Supreme Court, *can* serve as a moral and constitutional tutor to public opinion and to the other branches of government. On the other hand, its decisions are not self-enforcing. In the *Brown* decision the Supreme Court recognized its own weakness in this respect. It knew that the decision in this case, that separate public schools were inherently unequal, would be resisted, particularly in the southern states. So, not wishing to adopt an excessively accusatory tone against the South or against its own precedents, it did not condemn the *Plessy* doctrine of 'separate but equal' as a clear error of construction of the Fourteenth Amendment, but relied instead on psychological findings (a 'modern authority' not available when *Plessy* was decided) that racial segregation 'generates a feeling of inferiority' which harms black children's education. In addition to its choice of an inoffensive argument, the Court recognized its limited power by calling (in the second *Brown* case, in 1955) for school desegregation to be undertaken 'with all deliberate speed'. That formula left much room for manœuvre and delay. Ten years after *Brown*, only 2 per cent of black school children in the South attended schools that white children also attended.

Resistance to integration of schools took forms other than judicially-sanctioned 'deliberate speed'. The *Brown* decision had boosted attendance at private schools. There was also a trend towards 'white flight' away from areas in which desegregation meant mixed-race schools. Running counter to this trend was a policy adopted in some school districts of cross-town busing in order to achieve racial integration. The Court approved this practice in cases where school districts have deliberately segregated students by race (*Swann v. Charlotte-Mecklenburg Board of Education*, 402 US 1, 1971). However, there has been an acrimonious debate over the merits of busing. (One of Linda Brown's complaints in the 1954 case had been that, having been denied admission to a nearby but all-white school, she had had to take a bus to an all-black school.) The Court has, in its way, responded to this debate. In 1974 (*Milliken v. Bradley*, 418 US 717) the Court disapproved a 'metropolitan' busing plan, that would have encompassed Detroit and its suburbs. In the 1980s the Court started allowing some school districts to discontinue busing, emphasizing that a district is not responsible for correcting any resegregation that occurs as a result of demographic changes, as long as deliberate segregation by the district is no longer involved.

In the late 1950s and early 1960s, non-violent 'direct action' (boycotts, sit-ins, marches, demonstrations, etc.) took its place alongside legal briefs in the civil rights armoury. Direct action was a tactic suited to the urban environment in which more and more blacks lived. Often such direct action followed up favourable legislation or judicial decisions, testing how well — or how badly — they were being followed up in practice. But direct action also served to dramatize and to publicize situations in a way that a legal case on its own never could. The growing importance of television and the national news media in American politics during this period helped to publicize and to nationalize the civil rights struggle. One of the most spectacularly successful and memorable direct actions was the boycott of the buses in Montgomery, Alabama, following the arrest of Rosa Parks in 1955 for her refusal to move to the 'colored' section at the back of the bus. This was the action that made Martin Luther King, Jr., then a 27-year-old Baptist minister, a nationally prominent civil rights leader.

This direct action displayed very clearly and openly the ugliness of racial segregation and of the violence of its champions. Public opinion was mobilized and politicians felt obliged to respond. The presidential branch of government responded more quickly than Congress, which always faced southern filibusters against strong civil rights bills. Rather ineffective Civil Rights Acts passed Congress in 1957 and 1960 (establishing the Civil Rights Commission and a civil rights division in the Justice Department, and giving the Justice Department the right to sue to protect voting rights). Both the Democratic and the Republican presidential candidates in 1960 were 'men identified with activism on civil rights' (Sundquist, 1968, p.251). After the election of the Democrat, John Kennedy — and after he was assassinated, and was replaced by Lyndon Johnson, an astute congressional politico, anxious to prove that a southern President could do the right thing on racial policy — came the more significant Civil Rights Act of 1964, and Voting Rights Act of 1965. These Acts came on the heels of well-publicized violent resistance to non-violent protests. The violence was an important ingredient:

> King had failed miserably in his major desegregation campaign in Albany, Georgia, in 1961 and 1962. There police chief Laurie Pritchett had politely arrested and jailed all civil disobeyers, thereby providing little martyrdom and small inducement for television news cameras. But not so in Birmingham in 1963, where Bull Connor played the perfect foil, and the chief result was the Civil Rights Act of 1964. King needed a similarly inhospitable environment to dramatize the need for radical federal intervention to enfranchise southern blacks, and he found it in Selma.
>
> (Graham, 1990, p.165)

As originally designed and interpreted, these two Acts continued the integrationist, equal opportunities vision of civil rights, although both of them were soon to be reinterpreted, during the second phase of the Civil Rights era, in terms that gave more attention to equality of results and anticipated a less colour blind, more emphatically plural polity. The 1964 Act tightened rules against discrimination in voter registration, outlawed discrimination in public accommodations (where their operations affected interstate commerce or the discrimination was supported by state laws or customs), gave the federal government the authority to sue to compel desegregation, banned discrimination in any activity (for example, many university courses) in receipt of federal money, and established a right to equal opportunity in employment, to be pursued by the Equal Employment Opportunity Commission (EEOC). The Voting Rights Act of 1965 outlawed discriminatory voter registration tests and authorized federal officials temporarily to take over voter registration in areas (mainly in the South) where voting registration or actual voting in presidential elections included fewer than 50 per cent of the voting-age population.

Like virtually all important legislation in the United States, the 1964 and 1965 Acts incorporated compromises hammered out during lengthy deliberations. However, in these compromises, southern concerns were given less deference than northern fears about the effects of the Acts; for example, the Senate minority leader, Everett Dirksen (of Illinois), was able to insert amendments to the 1964 Act (e.g. weakening the EEOC's power to initiate legal proceedings against employers) that addressed northern fears about the breadth of the employment opportunity provisions of the Act. Only by making the Act appear to be directed mainly at the obvious injustices in the South could the coalition of liberal Democrats and liberal Republicans defeat the filibuster by conservative Senators (Graham, 1990, pp.145–52). In their most unambiguous effects, both the 1964 and 1965 Acts have indeed affected the South more than the rest of the country. The bold public accommodations section of the 1964 Act destroyed 'Jim Crow' practices 'with surprising speed and virtually self-executing finality' (ibid., p.152). And the Voting Rights Act has transformed politics in the South; few politicians there can now afford to ignore the votes of black citizens.

Perhaps the 1964 and 1965 Acts, then, can serve as a good example of the theory of *The Federalist* No.51 (discussed in Section 2.1) working as intended, with the large republic taking a step towards 'justice and the general good' that smaller territories on their own would not have taken. On the other hand, the federal government acted less quickly than had some states. Besides, the role of public opinion and the presidency as the tribune of the people is a modern addition to Madison's theory. At any rate, the Acts were clearly a good example of majoritarian politics and solid electoral calculations. Those relatively few southern Democrats who voted for the Acts represented urban districts, with substantial numbers of black voters (Graham, 1990, p.173). Moreover:

> The singular fact to emerge from the election of 1960 was that the solid vote of urban blacks for Kennedy accounted for the narrow margin of victory over Nixon. Since this same urban vote had gone for Eisenhower in 1956, the evident political strategy for the Democrats in the 1960s was to consolidate this vote in the Democratic camp. The Civil Rights Act of 1964 and the Voting Rights Act of 1965, whatever altruism they may have displayed as remedies for

'historic' discrimination, were a large part of the attempt to keep the urban black vote solidly Democratic. They were thus ... a recognition that blacks had become a significant and crucial part of the governing majority.

(Erler, 1982, p.443)

3.2   FRAGMENTATION OF POLICY AND POLICY MAKING IN THE SECOND PHASE OF THE CIVIL RIGHTS ERA

A noticeable decline in this majoritarian character of policy making came with the second phase of the Civil Rights era. During the 1970s and 1980s a more fragmented policy process accompanied a more fragmenting vision of ethnic and racial policy. This strategic and procedural fragmentation continued into the 1990s, so to understand today's civil rights controversies we need to understand the genesis of this newer and more pluralistic approach.

This fragmenting vision first appeared as a way of justifying and transforming the federal government's civil rights policies in the 1960s and 1970s, in executive orders and bureaucratic activities reviewed by courts, rather than in publicly-debated legislation. It is arguable that adopting such a vision is in fact inevitable when one turns from drafting general laws to implementing and enforcing them (Graham, 1990, pp.456–8). For example, how can one know whom to prosecute for racial discrimination if one does not to some extent 'count by race', thereby adopting and encouraging a less colour-blind approach to politics and business? But this shift away from the 'political' (elective) branches of government towards the 'non-political' governmental bodies (bureaucratic and judicial) also reflects a deeper and widespread feature of the American polity during the last three decades. Furthermore, the adoption of the more fragmenting vision of 'affirmative action' came out of the changing political circumstances of the later 1960s, a period in which an air of social crisis and desperation made desperate measures seem appropriate. Like busing, affirmative action is generally unpopular in opinion polls (even among its 'beneficiaries'), but various policy élites, for various reasons, have found it attractive.

'Affirmative action' is the generic term applied in the United States to the proactive pursuit of civil rights. It can take rather mild, uncontroversial forms, such as ensuring wide publicity to job vacancies, but it also includes the much more controversial practice of preferential treatment to members of groups 'protected' by civil rights legislation. In other words, it can shift over into a strategy of protecting *group* rights rather than *individual* rights, and a focus on equalization of *results* rather than of *opportunities*. This is the heart of some of the most heated civil rights controversies of recent years. The Supreme Court, itself a much more fragmented body in the 1970s and 1980s, has been unable or unwilling to decide this matter. The Reagan and (less strenuously) the Bush Administrations tried, inconsistently, to combat the shift towards affirmative action as group rights, but their mixed success left this controversy still on the agenda of American politics as the Democrats reclaimed the presidency in 1992 (Peele, 1992).

Jesse Jackson at the Supreme Court in 1989, protesting against the Court's decisions on 'affirmative action' (soon to be reversed by the Civil Rights Act of 1991) that made it more difficult for employees to prove charges of racial discrimination against employers. Jackson was a candidate for the Democratic Party's presidential nomination in 1984 and 1988; in 1988 he received 95 per cent of the black vote in the Party's primary elections

Even before the civil rights laws of 1964 and 1965 were enacted, there were many civil rights activists and some politicians who favoured race-conscious treatment of blacks and other minority groups as the best way of addressing the problem of past and present discrimination. Those laws were immediately reinterpreted by some civil rights lawyers as allowing and even requiring a race-conscious approach to determining when and where discrimination had occurred, and the courts and executive agencies responsible for enforcing those laws moved in that direction. In this way, 'A political decision was made to revive race as a criterion of public policy in the belief that race-based decision making, when employed in the service of a good cause and used not to stigmatize or offend those whose rights are thereby denied, has no corrupting effect, but rather is consistent with democratic justice.' (Belz, 1991, p.41.)

As noted above (in Section 3.1), non-violent demonstrations, bipartisan coalitions and majoritarian party calculations played a large role in the making of the Civil Rights Act of 1964 and the Voting Rights Act of 1965, both of which embodied the integrationist principles of equality of individual opportunity. The shift towards a policy of equalization of group results was encouraged by notably different political conditions. An increasingly out-

spoken Black Power movement, coupled with violent urban riots — perceived and described by some as 'race riots' — in the summers from 1964 to
1968, helped make it possible to justify emergency policies with more
immediate results than the Civil Rights Acts (as originally designed) could
promise. In this crisis atmosphere, bipartisanship in the civil rights field
became more rare, and Congress became happier to let the administrative
agencies and the courts take over the initiative in civil rights policy, so it
could avoid partisan controversy. On the other hand, partisan calculations
were still made, of course, and on the whole these favoured the continued
development of hard affirmative action policies. The election of a Republican President, Richard Nixon, in 1968, merely shifted the emphasis on this
new 'liberal' civil rights policy away from schools and the South and
towards employment discrimination, to force a wedge between the Democratic Party's civil rights sentiments and supporters on the one hand and, on
the other, their labour union supporters (historically quite racist, and generally opposed to affirmative action) (Belz, 1991, pp.34–41). (The Democratic
Party did obligingly split largely in the desired manner. Not before the 1992
presidential election has there been much evidence of that split having been
healed, and it remains to be seen whether the biracial unity seen among the
Democrats in 1992 will endure.)

The agencies most responsible for shifting the civil rights agenda into the
second phase were the Equal Employment Opportunity Commission, established by the Civil Rights Act of 1964, and the Office of Federal Contract
Compliance (OFCC). The OFCC, part of the Labor Department, followed
from an executive order of President Johnson in 1965. It wielded the power
of the federal purse, a not inconsiderable weapon in civil rights enforcement, which had been used by the federal government as long ago as the
1940s (during the Second World War) in order to encourage businesses with
federal contracts — and the unions that organized their labour — to end
racial discrimination. Under the presidency of Richard Nixon, the OFCC
began pursuing an ambitious policy of insisting on firm percentages of
'minority' workers being employed on federally-funded projects. Both the
EEOC and the OFCC can be compared to other 'new social regulation' agencies that emerged in the 1960s and 1970s: for example, the Occupational
Safety and Health Administration, the Environmental Protection Agency,
and the Consumer Product Safety Commission. These agencies all dealt with
issues that cut across several (or all) sectors of the economy, so differed from
the classic 'iron triangle' type of regulation in which cosy and well-defined
relationships between regulators and regulated had grown up. The 'issue
networks' of the 'new regulation' are less tightly defined, and therefore
more open to controversy, although their controversies are often couched in
technocratic jargon. The new regulators have wide discretionary powers
delegated to them by Congress, and they in turn issue broad regulations,
applying to a wide range of activities. They address the problems that they
are asked to solve less with specific cease-and-desist orders directed at
single offenders than with detailed but general rule making, swelling the
Federal Register with proposed and final guidelines and standards. But there
is a difference between the civil rights agencies and the other new social
regulators:

For the consumer–environment regulators, all citizens deserved equal protection from the harms of polluted environs or dangerous products and services. The reach of these new protections was determined by statutory and administrative policy rather than by constitutional guarantees. The civil rights regulators, however, diverged from the equal treatment tradition after 1965, and shifted to an equal-results approach based on a model of proportional representation grounded in group rights theory. This ... set them against the American constitutional tradition of equal individual rights, and as a result the minority preferences required by the civil rights agencies drew them, unlike the other social regulators — the anti-pollution monitors and the safe toy police — into thorny controversies like the constitutional suits over reverse discrimination.

(Graham, 1990, p.468)

Thus, the shift away from integrationist policy in the second phase of civil rights was a conscious decision by some important actors in the political system, but it also fits very closely with two more general changes in the American polity in the 1970s and 1980s: the continued rise of federal courts and bureaucracies as rivals to Congress in social policy making, and the movement of federal bureaucracies away from specific and limited areas of responsibility towards general, society-wide terms of reference. Both of these changes involved an increase in public controversy and more acrimonious confrontations among the various elements of the political system. A more fragmented political system has thus dealt with ethnic and racial policy at the same time that a fragmenting vision of ethnic and racial relations has become more dominant.

SUMMARY

During the 1950s and 1960s, the black Civil Rights movement advanced integrationist arguments, to which American public opinion and the political process gradually responded. The American political system thus demonstrated its capacity for deliberative majoritarian politics.

In the last two decades, minoritarian politics has been more evident, with a new emphasis on group rights and a more fragmented policy process.

4   CONCLUSION

The two basic strategies of ethnic politics in America — the integrationist and the separatist strategies — are antagonistic, but they are not mutually exclusive. They can be seen as parts of a dialectical process. As noted in Section 2.4, some Black Power theorists have suggested that separation is a necessary precursor to integration. However, there are dangers in relying on the workings of a dialectical process. The advance of the case for separatism from the late 1960s does seem to have threatened the capacity of the American political system to work towards integration: a minoritarian politics and a more fragmented polity have threatened to replace the more traditional majoritarian politics characteristic of the first phase of the Civil Rights era (as described in Section 3.1). At the same time, nostalgia for an allegedly more innocent and integrated past, as well as genuine appreciation of the shortcomings of fragmented politics, have posed substantial obstacles to ethnic or racial separatism, even while not articulating very clearly any tenable grounds for a stronger sense of liberal citizenship and community. America's progress towards justice in matters of ethnicity and 'race' thus remains ambiguous and controversial. Americans remain divided on what would constitute the right mixture of separation and integration, of plurality and unity. And in any case the liberal creed that has served in the past as a basis for cultivating unity seems less credible in an age of postmodern doubts about universal truths.

Perhaps one of the practical consequences of the simultaneous workings of both the integrationist and the separatist strategies is the creation of two black Americas: a large middle class (now two-thirds of the total black population) and a smaller but worryingly self-perpetuating lower class. Or perhaps ethnic policies and strategies have only marginal effects on this: perhaps the political problems of class run deeper, after all, than those of ethnicity and 'race', in modern urban America.

REFERENCES

Basler, R.P. (ed.) (1953–5) *The Collected Works of Abraham Lincoln*, 9 vols, New Brunswick, Rutgers University Press.

Belz, H. (1991) *Equality Transformed: a Quarter-Century of Affirmative Action*, New Brunswick, Transaction Publishers.

Epps, A. (ed.) (1969) *The Speeches of Malcolm X*, London, Peter Owen.

Erler, E.J. (1982) 'Equal protection and personal rights: the regime of the "discrete and insular minority"', *Georgia Law Review*, vol.16, pp.407–44.

Fukuyama, F. (1992) *The End of History and the Last Man*, London, Hamish Hamilton.

Graham, H.D. (1990) *The Civil Rights Era: Origins and Development of National Policy, 1960–1972*, New York, Oxford University Press.

Hartmann, E.G. (1948) *The Movement to Americanize the Immigrant*, New York, Columbia University Press.

Kallen, H. (1970) *Culture and Democracy in the United States: Studies in the Group Psychology of the American Peoples*, New York, Arno (reprint of 1924 edn).

Lijphart, A. (1977) *Democracy in Plural Societies*, New Haven, Yale University Press.

Mann, A. (1979) *The One and the Many: Reflections on American Identity*, Chicago, University of Chicago Press.

Novak, M. (1980) 'Pluralism: a humanistic perspective' in Thernstrom, S. (ed.) *The Harvard Encyclopedia of American Ethnic Groups*, New Haven, Harvard University Press.

Peele, G. (1992) 'Civil rights and the Bush presidency' in Peele, G., Bailey, C.J. and Cain, B. (eds) *Developments in American Politics*, London, Macmillan.

Storing, H.J. (ed.) (1970) *What Country Have I? Political Writings by Black Americans*, New York, St. Martin's Press.

Sundquist, J.L. (1968) *Politics and Policy: the Eisenhower, Kennedy, and Johnson Years*, Washington, DC, The Brookings Institution.

Williams, J. (1987) *Eyes on the Prize: America's Civil Rights Years, 1954–1965*, New York, Viking Penguin.

FURTHER READING

See Belz (1991), Graham (1990), Mann (1979), Storing (1970), Sundquist (1968) and Williams (1987) in the references.

AN AMERICAN WELFARE STATE?

John Clarke ★

1   THE POLITICS OF WELFARE

From a European perspective, the organization of social welfare in the United States has always looked strikingly different. Particular attention has focused on the absence of a strong centralized welfare state, co-ordinating and providing a wide range of more or less universal benefits and services, to the extent that some commentators have questioned whether the term 'welfare state' can be meaningfully used in the American context. The European view of welfare states has been contrasted with the American experience of a much more complex set of relationships between federal and state governments in organizing welfare, and with the predominance of private and philanthropic routes to welfare provision rather than publicly provided welfare. The organization of health care in the US, with its elaborate mixture of private for-profit, not-for-profit and public facilities and the absence of a national system of universal health insurance has provided the sharpest exemplification of this sense of difference.

There are a range of explanations which have been offered for the different development of welfare in the US (Pierson, 1990). One recurrent theme in the comparative analysis of welfare has focused on the relationship between the development of welfare and the role of political parties. In the case of the US, this argument links the underdevelopment of state welfare with the underdevelopment of an organized labour movement. This type of analysis highlights the absence of socialist or social-democratic political parties whose exercise of political power is elsewhere associated with the development and expansion of state welfare (Castles, 1989; Esping-Andersen, 1990).

There are some problems associated with the comparative analysis of welfare states. One is that they tend to look for and highlight differences at the expense of similarities. While the European perspective points to the relatively low level of development of state welfare in the US, such differences are significant in the context of comparisons being made among the advanced capitalist societies of the West. If comparisons are extended beyond this block of nations, the similarities between the US and European patterns of public welfare spending look much more significant than the differences. As Table 8.1 indicates, although starting from a lower level, the

United States' welfare spending grew significantly in parallel with other Western countries between 1960 and 1981. Some authors have suggested that, in the period following the Second World War, all of the advanced capitalist societies had found it necessary to develop some form of welfare state.

Table 8.1 Social expenditure as per cent of Gross National Product

	1960	1981
United States	10.9	20.8
United Kingdom	13.9	23.7
West Germany	20.5	31.5
Sweden	14.5	33.4

(Source: Organization for Economic Co-operation and Development, 1985)

Such arguments point to the role which welfare has played in promoting social and political integration and stability as part of the greater political management of such societies and their economies in the post-war era. The spread of Keynesian techniques of economic management by governments was, according to these accounts, matched by the development of 'Keynesian welfare states'. Keynesian approaches to economic management aimed to stabilize — or at least smooth the impact of — cycles of boom and slump. Keynesian welfare states aimed to minimize the social and political disruptions attendant on the workings of unregulated markets: the poverty and distress caused by loss of income, whether through unemployment, ill health or old age.

In this context, the differences between welfare states in the Western capitalist societies appear as variants — different routes — within a general convergence around the necessity of providing welfare. Societies found different ways of integrating welfare into the organization of their economic, social and political structures. Here, political differences once again take on some significance; distinguishing the highly developed 'social democratic' welfare states of Scandinavia from the underdeveloped welfare provision of the US. One of the most influential of recent comparative studies of welfare has been that undertaken by Esping-Andersen (1990). He has argued that it is possible to identify 'three worlds of welfare capitalism' — types of welfare development to which particular societies more or less correspond. He distinguishes the 'corporatist', the 'social-democratic' and the 'liberal' welfare states.

Corporatist welfare states are associated with extensive welfare provision which seeks to preserve 'status differentials' in the society (e.g. replicating income levels in the levels of benefits provided). They are likely to have a strong religious/voluntary involvement in the provision of welfare services and welfare policies are likely to promote traditional family arrangements (e.g. assuming that mothers will not be in paid employment). Germany provides an example of corporatist welfare. Social-democratic welfare states promote universalism through welfare, providing equal access to all citizens to high levels of benefits and services. The state is likely to be the primary provider of both benefits and services and welfare is likely to equalize social rights between men and women. Sweden exemplifies this model of welfare. Finally, the liberal welfare state is organized around the provision of a minimal welfare 'safety-net' with greater weight given to the individual's own responsibility to provide welfare (through insurance, for example). It embodies the 'poor relief' tradition, aimed at ensuring that welfare does not undermine the incentives to work and to provide for oneself and one's family. For Esping-Andersen, the US best exemplifies this model of welfare. Esping-Andersen's study highlights a close fit between different welfare types and forms of political organization in the Western capitalist societies, in particular the degree of power held by parties of the left, or parties of the working class.

1.1   WELFARE REGIMES: STATE, MARKET AND FAMILY

Esping-Andersen's work, and much of the rest of comparative studies of welfare, is concerned with the relationship between the state and the market. In societies based on market economies, the development of state welfare addresses the potential limitations and failures of the market as the mechanism for distributing social goods. Unemployment, disability, ill health and old age remove people from the opportunity to earn incomes, such that the central issue for state welfare is the extent to which, and the conditions under which, the state is willing to compensate for the inability to be a wage earner.

Table 8.2   The rank-order of welfare states in terms of combined decommodification, 1980

	Decommodification score		Decommodification score
Australia	13.0	West Germany	27.7
United States	13.8	Finland	29.2
New Zealand	17.1	Switzerland	29.8
Canada	22.0	Austria	31.1
Ireland	23.3	Belgium	32.4
United Kingdom	23.4	The Netherlands	32.4
Italy	24.1	Denmark	38.1
Japan	27.1	Norway	38.3
France	27.5	Sweden	39.1
Mean	27.2		
Standard deviation	7.7		

(Source: adapted from Esping-Andersen, 1990)

In Esping-Andersen's terms, this involves the extent to which the state 'decommodifies' such compensation. He argues that the predominant social relationships of market economies are 'commodified'; that is, they are based on contracts of monetary exchange. Goods, services and labour are subject to being treated as commodities, to be bought and sold. Decommodification refers to the process of taking some goods, services and benefits out of the field of contractual exchange and providing them as of right — as the entitlement of citizens. He compared different welfare states in terms of their extent of 'decommodification' (see Table 8.2), by developing a measure of the extent to which a range of welfare benefits were available to citizens as rights rather than being conditional on other statuses (such as employment history).

The United States' place in this ranking confirms the limited extent of state welfare and the predominance of the market (or commodified relationships) over state provision. However, before proceeding to look in more detail at the nature of this American welfare state, it is worth considering one limitation of Esping-Andersen's approach to welfare which has considerable significance for what follows in this chapter. His approach rests on identifying welfare in the mix of relationships between the market and the state as indicated in Figure 8.1.

Market	State
(commodified relationships)	(decommodified relationships)

Figure 8.1

A number of writers on social welfare have pointed out that this view of welfare omits a crucial dimension of how welfare is in practice organized and delivered; that is, within the family or kin networks (Gordon, 1991; Williams, 1989). Characteristically in Western societies, there is a presumption that much welfare is promoted by and delivered through the activities of women as wives, mothers and sisters. Such activities, ranging from child care to the care of elderly or sick relatives, do not fit into the distinction between the state and the market. They represent invisible welfare work, subject to neither the contractual relations of commodification nor the citizenship rights of decommodification. Yet the organization of social welfare in these societies is unimaginable without this gendered familial structure. Rather than the two-dimensional model used by Esping-Andersen, we need to view welfare as located within a three-dimensional network of relationships, in which the third dimension is that of family relationships. These might tentatively be described as 'pre-commodified', referring to their existence before and outside of the network of market and state relationships. They involve 'labours of love' — built into patterns of assumptions about gender, duty and obligation in personal relationships — rather than contractual or legal duties (see Figure 8.2).

Family	
(pre-commodified relationships)	
Market	**State**
(commodified relationships)	(decommodified relationships)

Figure 8.2

Rather than simply referring to welfare states, some writers have suggested that it is more useful to think about the social organization of welfare in terms of welfare regimes in which the mix and balance of these three different aspects of welfare provision are examined (Cochrane and Clarke, 1993). This points to the significance of elements beside state provision in the creation and delivery of welfare. It also helps to move the focus away from definitional arguments about whether a particular society such as the United States' has a welfare state or not. There is a further problem about the word 'state' in this context. Although this is generally taken to refer to the 'nation state', it does not imply that the only public agency which can deliver or provide welfare is the national government. In most Western societies, welfare functions are divided between national and local governments: in Britain between the centre and local authorities, in Germany and the US between the federal government and state governments, for example. In the latter two cases, the balance of powers and duties between federal and local authorities has a basis in constitutional arrangements. Despite such complicated layerings of local–national relationships, it is still worth distinguishing between state and non-state dimensions of welfare. In the rest of this chapter, I will be considering the US in terms of this pattern of relationships between market, state and family.

1.2 WELFARE: POLITICS AND IDEOLOGY

Introducing the family and gender into the discussion of welfare immediately has the effect of making questions of the connections between politics and welfare more complicated. For the most part, discussions of the politics of welfare have been conducted in terms of class; for example, the link between working-class organization in social-democratic parties. Such discussions have paid little attention to gender, assuming a unity of interests between working-class men and women over welfare issues. Closer examination suggests that such unity is doubtful. Women's campaigns over welfare have tended to stress very different issues from those of male dominated trade unions or parties of the left. For example, they have pursued demands for policies such as the public provision of child care or the payment of benefits for children directly to women rather than through the assumed male 'head of household'. As a consequence, the assessment of the politics of welfare requires us to look at the dimensions of both class and gender, both in terms of campaigns for particular welfare policies and the outcomes or consequences of welfare policies. For example, campaigns for full employment rights or unemployment insurance have tended to treat employment as a male phenomenon, assuming that women as wives and mothers will be outside of the labour market.

A further dimension of social organization which is particularly (although by no means exclusively) significant for welfare in the US is that of 'race'. Where racialized patterns of inequality play a major role in employment, income, housing and access to other social goods, we need to be attentive to the relationships between these wider patterns of inequality and welfare provision. Again, this needs to be considered both in relation to welfare outcomes (does welfare provision reproduce or remedy social inequalities?) and in terms of the politics of welfare development and reform. Just as organized politics have tended to be dominated by men rather than women, so too they have tended to be dominated by white rather than black people — and again a unity of interests based on class cannot be assumed.

Attention to these dimensions makes the assessment of welfare politics more difficult than assuming that they are merely the subject of gains and losses by different classes. But it also makes welfare more significant in one other respect. For the most part, the assessment of welfare outcomes has tended to focus on the directly measurable products or outputs of welfare systems: what sort of benefits or services, provided to what sorts of people, under what conditions? Have benefits increased or decreased? Have conditions of eligibility for benefits or services widened or narrowed? While such issues are important, they underestimate the wider political and ideological consequences of welfare provision. For example, assumptions about a 'woman's place' which are built into welfare systems have consequences both for individual women and for the wider ideologies about gender differences and roles that predominate in that society. Welfare produces not only particular outcomes in terms of benefits or services but also contributes to what we might call 'social positioning' — the allocation of places and identities in the social structure and the ideologies which surround it. The rest of this chapter examines the development of welfare in the US in the context of this concern with the social relations of welfare: the interconnections between welfare and 'race', gender and class.

SUMMARY

The organization of welfare involves more than just the role of the state. The idea of a welfare regime points to the relationships between the state, the market and the family in the provision of social welfare. The study of welfare must pay attention not just to the specific outcome of welfare policies (in terms of particular benefits and services) but also to the ways in which welfare intersects with wider social relations such as those of gender, 'race' and class. The effects of welfare in creating, reinforcing or changing patterns of 'social positioning' is particularly significant.

2 FROM NEW DEAL TO GREAT SOCIETY: THE ELEMENTS OF US WELFARE

Rather than trying to provide a complete history of the development of welfare policy in the United States, this section focuses on two periods of major welfare reform and innovation: the 1930s and the 1960s. There are two reasons for taking this route. The first is that these two periods feature in most accounts of US welfare as formative periods, where the major structural changes in the organization and provision of welfare took place. The second is that the two periods acquired a politicized significance in later controversies about welfare in the US. As we shall see in Section 3, the distinction between the 'New Deal' and the 'Great Society' welfare programmes emerged as a central feature of the politics of welfare in the 1980s.

2.1 THE NEW DEAL AND SOCIAL RECONSTRUCTION

Prior to the 1930s, welfare was organized and delivered at local level, through the states and cities and through voluntary and philanthropic agencies, with the exception of Civil War Veterans' pensions (Amenta and Skocpol, 1989). The economic depression of the 1930s exposed the limitations of this patchwork and highly differentiated pattern of welfare. The scale of unemployment and the resulting poverty rapidly outran the capacity of philanthropy and local state arrangements to cope. This failure of welfare evoked substantial social movements among the poor and unemployed, demanding public intervention to remedy unemployment and relieve poverty.

The Roosevelt Administration's 'New Deal' combined temporary measures to remedy unemployment through public works schemes supported by federal funds, with longer term programmes establishing more systematic and more rigorously administered welfare benefits. The creation of the Public Works Administration in 1933 was followed by the Social Security Act of 1935 which provided the foundation for the structure of US welfare benefits. Its core component was the creation of a system of social insurance to provide benefits for old age and federal support for state schemes for unemployment insurance. It was subsequently extended in respect of survivors (widows and their dependants), sickness and disability. Like other insurance schemes elsewhere, its central principle was the accumulation of a record of insurance contributions through employment. It also established the principle of reproducing labour market inequalities in welfare by paying benefits at differential levels, linked to income levels in previous employment. Many occupations, including many of those in which black people and female workers were concentrated such as agriculture and domestic work, were excluded from the scheme. Others involved levels of pay too low to qualify for insurance payments and benefits, again disproportionately affecting both white women and black workers.

In August 1935, on signing the Social Security Act, Roosevelt noted: 'Today a hope of many years' standing is fulfilled ... We can never insure 100 per cent of the population against 100 per cent of the hazards and vicissitudes of life, but we have tried to frame a law which will give some measure of protection to the average citizen and to his family against the loss of a job and against poverty-ridden old age.' (Quoted in Alsop, 1982, p.127)

Socialized, rather than individual, insurance had been established as a core principle of welfare provision in Europe much earlier. Its introduction into the US had been consistently resisted by politicians and employers' organizations as a development which would undermine both the workings of the market and the incentives to individuals to make provision for their own needs (Skocpol and Ikenberry, 1983). One indicator of the scale of social dislocation created by the Depression was the sudden acceptance of the need to supplement local public and philanthropic assistance with a more integrated system of social insurance. The insurance model adopted, however, was one which was closely geared to the labour market and which sought to maintain proper incentives to work. The insurance model for social security embodied three core principles:

1   That social insurance should not be directed at the elimination of all hardship, but only be concerned with a limited range of specified risks (unemployment, ill health, old age and widowhood) which were not voluntary conditions.

2   That workers should see the connection between their income, their insurance payments and the benefits which they received, avoiding expectations of high benefit levels and maintaining work incentives.

3   That the scheme should be clearly distinguished from public assistance; such that its benefits were 'earned' as a right through a contribution record rather than being a stigmatizing and means-tested relief from the public purse or private charity (see Katz, 1986, pp.236–7).

The Committee on Economic Security, which oversaw the development of social security, was concerned that the development of new welfare measures should not blur the line between insurance based provision and 'public assistance' (the locally provided, means tested, support for those in poverty). Only two initiatives of the New Deal risked this effect. The first was the decision to pay old age pensions immediately to those who had no contribution record, but this was a temporary arrangement intended to last only until the scheme was fully established. Subsequently, a means test for those not insured was reintroduced.

The second initiative was the creation of ADC (Aid to Dependent Children) in the 1935 Act, which allowed the federal government to contribute to the costs of states' programmes for benefits to be paid to families in poverty for the maintenance of children. ADC itself was based on the 'mothers' pensions' programmes which a number of states had developed in the 1920s to provide some assistance to widowed or deserted mothers with young children. ADC's federal funding moved public assistance part way to being a national scheme, although the administration of such schemes remained at local level.

ADC provides a paradigm of the interrelationship between welfare, 'race', class and gender in the US. Where social insurance was earnings related, ADC was available if the candidate family passed a series of 'tests', of which the means test was only one. The legislation also included a 'suitable home' provision, which allowed benefits not to be paid if investigation showed that children were being brought up in an unsuitable environment. This provision effectively became a 'morals test' to be applied to mothers seeking assistance. It drew on well-established assumptions about 'moral fitness' developed in the administration of mothers' pensions schemes:

'Moral fitness' was encoded with Anglo-Saxon biases — for temperance, nuclear-family households, American cooking ... wide discretion was ordinarily delegated to administrators and social workers — most of whom were white and middle class. Discretion allowed for the imposition of Anglo-Saxon criteria, as well as for racial exclusion where uplift was seen as either undesirable or impossible. Discretion meant, for example, that black mothers, barred from eligibility in some southern states, were elsewhere denied entitlement by policy managers. Further, both law and discretion invited pension agencies to police their clients regularly to enforce fitness: evidence of smoking, lack of church attendance, poor hygiene, male boarders or faulty budgeting could result in withdrawal of a mother's allowance.

(Mink, 1991, p.110)

For the United States, the New Deal was a small and partial revolution — the founding of what Katz (1986) calls a 'semi-welfare state'. Although it maintained the formal separation between federal and state or city administration of different aspects of welfare, it nevertheless changed the balance between national and local through the development of some national schemes and the greater use of federal funding to support the delivery of locally based welfare. It laid the foundation for a nationally co-ordinated system of social insurance, with benefits and entitlements for limited categories of the population. The creation of an insurance system aligned the US with other Western societies in the decommodification of limited welfare rights in relation to unemployment, old age, disability and ill health. Because of the insurance principle, however, such decommodification was limited in its impact to those with a record of contributions earned through employment. For those inside the insurance system, the New Deal represented a considerable step forward. But the combination of social insurance with the preservation of local systems of public assistance created a 'two tier' welfare state in which those outside the insurance system had to prove both need and moral worth in order to receive assistance. This categorization of those entitled to welfare reflected the wider structures of the inequality of American society. Mink argues that:

> the New Deal welfare state perpetuated gender and race distinctions among citizens by entrenching gender and race distinctions in entitlements. Women's entitlements and women's exclusions were tied to 'mother's needs' and women's economic dependence on men. Minority men's entitlements and exclusions varied with their conformity to the work, war, union and income experience of white men. ... While minority men were folded into the Social Security system and covered by New Deal labor policies if employed in covered occupations, they fell out of coverage disproportionately in comparison to white men because they could not meet occupational or minimum income eligibility criteria.
>
> (Mink, 1991, p.113)

However partial the changes wrought by the New Deal, they dominated the pattern of US welfare through to the 1960s and created the conditions from which the subsequent wave of welfare reform developed. In particular, they established within the welfare regime the distinction between insurance-based benefits and public assistance which overshadowed the later politics of welfare in the US.

2.2 THE GREAT SOCIETY: A WAR AGAINST POVERTY?

The 'Great Society' programmes of welfare reform are associated with the Kennedy and Johnson presidencies. They also need to be understood in the context of the social movements which generated the impetus and demand for reform — particularly the Civil Rights movement. Katz presents a summary of the pressures to welfare reform which indicate how traditional concerns about welfare intersected with changing social conditions, political circumstances and social movements in the early 1960s:

> Racial conflict, urban riots, militant welfare clients and increased out-of-wedlock births among black women impelled a search for new ways to preserve social order and discipline. Unemployment induced by technology, functional illiteracy, or inadequate education; fear of Soviet competition; new manpower theories; and the realization that welfare regulations discouraged work, all encouraged the use of welfare policy to shape and regulate labor markets. The increased Democratic dependence on the votes of urban blacks insured the continued use of welfare as a source of political mobilization, and the shock and outrage aroused by the rediscovery of poverty, hunger and malnutrition in the early 1960s spurred the improvement and extension of social welfare to relieve human suffering. To these conventional uses of welfare, the civil rights movement added a new element: for the first time, social welfare policy became one strategy for attacking the consequences of racism in America.
>
> (Katz, 1986, pp.251–2)

Of particular significance were the Civil Rights attacks on existing patterns of welfare. Movement activists combined with anti-poverty workers in challenging the 'suitable home' provisions of the Aid to Dependent Children scheme which many states had used as a racially exclusionary mechanism (Bell, 1965). Such alliances played a significant role in focusing political attention on the urgency of welfare reform and in shaping some of the policies which increased the resources of the poorest families through food stamp, nutritional and health programmes (West, 1981).

The policy responses to these challenges were dominated by a view of poverty which saw it as the result of 'blocked opportunities'. Poverty was not seen as the result of structured economic inequality, but as the inadvertent effect of historically-created barriers which inhibited people from taking advantage of the opportunities which the US presented to its citizens. Theories of 'cultural deficit' or 'cultural deprivation' among the poor played a leading role in shaping the policy responses (Katz, 1989). As a consequence, policy initiatives such as the Office of Economic Opportunity (OEO) (employment) and Operation Headstart (education) were designed to overcome barriers to participation in the opportunity structures of America by enhancing the skills and capacities of the poor.

Specific programmes developed during this period targeted particular aspects of social life in poor communities such as juvenile delinquency, civil rights, job training and education. For a brief period at least, one of the most salient features of these initiatives was the role given to community action, which stressed that community programmes should develop the 'maximum feasible participation' of the residents (Title II of the Economic Opportunity Act). This stress on the need for programmes to be carried out *by* the community rather than *for* the community identified state and city politicians and welfare agencies as part of the problem to be overcome (Marris and Rein, 1967). In fact, the attempt to make funding by-pass existing power structures was very quickly curtailed, with political resistance leading to restrictions on the Office of Economic Opportunity's ability to fund community groups directly. The programme was ended in 1974 when the Nixon Administration closed the OEO and transferred its responsibilities to other government departments.

Such projects were part of a wider 'war on poverty', conceived in the Kennedy Administration, carried through by Johnson's and even continued in the Republican Administration of Richard Nixon. Beginning with the Public Welfare Amendments of 1962 and ending with the Social Security Amendments of 1974, the period saw a major restructuring and expansion of US welfare. Between 1965 and 1972, federal spending on welfare rose from $75 billion to $185 billion, rising from 7.7 per cent of America's Gross National Product in 1960 to 16 per cent by 1974. This expansion had three main features:

1   the expansion of those eligible for welfare services and benefits,

2   the changing balance between services and benefits, and

3   the relationship between social security and public assistance.

The reforms expanded the numbers of people eligible for welfare services and benefits in two main respects. The most visible was the reduction in racially discriminatory administration of welfare programmes, particularly in the change of ADC to AFDC (Aid to Families with Dependent Children). The less visible, but numerically more significant, was the withdrawal or reduction of means testing across a range of welfare services, which turned them from a conditional entitlement into an unconditional right. This change in the criteria of access had some effect in destigmatizing public services and affected their ethos, turning them away from a focus on assessing, investigating and supervising the poor towards seeing them as means of promoting greater social integration and participation.

Secondly, the reforms changed the nature of welfare provision to a greater emphasis on the provision of services (e.g. health care, housing and access to legal services) rather than on direct cash payments (or 'transfer payments', as money benefits are conventionally known). A variety of initiatives provided 'matching funding' from the federal government to states' social service schemes and provided funding for the purchase of service from private sources (including voluntary and not-for-profit agencies as well as commercial providers). Between 1964 and 1974, federal spending on 'in-kind' programmes increased from 3 per cent to 20 per cent of social welfare costs (Katz, 1986, p.265). The most significant of these developments related to public housing, nutritional programmes (particularly the provision of food stamps to poor families) and health services.

Health services were a particular focus of attention. The costs of health care (either directly for services or indirectly through private insurance) had effectively excluded many Americans from such services. At the same time, however, the costs of socializing health care were thought politically prohibitive and were forcefully presented as such by the health and insurance industry lobby groups. What emerged instead was a package of measures which aimed to subsidize health costs among those in need, and which reflected the social insurance–public assistance distinction in other welfare programmes. The Medicare and Medicaid schemes provided public funding for health costs among eligible groups, but the creation of the two schemes reproduced the different logics of social security and public assistance:

> Though adopted together, Medicare and Medicaid reflected sharply different traditions. Medicare was buoyed by popular approval and the acknowledged dignity of Social Security; Medicaid was burdened by the stigma of public assistance. While Medicare had uniform national standards for eligibility and benefits, Medicaid left states to decide how extensive their programs would be. Medicare allowed the physician to charge above what the programme would pay; Medicaid did not and participation among physicians was far more limited. The objective of Medicaid was to allow the poor to buy into the 'mainstream' of medicine, but neither the federal government nor the states were willing to spend the money that would have been required.
>
> (Starr, 1982, p.370)

This split in the approach to the funding of health costs reflected the continuing salience of the distinction between social security and public assistance in US welfare. The two programmes remained the core of US welfare policy and spending and played a major role in its expansion during the 1960s and early 1970s. In relation to public assistance, AFDC played the leading role with the numbers covered by the scheme increasing from 3.1 million in 1960, 4.3 million in 1965, 6.1 million in 1969 to 10.8 million in 1974 (Patterson, 1981, p.171). Popular challenges to entitlement restrictions combined with federal and state relaxations of conditions to increase both the numbers of families eligible and the rate of take up amongst those eligible.

Despite the dramatic increase in AFDC assistance, it was social security which grew most in the period, partly through demographic trends affecting the numbers eligible for insured benefits, particularly the elderly. But, as Katz argues, its demography was less significant than its social and political base:

> Social security cut across class lines. Like public education, it offered at least as much to the middle classes as to the poor. Its constituency, therefore, was broad articulate, effective and, above all, respectable. In 1970, social security payments to the elderly, $30.3 billion, were about ten times higher than federal payments for AFDC, $2.5 billion. By 1975, the gap had widened: social security cost $64.7 billion and AFDC, $5.1 billion. Throughout the late 1970s and early 1980s the disparities increased even more: in 1984, social security spending, which was indexed to inflation, had mushroomed to $180.9 billion while AFDC, which was not, had risen only to $8.3 billion.
>
> (Katz, 1986, p.267)

Social security emerged as the dominant feature of US welfare, combining income benefits for the elderly, disabled people, and the unemployed with the insurance of health costs for eligible groups. The value of social security benefits was enhanced by changes throughout the late 1960s and 1970s which increased benefits beyond the cost of inflation and extended welfare to the 'non-poor'. Attempts by Presidents Nixon and Carter to reform welfare further towards a closer integration of insurance and assistance based schemes through proposals for a guaranteed family income failed because, Katz argues, they threatened the underlying distinction between the deserving and undeserving poor which was embodied in the split between insurance and assistance (Katz, 1986, p.269). As we shall see in the next section, this distinction between the programmes was to be a major issue in the politics of welfare in the 1980s.

Before leaving this period, however, it is worth noting some wider issues in relation to the reconstruction of US welfare. Although this account has focused on the domestic conditions of reform and expansion, the pattern is one which is shared more widely by Western capitalist societies. The period of the early 1960s to the mid-1970s is one which sees a considerable expansion of welfare state spending in most of the major Western societies. It appears to be associated with the peak of the long post-war boom in the world economy and with a greater role for the state in both social and economic planning. In fact, US welfare spending grew faster than the OECD average in this period, although from a much smaller base. While the US participated in these wider trends, the shape of the reforms and the nature of the welfare regime created was distinctively American.

SUMMARY

These two distinctive periods of welfare innovation — the 'New Deal' and the 'Great Society' — constructed the main dimensions of welfare provision in the US. In both, welfare was developed in the context of social dislocation and popular movements demanding reform. Throughout, the social relations of class, 'race' and gender played a significant part in shaping welfare provision. Finally, in both periods the distinction between insurance and assistance was a central feature of the public provision of welfare.

3   THE WELFARE BACKLASH: THE NEW RIGHT IN THE 1980s

> The Soviet Union is the immediate danger perceived by Americans. Yet it is not the real threat to our national security. The real threat is the welfare state ...
>
> (Friedman and Friedman, 1984, p.73)

As the quotation from the Friedmans suggests, welfare came to play a central role in the New Right's agenda for the reconstruction of the US in the 1980s. Its centrality reflected the ability of welfare to condense a variety of themes about the economy, the state, the family, 'race' and gender that were essential to the New Right's diagnosis of America's fall from grace and its prescriptions for a return to greatness. Just as the period of welfare expansion is one which the US shared with other Western societies, so, too, the period of welfare backlash and retrenchment is one which links the US to other societies, with Britain an obvious example. Where the long post-war boom underpinned welfare expansion, so the onset of world recession from the mid-1970s provided a starting point for challenges to the costs of welfare. In part, this appears as a simple question of economics: 'can we afford welfare?' But it is also caught up in how economic and political crises are represented — the ideologies through which such crises are identified, their causes explained and their remedies defined. The apparently simple question 'can we afford welfare?' was itself part of the changing ideological framework, since it defined welfare as an 'unproductive' cost on national economies which made them less competitive. In the 1960s welfare was, at least in part, viewed as an expenditure necessary to modernize societies and make them more competitive, as well as more harmonious and more socially just.

Again, although the US shared some common features with other societies during the 1980s, the particular route taken was the product of domestic political forces and alliances. At the heart of this was the reshaping of the right in American politics. A new alliance, composed of different social and ideological groupings, came to dominate the Republican Party and supported the Reagan presidencies (Saloma, 1984). Combined in this alliance were neo-liberalism, neo-conservatism and the radical right. Neo-liberalism provided an economic rationale for change, identifying an over-regulatory, over-interfering and over-taxing state as a major cause of America's declining competitiveness. Individual and corporate 'enterprise' needed to be liberated from the state. Neo-conservatism provided a political rationale for change, arguing that the 'élite liberalism' of the 1960s and 1970s had gone too far, producing an over-extended state and a collapse of political and moral leadership. The radical right (itself a messy confederation of moral majoritarians, anti-communists and white supremacist groupings) provided a moral rationale for change: arguing that the liberalism of the 1960s had undermined fundamental American values, denied fundamental American freedoms (e.g. through enforced desegregation of schooling) and created a moral vacuum (Clarke, 1991, ch.5).

This alliance of apparently rather ill-matched interests and agendas contained sufficient focal points of agreement — or at least overlap — to hold them together in their support for Reaganite republicanism. One of these focal points was the state of welfare. Welfare provided a demonstration of the neo-liberal economic agenda, the neo-conservative political critique and the radical right's moral concerns. No wonder, then, that the Friedmans could so self-confidently identify it as the 'real threat'. In what follows I have focused on three main themes for the New Right's attack on welfare: the problem of the state, the problem of dependency, and the problem of the underclass.

3.1   THE WAR ON WELFARE: THE PROBLEM OF THE STATE

The most obvious feature of the threat to welfare was to be found in the role of the state. The expansion of welfare in the 1960s and early 1970s took an expanding share of the federal budget. For the New Right, the economics of welfare had three significant consequences. First, it promoted economic decline and de-industrialization by diverting resources from the productive to the unproductive sectors of the economy. It was paid for by taxation, or 'legalized robbery' as some New Right proponents preferred to refer to it, and as a consequence had a disincentive effect on enterprise. Secondly, it created further disincentives by encouraging people to use welfare as an alternative to work. This second effect will be looked at in more detail in the following section, but for now it is worth noting that these neo-liberal economics of welfare created a logic of reduced public spending on welfare. Reduced taxation is necessary to encourage the rich to be more enterprising, while reduced welfare spending is necessary to get the poor to be more enterprising. Thirdly, state employees were themselves a social and political 'interest', with a stake in maintaining or expanding welfare programmes.

This last point is worth pursuing in more detail. The New Right argued that public employees had to be counted among the beneficiaries of public spending. Public employees had an interest in the maintenance and growth of the state both in terms of keeping their employment and in terms of their development of professional or bureaucratic empires. Drawing on analyses of the social organization of communist regimes, the New Right identified public employees as a 'new class' (Djilas, 1957; Ehrenreich, 1987). The designation of public employees as a 'class' made a link between their material interests (the continuation of state sponsored employment) and their engagement in wider political and ideological commitments in favour of greater state intervention: 'social engineering' and the promotion of liberal values. Liberal values in this context meant a mixture of 'system blaming' views of disadvantage (rather than promoting individual responsibility); a commitment to rights and equalities at the expense of individual freedom and a degree of 'cultural relativism' rather than moral absolutes (Hunter, 1981). One characteristic statement of the supposedly noxious influence of the new class on American life is provided in this quotation from Howard Phillips:

> According to the Bible, God has charged parents, not civil governments, with responsibility for the rearing of children. All education

is rooted in values. The question is whose values shall prevail? Those of the parent, or those of the State? In a free society, the family, rather than the state, ought to determine whether children shall be subjected to pornography, amorally premised sex education, atheistically based textbooks and curriculum, or proselytization for doctrines of homosexuality, abortion and extra-marital sex.

(Howard Phillips, leader of the Moral Majority, in a statement to the White House Conference on Families, quoted in Young, 1982, p.115)

One of the effects of these arguments was to produce significant cut-backs in public sector employment during the Reagan presidencies. Such reductions intersected in a complex way with the wider politics of welfare in the US, since the growth of welfare agencies from the mid-1960s had been one of the main routes for both employment and career development for white women and black people. Joel Krieger argues that this gave a particular set of social consequences to the apparently gender- and race-blind language of cost-cutting or 'downsizing' in public services:

Between 1969 and 1980 the social welfare economy (both government and private contract work) accounted for 39 per cent of all new jobs for women, for black women it accounted for fully 58 per cent of the jobs gained during this period. As a result, women, blacks, and especially black women have been disproportionately harmed by the reductions in force (RIFs) mandated by the cuts.

(Krieger, 1987, p.192)

The expansion of welfare in the 1960s and 1970s did not just affect poverty by virtue of the services and benefits provided but by providing employment routes for those social groups most vulnerable to poverty (black women in particular). The restructuring of welfare in the 1980s had reciprocal effects, not merely on the level and nature of benefits and services, but also on patterns of employment and unemployment (Malveaux, 1987). At the same time, of course, cuts in welfare spending also affected the provision of services and benefits.

Beginning with Reagan's Omnibus Budget Reconciliation Act (OBRA) of 1981, a variety of measures reduced eligibility for benefits, levels of provision, transferred costs to states from the federal government and promoted both 'availability for work' tests and 'workfare' programmes (benefits being conditional on either taking part in public works schemes or attending work training). Such measures have tended to affect women with dependent children most (Sidel, 1992), which is of considerable significance given the growth in the number of lone parent households headed by women. The changing consequences of the politics of welfare combined with wider social and economic changes (particularly the growth of unemployment) can be seen in Table 8.3 (Ginsburg, 1991, p.104). This shows both the reduction in family poverty effected by changes in the 1960s and 1970s and the subsequent growth during the 1980s.

Table 8.3   Percentage of families below and just above the poverty line in the US

	All families	White	Black	Hispanic	Lone mother
Below the poverty line					
1960	18.5	15.2	48.1	n/a	n/a
1970	9.7	7.7	27.9	n/a	32.7
1980	9.2	6.9	27.8	20.3	30.4
1986	11.4	9.1	28.7	25.5	34.0
Within 125% of the poverty line					
1986	15.3	12.7	35.8	n/a	40.8

(Source: US Bureau of the Census, 1987, Tables 746, 749)

At the same time, tax cuts in the early years of the first Reagan presidency promoted a widening gap between rich and poor (Phillips, 1990; Ginsburg, 1991, p.103). Between 1980 and 1984, changes in income tax policy and increases in social security taxes left families with a net income of below $10,000 a year with a net $95 loss; by contrast, families with a $75,000–$100,000 income gained $403. Those with an income above $200,000, gained $17,403. At least in broad terms, the New Right agenda for welfare got off to a flying start, driving reductions in both taxation and welfare spending. However, the agenda was never simply an economic matter. It was also concerned with the social consequences of welfare, and here the distinction between social security and public assistance had a central role to play.

3.2   THE WAR ON WELFARE: THE PROBLEM OF DEPENDENCY

For the New Right, the major mistake of welfare expansion in the 1960s and 1970s was to be found in its effects on the poor. Where social security programmes, for the main part, could be seen as promoting independence by virtue of earning the benefits one received, public assistance (Aid to Families with Dependent Children, in particular) had the effect of undermining independence and creating a culture of 'demoralization'. The basic components of this view are familiar given that they stretch back to the nineteenth-century beliefs embodied in the Poor Law and public relief programmes. Giving people welfare stops them trying to help themselves, makes them dependent on the benefits they receive, and undermines the will to self-improvement. The more particular version of this theme in relation to AFDC pointed to the growth of lone parent families, arguing that the existence of AFDC meant that men could father children without taking financial responsibility and women were freed from the responsibility of trying to keep men in the household and in employment. As such the existence of the benefit creates 'perverse incentives' which lead to inappropriate behaviour being rewarded.

Among the storm of New Right criticism which descended on public assistance (which in the US was equated with 'welfare' in a way that social security was not), one particular blast stands out. Charles Murray's *Losing Ground* (1984) was a huge and apparently well documented survey on the impact of welfare on employment, family life and achievement among black people in the US. It was significant in its own right and influential far beyond America in its critique of welfare and in the way it linked welfare to the emergence of an 'underclass'.

Murray used four key indicators to demonstrate the demoralizing effects of poverty programmes:

1   labour force participation (very low for young black males),

2   illegitimate births (very high for young black females),

3   the number of lone parent families (very high among black people), and

4   the number of homicide victims (very high among young black males).

Together, these indices mapped a section of the population which had become demoralized and dependent.

Murray argued that these declining fortunes among black people reflected the impact of the Great Society welfare reforms which had increased access to welfare benefits. In the process the distinction between the 'deserving' and 'undeserving' poor was destroyed, and 'status rewards' previously attached to striving for mobility and self-improvement were removed. This destruction was the result of 'élite liberal' thinking which engaged in system blaming rather than encouraging people to take responsibility for themselves. Murray concluded that this disastrous tale demonstrated the failure of 'élite liberalism' and the necessity to bring welfare policy closer to 'popular wisdom':

> The popular wisdom is characterized by hostility to welfare (it makes people lazy), towards lenient judges (they encourage crime), and towards socially conscious schools (too busy busing kids to teach them how to read). The popular wisdom disapproves of favoritism towards blacks and of too many written in rights for minorities of all sorts. It says that the government is meddling far too much in things that are none of its business.

> (Murray, 1984, p.146)

Although Murray's study has been subject to a wide range of criticisms which suggest that his claims about the relationship between welfare policy and its effects cannot be sustained, the quotation above indicates that its empirical truth was rather less significant that its political and ideological reverberations. Murray's description of 'popular wisdom' bears a striking similarity to the New Right's social and political agenda. Indeed, the similarity is intentional, for the New Right has consistently claimed to be able to speak for the 'silent majority'. There is, though, a peculiar paradox in Murray's relationship to this 'popular wisdom'. Having constructed it for us, he then suggests that it has unpleasant features — it is mean-spirited and racist. Only if it were to lose such features, he argued, would it be a reasonable basis for politics and policy. This is rather disingenuous, given that the entire book was constructed around a distinctively New Right premise about the relation between 'race' and welfare.

Murray used statistical comparison about the fortunes of black and white people in the US as the basis for his arguments about poverty, despite the fact that there were twice as many white people living in poverty as black. Claiming that there is no usable data about the poor, he insisted that black people provide a satisfactory 'proxy' for poor people. The effect of this device was to construct an elision between the categories of 'poor' and 'black' and to tell the story of black America only from the standpoint of welfare. Such constructions were endemic to the New Right's attack on welfare to the extent that many commentators argued that 'welfare' became simply a synonym for 'race' in US politics during the 1980s. The culmination of this connection was to be found in the idea of the 'underclass'.

3.3 THE WAR ON WELFARE: THE PROBLEM OF THE UNDERCLASS

Murray's analysis linked with wider discussions about the emergence of an urban 'underclass' — a category of people living a semi-detached existence from the rest of the society, marked by their disengagement from normal patterns of behaviour in employment and in family life. Murray's contribution to the development and popularization of this idea has been to link it explicitly to the perverse and demoralizing effects of welfare policy. One characteristic description of the underclass is provided by Auletta who identified four different components:

> (a) the passive poor, usually long term welfare recipients; (b) the hostile street criminals who terrorize most cities, and who are often school dropouts and drug addicts; (c) the hustlers, who, like street criminals, may not be poor and who earn their livelihood in an underground economy, but rarely commit violent crimes; (d) the traumatized drunks, drifters, homeless, shopping bag ladies and released mental patients who frequently roam or collapse on city streets.

> (Auletta, 1982, p.xvi)

The underclass has proved to be an enormously powerful social metaphor, although its empirical basis and forms of explanation are considerably more shaky. What it provided was a stark and striking image of urban collapse and urban fear — inscribing a profound distinction between the 'we' who belong to the mainstream and the dangerous 'other'. The underclass, claimed the New Right, was the outcome of the misguided reforms of the 1960s which have undermined authority, values and respectability and substituted lawlessness, immorality and dependency in their place. The underclass also repeats the elision of 'race' and welfare, for the underclass is above all a black underclass. The visibility of 'race' in this context owes much to the shifting patterns of urbanization and suburbanization of the 1960s and 1970s in which a growing black population in the cities coincided with 'white flight' to the suburbs.

The complex mixture of the metaphors of a 'dependency culture' and the 'underclass' in the New Right's demonology of welfare underpinned the retreat from welfare spending in the 1980s: the toughening up of welfare eligibility and conditions and a greater concern with the use of welfare as a way of controlling the poor. In the 1980s, welfare came under attack at all levels — federal, state and city — through budget trimming practices and changing regulations. This attack was concentrated on public assistance rather than social security, given their different political constituencies. The exception was benefits to disabled people under the Social Security Act. Congress amended the Act in 1980 to require a periodic review of all cases, which the Reagan Administration accelerated. Katz notes that, between March 1981 and April 1982, 400,000 cases were reviewed from which 190,948 cases were ruled ineligible (Katz, 1986, p.286). The major assault, however, was on public assistance and social service programmes:

> by 1983, under complex, new regulations, 408,000 people had lost their eligibility for AFDC and 299,000 had lost their benefits ... Through these reductions federal and state governments saved $1.1 billion in fiscal 1983. Other regulations restricted eligibility for food stamps and sliced $2 billion out of the program's $12 billion budget ... Spending on Medicaid dropped 3 per cent in fiscal year 1982 ... The social services block grant to the states was chopped by 20 per cent in 1981 ...
>
> (Katz, 1986, p.287)

The cumulative effect of these and other changes are shown in alterations in spending as a result of government action on a number of programmes between 1982 and 1985 (Table 8.4).

Table 8.4 Reductions in spending on selected welfare programmes, 1982–5

AFDC:	12.7%
Food stamps:	12.6%
Child nutrition:	27.7%
Housing assistance:	4.4%
Low income energy assistance:	8.3%

(Source: Katz, 1986, p.288)

These changes set the tone for welfare in the 1980s. Although the Reagan Administrations did not 'abolish the welfare state', as some of the New Right ideologists would have wished, its programmes, staffing and its resourcing were significantly diminished — albeit selectively — by the 1990s. The brunt of the 'war on welfare' was borne by the poorest — those dependent on public assistance programmes rather than social insurance.

SUMMARY

The New Right focused its attacks on public spending on welfare. They identified the economic costs, the political ideology and the social and moral consequences of welfare programmes as profoundly damaging to American society. They concentrated, as did the spending reductions of the Reagan era, on public assistance programmes such as AFDC in particular. In the process, they gave new salience to the social relations of 'race' and gender in the politics of welfare.

4 CLASS, 'RACE' AND GENDER IN THE POLITICS OF WELFARE

One simple way of reviewing the effect of the politics of welfare in the 1980s is to state that differentials widened. In class terms, the gap between rich and poor (whether working or non-working) grew substantially. In gender terms, although women's share of employment and their average wage in proportion to the average male wage increased, so too did their share of poverty — what came to be referred to as the 'feminization of poverty'. In terms of 'race', the income of the average black family stood at 56.1 per cent of that of the average white family — the lowest proportion since the early 1960s (Phillips, 1990, p.207). In some ways, it is tempting to leave it at these bare statements. After all, they seem to accurately reflect the class, gender and racial politics of the New Right so one might expect them as the outcomes of those politics.

Yet to do so would be to treat class, gender and 'race' as separate dimensions of inequality when in fact it is their interconnectedness which is most significant. What happens when one looks at this interconnectedness? Working class women suffered more from the Reagan years than did middle class women, but in either case being lone parents exacerbated the situation. Among black households, the gap between upper and lower income groups widened considerably, partly as a result of the emergence of a small black middle class and two-earner households and partly as a result of the disproportionate impact of unemployment and welfare benefits cuts on the lower income section. Here, too, woman-headed households meant increased poverty. Gender, class and 'race' intersected in complex ways in what Phillips (1990) has called the 'politics of rich and poor' in the 1980s.

But such politics are not just about the distribution of income and wealth, significant though they are. They are also about the ideologies which both shape and legitimate such patterns of inequality — providing the normative judgements of worthiness and blame. It is worth reminding ourselves here that welfare policy is not just a matter of benefits and services and the administrative principles of their distribution, but also concerns the social assumptions which underpin and motivate those principles. It is here that the politics of rich and poor, and the politics of class, 'race' and gender meet. Above all, the 1980s saw a political challenge to gains that had been made in the 1960s and 1970s in US welfare and to the ideologies which had driven and supported those gains. The 1980s featured a 'class politics' of reverse redistribution, which challenged the tenuous notions of social justice created in the 1960s. Neo-liberal 'trickle down' theories of wealth creation claimed that, rather than trying to distribute income more evenly, it was economically more effective to concentrate wealth. The rich would then spend their wealth, enabling it to make its way through the circuits of the economy and, eventually, pass into the hands of poor through either employment or philanthropy. The evidence suggests that it got held up somewhere on the way.

The politics of the 'gender backlash' are more complicated. The moral majority's reassertion of family values and visions of feminine domesticity coincided with a continuing rise in women's employment and (small) improvements in women's earnings relative to men's. At the same time, at least some versions of women's 'independence' carried greater penalties. The decline of welfare support of all kinds to families with children ensured that lone parent households faced the prospect of poverty, and since the vast majority of these were headed by females, the feminization of poverty proceeded apace (Sidel, 1992). Along with these changes was the emergence of an increasingly punitive public and political view of 'welfare mothers'. The attack on AFDC and the metaphor of the underclass combined in iden- tifying lone women parents as a major cause of social ills. Supposedly unable or unwilling to keep a man, and unable or unwilling to make sure he kept a job to support his family, the 'welfare mother' was identified as the root cause of moral collapse in the present generation (the feckless man she failed to domesticate) and in the future generation (young men without a role model because she couldn't keep her man). While such arguments are travesties of lone parent family life, they provided effective public vehicles for transferring blame away from wider social economic and political cir- cumstances onto an easier target.

As we have already seen, the 'welfare mother' and the underclass combined a distinctive pattern of racial and gender politics. In the eyes of the New Right, welfare policy, not racism, had produced the increasing dislocation of the black population from the 'American way of life'. Since black Americans had so signally failed to take advantage of the opportunities which America presented, they now had only themselves (or their mothers) to blame. At the same time, the New Right argued strenuously against the gains made in the 1960s in terms of equality initiatives, legal rights and affirmative action, claiming that such developments interfered with the natural workings of the 'free market' and individual choice.

In the 1980s, economic logics for dismantling welfare benefits and services, for dismantling protective and social legislation, and for dismantling welfare as a source of black and female employment combined with a political cul- ture, which was intensely hostile to the 'liberalism' of the 1960s, to restore some of the class, gender and racial inequalities which seemed to be essential for the 'American way of life' to flourish again. By the beginning of the 1990s, the levels of personal, economic and social dislocation which accompanied the New Right's reconstruction had led to a degree of disenchantment. George Bush, the apparent inheritor of the Reagan years, was denied a second term of office in the 1992 presidential elections. The return of a Democratic President posed new problems about the shape of the politics of welfare in the 1990s.

SUMMARY

The 'welfare backlash' of the 1980s linked economic, political and moral critiques of state welfare. In the process of 'rolling back the state' a new 'politics of rich and poor' emerged at the intersection of class, 'race' and gender. The New Right's concerns with the economic, social and moral costs of welfare highlighted issues of dependency and the underclass in ways which made explicit links between welfare, 'race' and gender.

5 NEGOTIATING THE CRISIS OF WELFARE: WELFARE IN THE 1990s

Three major dimensions have emerged as central to the politics of US welfare in the 1990s. These are:

1   how to respond to the welfare needs of the 1990s,

2   how to respond to the crisis of health care, and

3   how to shape the relationship between welfare and wider social and economic development.

These are hardly separate issues, but they do warrant a degree of separate attention since answers to one question have consequences for the others.

5.1   WELFARE NEEDS IN THE 1990s

One legacy of the 1980s is the depth and diversity of poverty in the United States. Although it is possible to identify its deepest points of concentration — among urban, female headed, lone parent households with children — the overall composition of poverty in the US is more complex. It embraces rural as well as urban poverty, black and white households, the elderly, sick, disabled and unemployed people who fall outside of, or who have exhausted, social security entitlements, not least the growing numbers who have contracted AIDS. In part, the growth of poverty in both its depth and spread is the result of welfare retrenchment in the 1980s. But it is also the product of wider social and economic reorganization over the same period: economic restructuring has led to widespread and prolonged unemployment (both rural and urban); average incomes have declined, particularly those in manual and service occupations, leading to an increasing reliance on dual incomes in those households with two people in employment. The growth of unemployment in the late 1980s, not least in its belated impact on white collar, professional and managerial jobs, has also created increasing welfare needs as unemployment also brings with it the loss of occupational benefits (such as health care entitlements).

Such social, economic and demographic changes have taken place during a period of continued financial restrictions on welfare at both federal and state level, resulting in an increasing tension between the demand for welfare services and benefits and the attempt to control or reduce costs. Again, this is a phenomenon which the US shares with most other Western societies where the containment of welfare costs has been an issue through the 1980s into the 1990s. The politics of welfare of the 1980s drove the US back towards a 'residual' view of welfare, making public assistance more punitive, shifting the costs to states and cities which themselves tried to drive down welfare costs in their competition to attract capital investment by creating low tax environments.

The problem for the 1990s is whether the other costs of a residual model outweigh the economic costs of moving away from residualism. One view of this issue suggests that residualism provides a way forward, surrendering large sections of the society to marginality and destitution, as the price to be paid for low taxation and economic competitiveness. An alternative suggests that the social, political and economic costs of such marginalization are so high that the US must move towards a more expanded welfare state, which rediscovers the commitment to social welfare as a vehicle for social integration and mobilization. But, as we shall see, such arguments do not include any prospect of returning to state welfare on the model of the 1960s. Almost no one argues that the expanded welfare state of that period could be reconstructed. The combination of New Right arguments in their hostility to welfare and the wider framing of the 'costs of welfare' has produced a political climate in which welfare spending is permanently 'under review'.

5.2 THE CRISIS OF HEALTH CARE

The field of welfare which emerged in the early 1990s as the focal point of political concern was health care. The most apparent feature of the US crisis of health care is the problem of how to contain rising costs. In this respect, it is similar to other health care systems in Western societies. All have faced rising costs in the context of rising demand, changing demography (with increasingly elderly populations) and the rising costs of medical services.

What is different is the organizational setting of these problems in the US, where direct public provision forms only a small part of health care. Most provision has been through private (for-profit and not-for-profit) organizations with payment for services financed though a variety of routes. The balance of funding has shifted from the original pattern of direct payments by users, supplemented by public assistance for the poor through the growth of non-profit mutual insurance schemes (organized by hospitals for their users, such as Blue Shield and Blue Cross), in the 1930s, to a situation which is dominated by employment based health insurance plans. By 1983, 58 per cent of Americans were covered by such employment based schemes; 12 per cent by Medicare and 8 per cent by Medicaid; 15 per cent of Americans had no health coverage (Staples, 1989, Table 1). Not surprisingly, health insurance follows the familiar patterns of employment stratification, reproducing labour market disadvantage in terms of race, gender and class.

The welfare cuts of the 1980s affected both Medicare and Medicaid coverage. Tighter limits were introduced on the insurance-based Medicare payments (usually involving the transfer of costs from the insurance scheme to patients themselves). In parallel with the restrictions on other aspects of public assistance, Medicaid payments became even more stringently restricted such as to discourage health providers from taking on Medicaid patients. At the same time, changes in its eligibility criteria and increased administrative complexity were such that around 60 per cent of the poor were either not eligible for or not receiving Medicaid (Ginsburg, 1991, p.131).

The supply of health care has operated through a complex of institutions, ranging from for-profit, through not-for-profit, to public hospitals. Two particular changes have affected this mix of provision. One is the growth of Health Maintenance Organizations (HMOs), which offer health care packages on the basis of an annual fee (which employers may pay or contribute to). The HMO then either provides direct services itself or contracts with other providers for services. By the late 1980s, Ginsburg estimates, HMOs covered about 12 per cent of the population (Ginsburg, 1991, p.129). The second major development has been the growth of 'for-profit' hospitals and health provision. This involves both a greater number and range of forms of private sector provision (including some HMOs) but also the growing 'incorporation' of health care as the basis of major corporate organizations, such as Humana and AMI (Wohl, 1984). Wohl coined the phrase 'the medical-industrial complex' to describe this trend towards the corporate domination of health care provision. The trend seems likely to create a tripartite division of health care, with the corporate sector 'creaming off' the most profitable patients, with a second layer of not-for-profit or smaller for-profit hospitals taking all but the uninsured and the bulk of Medicaid patients who will remain the province of an increasingly residual public hospital system (Ginsburg, 1991, p.129).

Within this complex network, cost containment takes on a very complex shape. For the most part, the system has been driven by the power of the medical profession who have resisted attempts to socialize the costs of health care through national health insurance from the 1940s through to the present. As a result of the complexity of the system, no alternative concentrations of power existed to check that of the medical profession given that payment for health care was distributed between state and federal governments, insurance schemes, employers (paying workers' health insurance) and private individuals. The 1980s, however, saw the beginnings of rather more concerted attempts to challenge the institutional dominance of the medical profession. There have been a variety of federal attempts to impose bureaucratic means of limiting medical costs (Bjorkman, 1989). These have been paralleled by pressures from insurance companies and schemes, and from employers, for greater cost containment. Both of these have been, so to speak, external attempts to put pressure on the medical profession. But the growth of corporate health care suggests a third source of financial pressure — the wish of the corporations to rationalize costs and increase profits. Wohl (1984) and Starr (1982) have both argued that the corporate pressure and the ability of the corporations to exercise greater control over doctors who are employees rather than independent professionals may be the most significant long-term development in cost containment.

In the shorter term, arguments over both the cost and the organization of health care have attracted increasing public and political attention. In particular, arguments for a more nationally rationalized system of provision and for some form of national health insurance have been revived. Such arguments are addressed to the cost containment issues, but are also explicitly directed at the crisis of health insurance. This has a number of elements: employers are concerned about the rising cost of insuring their employees; the insured are increasingly concerned about exemptions in their coverage as both insurers and employers look to reduce the risks covered to control costs; and the declining value and extent of Medicare and Medicaid coverage has made more people vulnerable to the costs of ill health or to the risks of not seeking health care itself. Perhaps the most powerful twist has been given by the growth of white collar and managerial unemployment in the early 1990s as such groups find themselves without health insurance coverage for the first time.

This public significance of health care was reflected in the speed with which President Clinton established a task force (headed by Hillary Clinton) to make proposals on health care reform. This group has explored a variety of public and private sector 'mixes' for the reshaping of both health insurance and the provision of services (e.g. from the creation of a nationalized system of health insurance through to a 'managed market' based around the HMO model). At the time of writing, however, the political urgency of the task seemed to have become bogged down in the complex politics of different and conflicting interests in the field of health care. In particular, most of the existing major agents in the field (such as the American Medical Association, the health corporations and the insurance companies) were all striving to keep or advance their 'market position' and resist proposals which would undermine their influence.

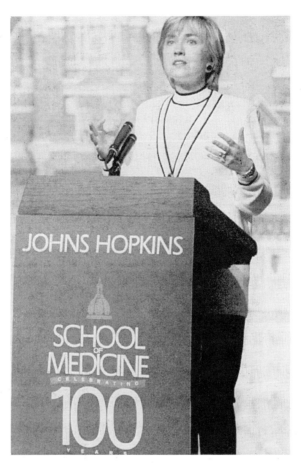

First Lady Hillary Rodham Clinton addresses a symposium on health care reform, June 1993. She said an over abundance of high-priced medical specialists has left much of the urban and rural areas without adequate health care

5.3 WHAT ROLE FOR WELFARE?

Just as I started this chapter by noting that some form of welfare state appeared to be a common feature of all the post-war Western capitalist societies, so it is possible to conclude it by saying that in all those societies there is now a crisis of the welfare state. While each society will no doubt make its own way through the dilemmas and choices about the future of welfare, it is nevertheless possible to suggest that those dilemmas and choices are framed by some common themes. These concern the role welfare is expected to play in the future development of these societies. None is likely to abolish welfare in its entirety but equally none looks likely to aspire to a fully developed 'welfare society' in which fully socialized funding underpins a wide array of citizenship rights for all its members. At present, the choice seems to be polarized between a 'residual' model (which the US has, of course, exemplified) and a 'social investment' model, where welfare is seen as an investment in national modernization and improved competitiveness.

Both of these choices are framed by a view of the world as composed of competing national, regional and local entities each striving to find a competitive 'edge' or advantage in relation to the others. Welfare, in such a context, cannot be justified by reference to non-competitive criteria such as egalitarianism, social justice or social improvement for the disadvantaged. It is worth briefly exploring the implications of this framework for the two models I mentioned.

The place of the 'residual' model in this framework should be relatively clear. It was, after all, the place sought explicitly in New Right politics in the 1980s. Welfare is a cost, pure and simple. High welfare costs bring competitive disadvantage (by virtue of individual and corporate taxation) which leads investors to look elsewhere for a 'better business environment'. As a consequence, being competitive means driving down the costs of welfare to the minimum achievable. If costs can be cut, the nation (or state) will be better placed to attract investment, which will create more jobs and wealth, which will reduce the demands for welfare. The public provision of welfare should supplant only in this last instance the responsibility of individuals and families to provide for themselves and their future. The hidden side of this argument is that if there are non-economic costs to be borne as part of this strategy, they will fall on the marginal and politically ineffective groups who, it is assumed, can do little about it.

The 'social investment' model is rather different. It views welfare as an investment rather than a cost and sees it as potentially giving rise to competitive advantage — at least if it is invested wisely. That is, welfare may help to produce a society which can, so to speak, compete by virtue of quality rather than on cost. In this model, welfare means investment in labour forces: their health, training, willingness and ability to work. In some versions, it also stresses welfare as a way of promoting social integration or 'membership' (Reich, 1984). It might include public work programmes as a way to invest in infrastructure development and as a way of keeping the otherwise unemployed active. It might include family policies directed at both the health of children and at care services which allowed working mothers to rejoin the labour market effectively. The hidden side of this argument is that 'non-productive' investment is unlikely. So, it stresses 'workfare' as a way of proving willingness to work (and contribute) before benefits will be provided. It may not include family policies, since many of these responsibilities could, it is assumed, be left in the hands of mothers.

These are two very crude sketches of 'welfare futures'. But in crude terms they do frame the welfare politics of the US for the 1990s. On the one hand, the residual model is the inheritance both of the 1980s and of the longer history of US welfare. On the other hand, the 'social investment' model has played a significant part in Democratic politics in the late 1980s and early 1990s, not least in the thinking of President Clinton's economic adviser Robert Reich (e.g. Reich, 1984). Both are framed by the issue of welfare's role in America's competitive economic positioning, but view the contribution which welfare can make in very different terms.

What is striking is that the arguments around these two 'welfare futures' accept a common frame of reference — viewing welfare from the standpoint of international economic competitiveness. In the process, the 'politics of welfare' with which this chapter has been concerned have tended to disappear from public view. The debate over 'welfare futures' is not addressed to the issues of class, 'race', gender or other inequalities — indeed, the word 'inequality' itself seems like a throwback to the 1960s — despite all the evidence about how inequalities have deepened. Instead, the debates are dominated by arguments about the costs of welfare, how welfare can be delivered most efficiently and the contribution which welfare can make to national economic revival. The fact that the other politics of welfare have disappeared from view does not make them any less significant. Welfare is still bound up in the structure of inequalities and the social relations of class, 'race' and gender and is implicated in their reproduction. Those dimensions will not go away — even if they are not being talked about. They constitute the real social and political processes of welfare which stand behind the language of economics, efficiency and administration.

SUMMARY

The cost of health care has emerged as a political concern in the 1990s. This has been brought about by the increased cost of employers insuring their employees, concern over exemptions to that insurance as insurers look to reduce their costs, and the declining position of the residual public hospital system with many more people vulnerable to the risks of not being covered by health insurance.

The future role for welfare seems to be polarized between a 'residual' model and a 'social investment' model. Although different models they are both framed by the issue of welfare's role in America's competitive economic positioning within the world. This reflects the way in which arguments about the *costs* of welfare have come to dominate political and public debates about the future of welfare. This marks the legacy of the New Right's hostility to state welfare in the US.

REFERENCES

Alsop, J. (1982) *FDR 1882–1945: the Life and Times of Franklin D. Roosevelt*, London, Thames & Hudson.

Amenta, E. and Skocpol, T. (1989) 'Taking exception: explaining the distinctiveness of American public policies in the last century' in Castles, F.G. (ed.).

Auletta, K. (1982) *The Underclass*, New York, Random House.

Bell, W. (1965) *Aid to Dependent Children*, New York, Columbia University Press.

Bjorkman, J.W. (1989) 'Politicizing medicine and medicalizing politics: physician power in the US' in Freddi, G. and Bjorkman, J.W. (eds) *Controlling Medical Professionals*, London, Sage.

Castles, F.G. (ed.) (1989) *The Comparative History of Public Policy*, Cambridge, Polity Press.

Clarke, J. (1991) *New Times and Old Enemies: Essays on Cultural Studies and America*, London, HarperCollins.

Cochrane, A. and Clarke, J. (eds) (1993) *Comparing Welfare States: Britain in International Context*, London, Sage.

Djilas, M. (1957) *The New Class*, London, Unwin.

Ehrenreich, B. (1987) 'The New Right attack on social welfare' in Block, F. *et al.*, *The Mean Season: the Attack on the Welfare State*, New York, Pantheon.

Esping-Andersen, G. (1990) *The Three Worlds of Welfare Capitalism*, Cambridge, Polity Press.

Friedman, M. and Friedman, R. (1984) *The Tyranny of the Status Quo*, Orlando, Harcourt Brace Jovanovich.

Ginsburg, N. (1991) *Divisions of Welfare*, London, Sage.

Gordon, L. (ed.) (1991) *Women, Welfare and the State*, Madison, University of Wisconsin Press.

Hunter, A. (1981) 'The ideology of the New Right' in Union for Radical Political Economy, *Crisis in the Public Sector*, New York, Monthly Review Press.

Katz, J. (1986) *In the Shadow of the Poorhouse: a Social History of Welfare in America*, New York, Basic Books.

Katz, J. (1989) *The Undeserving Poor*, New York, Pantheon.

Krieger, J. (1987) 'Social policy in the age of Reagan and Thatcher' in Miliband, R. *et al.* (eds) *Socialist Register 1987*, London, Merlin Press.

Malveaux, J. (1987) 'The political economy of black women' in Davis, M. *et al.* (eds) *The Year Left 2*, London, Verso.

Marris, P. and Rein, M. (1967) *Dilemmas of Social Reform: Poverty and Community Action in the United States*, London, Routledge & Kegan Paul.

Mink, G. (1991) 'The Lady and the Tramp: gender and race in the formation of American welfare' in Gordon, L. (ed.).

Murray, C. (1984) *Losing Ground: American Social Policy, 1950–80*, New York, Basic Books.

Patterson, J.T. (1981) *America's Struggle Against Poverty*, Cambridge, Mass., Harvard University Press.

Phillips, K. (1990) *The Politics of Rich and Poor*, New York, HarperCollins.

Pierson, C. (1990) 'The exceptional United States: first new nation or last welfare state?', *Social Policy and Administration*, vol.24, no.3, pp.168–98.

Reich, R. (1984) *The Next American Frontier*, New York, Penguin.

Saloma, J.S. (1984) *Ominous Politics: the New Conservative Labyrinth*, New York, Hill & Wang.

Sidel, R. (1992) *Women and Children Last*, New York, Penguin (2nd edn).

Skocpol, T. and Ikenberry, J. (1983) 'The political formation of the welfare state. An historical and comparative perspective' in Tomasson, R.F. (ed.) *Comparative Social Research, 6*, London, Jai Press.

Staples, C. (1989) 'The politics of employment-based insurance in the United States', *International Journal of Health Services*, vol.19, no.3.

Starr, P. (1982) *The Social Transformation of American Medicine*, New York, Basic Books.

West, G. (1981) *The National Welfare Rights Movement: the Social Protest of Poor Women*, New York, Praeger.

Williams, F. (1989) *Social Policy: a Critical Introduction*, Cambridge, Polity Press.

Wohl, S. (1984) *The Medical-Industrial Complex*, New York, Harmony Books.

Young, P.D. (1982) *God's Bullies*, New York, Holt, Rinehart & Winston.

FURTHER READING

See Gordon (1991), Katz (1986) and Sidel (1992) in the references.

Jonathan Katz's *In the Shadow of the Poorhouse* provides an excellent and accessible critical history of American welfare policies towards poverty; the collection of readings edited by Linda Gordon, *Women, Welfare and the State*, offers a range of perspectives on the relation between gender and welfare in the US; and Ruth Sidel's *Women and Children Last* is an accessible account of the social and policy changes behind the 'feminization of poverty' and of its impact on family lives.

A NEW CONSTITUTION?

Richard Hodder-Williams ★

1   INTRODUCTION

The Constitution of the United States was signed in Philadelphia on 17 September 1787. Two hundred years later it was celebrated across the United States in a series of events which publicly expressed the nation's respect and reverence for the document and for its symbolic importance as a statement of the country's political values. President Ronald Reagan observed in his address commemorating the Bicentennial that the Constitution evoked not merely 'simple admiration, but also a feeling more of reverence' (*New York Times*, 18 September 1987). More than half a century earlier a distinguished scholar had referred to the Constitution as 'totem and fetish', implying its mystical, almost religious relationship to the American public (Lerner, 1945–6, p.1294). Most young school children still solemnly pledge their allegiance to it each morning, partly as an expression of social commitment and partly as an expression of genuine belief in its virtue.

Celebrating the Bicentennial of the Constitution reaffirmed the public commitment to its virtues. At the same time, however, it spawned a number of colloquia and a myriad of commentaries which questioned its perfection and challenged the appropriateness of some of its fundamental features. Although mainly the concern of intellectuals and legal scholars, the debate reflected a growing concern that a constitution fashioned in different times and under different pressures might no longer express the right priorities for the twenty-first century nor provide the most appropriate institutional structures to deal with problems in the current age (see Lobel, 1988; Marshall, 1987; Robinson, 1985; Sundquist, 1986).

The Constitution essentially incorporates three basic and fundamental features. First, it implies a division of powers between one central government and several state governments, a system which we now refer to as federal. Scholars have disputed the meaning of federal and federalism, but, in the context of an examination of a Constitution, a legalistic definition is most appropriate (see, especially, Wheare, 1963). In this view a federation is a single political unit in which sovereignty is divided such that the central government and the state governments each enjoy a degree of constitutional independence and autonomy. This does not mean that the various governments cannot *influence* the policies and practices of government at other levels; but it does mean that the central government cannot ultimately *control* what the state governments do, nor can the state governments ultimately *control* what the central government does. The 50 individual states thus enjoy a degree of genuine independence, but shared sovereignty means that neither they nor the federal government have the power to make the final authoritative decision on every matter with which government might be concerned. In Section 2 how the line is drawn between the powers of the national and the state governments is explored in more detail.

Soon after their deaths the Founding Fathers became venerated by the people. Here George Washington is pictured ascending to heaven

The second principle is the separation of powers. Authority within the central government is divided into three separated, yet interrelated, institutions: the legislature (the House of Representatives and the Senate), the executive (the President, the departments of state and regulatory agencies), and the judiciary (the Supreme Court and the lower federal courts). Article I of the

Constitution sets out the powers of the legislative branch, Article II the powers of the executive branch, and Article III the powers of the judicial branch. These institutions are separate in the senses that no individual can simultaneously be a member of more than one branch and to each branch is granted distinctive and different governmental functions. Simplifying a little, we could say that the legislative branch is responsible for rule making, the executive branch for rule implementation, and the judicial branch for rule adjudication.

The branches are, however, interrelated in that many of the functions of government can only be performed if two or more of the branches co-operate. Thus, the normal procedure for enacting a law is for the legislature to debate and propose a bill and for the President to sign it into law; a Justice of the Supreme Court is nominated by the President and confirmed by the Senate, but cannot be removed by the President unilaterally and only with great difficulty through the impeachment process by the legislature (which has never yet occurred); the President is Commander-in-Chief of the armed forces, but the legislature calls them into action, funds them, and has responsibility for their regulations. The various branches inevitably affect one another and provide checks and balances against any single institution exercising too much power. Section 3 examines how this separation of powers operates at the end of the twentieth century.

Third, in the words of Article VI of the Constitution, 'This Constitution, and the Laws of the United States which shall be made in Pursuance thereof ... shall be the supreme Law of the Land; and the Judges of every State shall be bound thereby, any Thing in the Constitution or Laws of any State to the Contrary notwithstanding.' (See Spaeth and Smith, 1991, for the Constitution and an excellent collection of material on it.) The original Constitution set down the basic principles and structure of government and the powers of its various parts. But many Americans were concerned that the new national government might be too powerful and so the first major action of the very first Congress was to propose a number of constitutional amendments which aimed to establish a set of individual rights upon which the national government could not encroach. Ten were accepted and ratified by the individual states and are usually referred to as the Bill of Rights. From almost the very beginning of the Republic, therefore, individuals and groups could go to court to thwart the will of an elected government or properly appointed official on the grounds that their laws or actions were contrary to the Constitution itself. Americans have not hesitated to claim their rights in this way and so the Constitution has had to be constantly interpreted and its words applied to an ever changing kaleidoscope of different disputes. The supremacy of the Constitution and a political system in which all power must be exercised within the rules of that Constitution provided the basis of the belief that the United States reflects the principle of 'a government of laws, not men'. Section 4 examines the process of constitutional adjudication and the problems it creates.

These three great principles — the division of powers, the separation of powers, and the primacy of a Constitution with a Bill of Rights — have in recent years been questioned. Perhaps the spark which fuelled the debate was an article published in the journal *Foreign Affairs* and written by President Jimmy Carter's legal counsel Lloyd Cutler (Cutler, 1980). It was called 'To form a government' and argued that the checks and balances in the Constitution made it virtually impossible to form a government that would be both responsible and representative. Cutler's chief concern related to the separation of powers principle. A little earlier a powerful attack on the 'imperial judiciary' had been made by Nathan Glazer and had provided the intellectual basis for a continuing critique of the Supreme Court's role in interpreting the Constitution (Glazer, 1975). And in 1985, Ronald Reagan's Attorney-General Edwin Meese III delivered a speech to the American Bar Association in which he lamented what he believed to be the end of federalism, blaming for the most part, the handiwork of the Supreme Court (Meese, 1985). All three of the Constitution's central principles, therefore, have been the subject of critical debate. Sometimes the principle itself has been challenged while on other occasions the dilution of that principle has been claimed; on yet others the concern has been about the effectiveness of the constitutional system to deal with the problems of the late twentieth century. But one thing is certain; the Bicentennial brought to the surface some serious doubts about the claimed perfection of the United States Constitution.

In this chapter, we look at these three great principles of the United States' constitutional system, examine how they have developed, and analyse the contemporary critiques of them. You will find that there is much disagreement and no simple answers to the questions posed by constitutional scholars. Much depends upon personal judgements about the purpose of government and the nature of democracy.

There is always tension between democracy in the sense of popular participation and efficiency in the sense of speedy decision-making. Defenders of the United States' system would argue, however, that efficient government is not primarily about the procedural effectiveness of devising and passing legislative responses to political problems rapidly and coherently. They would certainly include in the concept the idea that efficient government must reflect the various priorities and preferences of the people which government is supposed to serve. British observers might stress unfavourably the lack of coherence and the long drawn out process of decision-making in the US; American observers would stress unfavourably the small number of leaders involved in making policy in the United Kingdom and their distance from popular pressures. Thus, any appreciation of the United States' system of government needs to be clear about the meaning and relative weight to be given to concepts such as democracy and efficiency.

SUMMARY

The major principles of the US constitutional system directly affect the distribution of power within the country. Any examination of the political system will show that formal rules, even when as malleable as the US Constitution, have profound political consequences. The division of sovereign power, the different electoral bases for each house of the Congress and the President, and the existence of a Constitution as supreme law establish not only limits on politicians' powers but also a complex system in which there are multiple points of access to the decision-making powers and no obvious individual or group who can be thought of unproblematically as 'the Government'. The laws under which Americans live are the product of 51 legislatures, each of which separates the executive power from the legislative power, and in each of which (with the exception of Nebraska) the legislative power is itself divided between two chambers of approximately equal weight. The People obviously have many places in which they can attempt to rule; but it is difficult to place accountability unequivocally at the door of any institution in a system of such divided powers.

2   THE DIVISION OF POWERS: FEDERALISM IN THE UNITED STATES

The creation of the United States at the end of the eighteenth century brought together into a single union thirteen sovereign states, each of which had only recently achieved their independence from the British crown. Through the Articles of Confederation they had established a confederation (that is, a co-operative organization of states without any central sovereign power or authority) but many questioned its success as co-ordinated policies floundered upon the parochial interests of the states as well as upon a general economic decline in the region. Leading figures from several of the states met to discuss the economic problems facing the former colonies, but it seemed to most of those involved that the fundamental problem was political. So a Convention was called to revise the Articles of Confederation.

The Convention met in Philadelphia through the hot and sticky summer of 1787 without the current benefit of air-conditioning (for a very readable account, see Bowen, 1966). Despite the command to seek ways to improve the Articles of Confederation, those who attended the Convention in Philadelphia almost immediately saw their task as creating a quite new political system which would obviate the major problem of the Confederation, namely its inability either in law or reality to impose policies on those individual states which dissented from the majority view. The focus of the Convention, therefore, was almost entirely upon the type of central government that might be suitable and upon the particular powers it might be granted.

The underlying presumption, the unarticulated premise as it were, was that any such union would be composed of the existing states which already enjoyed sovereignty.

In the early years of the Union, the division of powers between the central government and the individual states was relatively unambiguous. The new national government was responsible for the defence of the United States and its foreign relations and it was charged with ensuring a free market of goods between the states. For the vast majority of day-to-day affairs the states remained the primary law-makers. This system, in which the two levels of government had their own specific areas of competence, came to be called dual federalism.

Towards the end of the nineteenth century, however, the nature of America's burgeoning capitalism persuaded many people that some regulation by government was needed. Laws began to be passed to set limits to the way in which trade was carried out and the forms of trade that were deemed appropriate. For example, the great railroads found themselves being super-vised by both state governments and the central government and some activities, such as prostitution or gambling, were for the fist time restrained by *national* laws. Little by little, therefore, more areas of human activity became subject to regulation by both levels of government.

It was not until the Great Depression of the 1930s and President Franklin Roosevelt's New Deal programme that the range of activities in which the federal government wanted to become involved grew dramatically. Many of the New Deal laws were designed to regulate commerce broadly defined; limitations on production were established, social welfare programmes set up, rights of workers created, and business freedoms curtailed. This was, in size and scope, quite new. It provided the basis for a widespread involve-ment by the government in Washington into areas which had hitherto been thought of as the prerogative of the individual states and was further extended as a result of the centralization caused by the military require-ments of the Second World War.

When Harold Laski, the socialist Professor of Government at the London School of Economics and Political Science, published a study of the United States in the late 1940s, he wrote of 'the obsolescence of the federal idea' (Laski, 1949, p.50). He had in mind both a normative argument (that is, he thought that federalism *ought* to be at the end of its useful life) and an empirical observation (that is, he thought federalism was *actually* collapsing in the US). His normative argument depended upon a firm belief in central planning, especially of the economy, in the primacy of economic activity over all other, and in the ultimate value of equality which could only be achieved through a single overarching government. Federalism, by preserv-ing the sovereignty of the individual states, obstructed rational central plan-ning and protected inequality in the southern states where racial segregation was the order of the day. But he also thought that the New Deal was, through its regulation of much economic activity and its equalizing policies

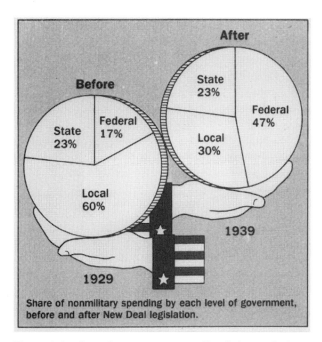

Figure 9.1   *Central government spending before and after the New Deal*

(Source: Welch *et al.*, 1992, p.60)

through the welfare programmes, sounding the death-knell for the autonomy of the individual states.

Laski was proved wrong. His normative argument, although some Americans favoured it, was broadly antagonistic to the major principles of the American belief system. Emergencies might temporarily give legitimacy to a degree of centralization, but the underlying commitment to a free market and to personal individualism unquestionably challenged ideas of central planning and policies determined by equality of outcome. And, as a matter of fact, the states retained their autonomy, although they became increasingly dependent upon central government funding for many of their activities. What emerged was a system characterized as co-operative federalism, in which the states worked alongside the Washington government to administer, and to contribute to various social policies. The ability of the states to play the major part in social policy remained, as the segregated practices of the southern states and the disparate educational systems and curricula throughout the country indicate.

In the 1960s the initiative shifted more obviously towards the national government, partly because it had greater financial resources and partly because many of the problems, such as civil rights, seemed national in scope. At any rate, the 1960s came to be seen as an era of creative federalism, in which the central government designed a range of policies, often targeted at political units smaller than the individual states, in order to deal with a range of social problems (inner city decay, poor transportation systems, the consequences of racial discrimination, educational conservatism) and provided the finances tailored to these specific programmes administered by civil servants from the centre. In many ways, it was an imaginative and liberal response to major social problems. But it seemed to reduce the significance of the states as the central players in social and economic policy yet further. Since many of the policies appeared to fail and the bureaucratization implicit in massive social engineering of the kind envisaged by the policy-makers lent support to the impression that the Washington government was usurping essentially state and local responsibilities, there were increasingly vocal protests against what was happening (see, generally, Wright, 1982).

At the same time, the Supreme Court was chipping away at the autonomy of the states in another area. The Fourteenth Amendment to the Constitution, ratified in 1868, held that 'No State shall make or enforce any law which shall abridge the privileges or immunities of citizens of the United States; nor shall any State deprive any person of life, liberty, or property, without due process of law; nor deny to any person within its jurisdiction the equal protection of the laws.' Precisely what the 'privileges' and 'immunities' of citizenship might be or what the 'equal protection of the laws' might reach or 'due process of law' might imply were litigated before the federal courts. Until the end of the First World War, this amendment appeared to have been interpreted as narrowly as possible to permit the states the maximum latitude in framing their laws. But from the decision in *Gitlow v. New York* in 1925 the Court slowly, but inexorably, began to interpret the amendment as protecting individuals, and some groups, from state intervention. The concept of due process of law shifted from a procedural meaning (that is, any law or official action is constitutional so long as the *procedures* from which they emanate are followed) to a substantive one (that is, the very idea of due process is deemed to include some *substantive* good practices and so can outlaw specific bad practices). In deciding what did, and did not, count as due process the Supreme Court moved cautiously forward towards a position which in fact, if never in explicit theory, incorporated into the four words 'due process of law' virtually all the rights set out in the Bill of Rights (see Abraham, 1988, pp.38–117).

The consequence of this jurisprudential revolution was to apply against the states the limitations, or obligations, set out in the first nine amendments to the Constitution. This had profound consequences. States found that their financial support for church schools was unconstitutional; that their requirement for prayers to begin the school day was unconstitutional; that their procedures for dealing with suspects and criminals were often unconstitutional; that their methods of obtaining evidence resulted in some evidence and confessions being excluded from trials; that they were obliged to provide counsel for the accused at trials; that their limitations on abortion laws were invalid; and that their prison systems and other state-supported institutions were often operating unconstitutionally. The Court's attempt to apply equally across the whole country its interpretation of the meaning of the Bill of Rights seemed to strike at the very heart of the federal idea.

Inevitably, the constitutional question which arose was this: what are the limits to central government involvement in state affairs? (See, generally, Hodder-Williams, 1989.) By the early 1940s the Supreme Court had virtually eviscerated the Tenth Amendment ('The powers not delegated to the United States by the Constitution, nor prohibited by it to the States, are reserved to the States respectively, or to the people.') and had allowed the interstate commerce clause and the general welfare clause to provide the constitutional underpinning to any social and economic policy which the Congress agreed upon. This increasingly worried both legal scholars and some politicians as they began to feel that state autonomy was a charade. This feeling was strengthened in the 1960s as a result of President Lyndon Johnson's Great Society programme — the engine of creative federalism — which differed from previous social initiatives by being unashamedly Washington led and administered.

It was Edwin Meese III who expressed this concern most pungently and most publicly. In a widely publicized address to the American Bar Association, he attacked a host of decisions made by the Supreme Court, especially those which incorporated, through the 'due process' clause of the Fourteenth Amendment, the substantive rights of the original Bill of Rights and made them applicable against state politicians. 'Nowhere else', he said, had 'the principle of federalism been dealt so politically violent and constitutionally suspect a blow as by the theory of incorporation' (Meese, 1985, p.704). While Meese almost certainly exaggerated the degree to which the sovereignty of the individual states had been reduced, he implicitly expressed a particular view of American federalism and American democracy.

Once again, it is necessary to go back to the creation of the Republic. The basic units of governance at that time were the town meeting and the state legislature. The conception of democracy — rule by the people — presumed a special view of who 'the people' were. The people were composed of autonomous, sovereign individuals with loyalties and links to local communities first and foremost. The practice of democracy was best observed, therefore, when the people took responsibility for their immediate concerns. In this view the locus of power ought to be close to the people affected by that power and only in special areas (notably national defence, trade policy and internal commerce) should power shift to the centre.

Such an assumption is very different from Harold Laski's view of divided power to which reference has already been made. The belief that power should be dispersed and that many decisions should be taken at a local level rather than centrally is well put, in both its normative and empirical forms, by the American political scientist Robert Dahl. He identified four positive virtues of federalism:

1   By reducing the workload of the national government, it makes democratic government at the national level more manageable;

2   By permitting diversity, it reduces conflict at the national level and thus makes democratic government at the national level more viable;

3   By providing numerous more or less independent or auton-
     omous centres of power throughout the system, it reinforces the
     principles of balanced authority and political pluralism;

4   By facilitating self-government at local levels, it greatly expands
     the opportunity for learning and practicing in the way of
     democratic government.

(Dahl, 1967, pp.172–3)

These propositions, both normative and empirical, are open to challenge, but
they encapsulate the family of arguments that need to be addressed in making a judgement about contemporary American federalism. It is clear that a
continental polity needs a degree of devolution from the centre; the question
is whether that devolution should be purely administrative (as in unitary
states) or political (as in federal states). It is also clear that multiple centres
of power reduce the possibility of one party or ideological persuasion from
playing an over-dominant role in a country. It is also clear that the dispersal
of sovereignty does diminish the possibility of a single, coherent conception
of public policy extending over the whole land. Federalism extols differences; and differences inevitably mean inequalities.

These inequalities may be the price to be paid for other, positive, characteristics of a federal system. More than 50 years ago Justice Louis Brandeis
wrote these words: 'It is one of the happy incidents of the federal system
that a single courageous state may, if its citizens choose, serve as a labora-
tory and try novel social and economic experiments without risk to the rest
of the country'. The same sentiments were expressed by a more recent Justice, Sandra Day O'Connor, when she wrote that one of the central functions
of the states was to act as 'laboratories for the development of new social,
economic and political ideas'. Indeed, there are plenty of examples of states
leading social change (e.g. on extending the franchise to women, on regulating working hours and conditions, on liberal forms of sentencing); but there
are also examples of states standing against change (e.g. by continuing
segregated schooling or outlawing the teaching of Darwin). But, just because
power is sometimes used in a way that is disapproved, it does not follow
that such a power is necessarily misplaced. If that was so, we would grant
no body and no institution authority over us; indeed, the pacifist anarchists
argue precisely that.

The first pillar of the US constitutional system thus poses a number of questions. The first set relates to the most appropriate way of organizing a large
and diverse country with a history, and culture, of local loyalties. This
points towards a system in which local political units, the states or even subdivisions of the states, exercise genuine power over matters of local concern
in line with the popular wishes of a locally defined population. The second
set relates to the balance between responsiveness and accountability to local
populations and co-ordinated nation-wide public policy. The Americans, by
and large, have valued strong, national government less than varied, state
governments, except at times of special crisis, such as the Great Depression
or the civil unrest of the 1960s. These are essentially normative questions.

A third set relates to the actual working of the division of powers. This has both a constitutional dimension and a political dimension. The constitutional dimension demands an answer to this question: what precisely are the areas of state responsibility which are outside the authority of the central government to regulate? The Constitution itself does not provide an answer. The Supreme Court has been the arbiter and has shifted the boundary over the years. In the decades after the New Deal, it tended to accept that, if the elected Congress (part of which — the Senate — was explicitly designed to protect state interests) and the elected President agreed to regulate the economy or society in a particular way, it was not the business of the Court to confound them unless the laws clearly fell foul of the Bill of Rights. However, in 1976 the Court decided by 5 to 4 in *National League of Cities v. Usery*, for the first time since the 1930s, that a Congressional Act did unconstitutionally trespass on an area of state priority. Many people thought that this might herald a new jurisprudence in which the demarcation between national and state power was to be redefined. This did not prove to be the case. In 1985, Justice Harry Blackmun, who had been the doubtful fifth vote in *Usery*, now changed his approach to the problem of drawing a line between what was uniquely a state matter and what was within the proper reach of the national government and so the Court reversed itself. By a different 5 to 4 vote, it decided in *Garcia v. San Antonio Transit Authority* that the political process should be sufficient to protect the interests of the individual states.

Blackmun had felt all along that there was no simple principle by which judges could distinguish between what was intrinsically a state matter and what was not and he had been concerned that any decisions taken would merely reflect the current whims of a majority of the Justices rather than a clear constitutional rule. Others before him had had this concern. So he adopted ideas propounded by legal scholars a generation or more earlier to argue that, since the states were represented in the Senate *as states*, that was the proper form for deciding when the national government was overstepping its authority. By passing legislation, the Senate was in effect saying that the states accepted the new reach of national government. It always had the opportunity to vote such laws down; not to do so must be interpreted as acquiescence in, or even support for, the power claimed.

The working of the federal system is thus, once again, a function of political forces within the United States. Three points may be made here. First, the government of the United States *is* ultimately to be characterized as a 'government of laws, not men'. The balance of power between the national government and the individual states must be legitimated by the Supreme Court as the final arbiter of the meaning of the Constitution. In the 1930s, the desires of the Congress, which reflected the majority will at the time, clashed with the understanding of the Constitution as then dominant (see Maidment, 1992). The change of personnel on the Court reinterpreted critical phrases of the Constitution so that laws, admittedly better drafted, which had earlier been found wanting now passed constitutional scrutiny. Again, in the 1970s and 1980s, the Court for a moment threatened to constrain Congress's authority (in *Usery*) but it backed away in *Garcia*. Over much the same period the Court steadily extended the Bill of Rights. These very major and, indeed, revolutionary changes were in line with much of the public opinion and the dominant political majorities in Washington; although the Supreme Court may be thought to have led in some areas, it was essentially in line with the majority (see Dahl, 1957).

Secondly, the shift in the relative power and influence of the states and the national government is, in the last analysis, a function of the political process. Blackmun's opinion in *Garcia* had noted that states have plenty of opportunities, through their elected representatives, to protect state autonomy from encroachment if they choose. The move from dual federalism through co-operative federalism to creative federalism flowed from major political movements and presidential responses to perceived crises in American life. Seen from this perspective, the Supreme Court has essentially legitimized the shifting contours of federalism in line with those favoured by the majorities of the day.

Thirdly, the argument that Washington has exceeded its constitutional powers and the states have been coerced into accepting a subordinate role is difficult to sustain. There is no doubt that the federal government's laws affect ordinary Americans in their everyday life a great deal more than they did in the 1920s or even the 1950s; but so, too, do the states' laws. The US, quite simply, has moved from a highly fragmented and individualistic state into what might be called an administrative state. Furthermore, the very people who pass the legislation which is said to impinge upon state autonomy are elected by, and accountable to, the voters of the several states. Especially in recent years, members of the Congress have felt it absolutely essential to reflect their constituents' interests and priorities in order to secure re-election. And they do get re-elected; over 90 per cent of members of the House of Representatives who stand for re-election are re-elected every other year. This suggests that there is not, in fact, a *popular* concern that the balance between national power exercised from Washington and state power exercised from the various state capitals is wrong. Indeed, it is possible to argue that the great majority of the American people accept the normative argument that divided sovereignty, for all its faults, is preferable to a unitary state and accept the empirical argument that the current balance between the two levels of government is satisfactory.

SUMMARY

In thinking about the division of power, three points need to be considered:

- The division of power between the central government and the individual states shifts over time in line with political pressures within the country and Supreme Court judgements.

- Divided sovereignty is a heritage bequeathed to the current generation of Americans by the Founding Fathers, nurtured in the states
  for 200 years, and inculcated in Americans as a natural and sensible form of government.

- In the abstract, the division of powers will result in different priorities and policies in different parts of the country (and, therefore,
  inequalities), but this may be the necessary price to be paid for
  both good governance and representation in a nation of 240 million
  people.

3   SEPARATION OF POWERS

Just as federalism raises both normative and empirical questions, so, too,
does the separation of powers. The Founding Fathers discovered that the
most difficult problem when writing a new constitutional structure was to
balance the need for a workable central government against the fear of a
central government that would be too powerful. Their solution, in James
Madison's words, was that 'Ambition must be made to counteract ambition'
and to divide the authority of the new government into three separate institutions (*The Federalist* No.51). This, they believed, would not only ensure
that the national government would be limited in its exercise of power but
would also protect the rights of individual citizens against any misuse of
national power. Too much power could be checked by institutional arrangements and the separated authority of legislature, executive and judiciary
would provide an ideal balance between competing institutions. Not everyone agreed. Indeed, the so-called anti-federalists argued that the Constitution as it emerged in September 1787 failed to constrain the proposed
national government enough and ratification was only achieved on the clear
understanding that a Bill of Rights specifically designed to protect individual rights against the new national government would be added to the Constitution at the earliest opportunity.

The argument for separation of powers depends upon two assumptions,
neither of which is free from challenge. The first is the normative belief that
governments ought to be limited and, therefore, the powers granted to a
government should be both restricted in range and bounded by institutional
restraints. Conservatives have generally held this view. The American political culture is a complex one, but one part of it has been the presumption
that the logical consequence of a commitment to individualism and personal
sovereignty is freedom in the political market-place as much as in the economic one. The belief in what Seymour Martin Lipset has called 'equalitari-
anism' (or equality of opportunity) leads logically to an acceptance of
inequality of outcome (Lipset, 1964). Different levels of effort, physical attri-
butes, fortune and friendship will naturally favour some individuals and

disfavour others. The purpose of government, within this paradigm, is to ensure that the context for individual competition is as open as possible; protection from outside, order within, and minimal regulation of social and economic activity become the central requirements of governments.

Radicalism in the United States has tended to stress the autonomy of the individual and the virtuous nature of the ordinary people as opposed to the intellectual strengths of élites. This populism exaggerates the virtue of local democracy and the vices of central government in particular. Radicalism in Europe, by contrast, has tended to emphasize collectivism rather than individualism, equality of condition rather than equality of opportunity. Its proponents have seen the state as the institution best suited to constraining private wealth and class advantages in the interests of the working poor through using its power to tax, regulate, distribute and provide for the welfare of people. It is argued that a proactive state of this kind needs a governmental structure which can ensure that the common interest is translated into law with the minimum of opportunities for minorities to restrain. A unified and centralized state is thus seen as the appropriate model.

The British pride themselves on strong government, where the executive is composed of the leading members of the legislature and where disciplined parties can ensure that policies offered to electors in the campaign can be turned into law without difficulty. The British, thus, emphasize efficiency over democracy and claim the virtues of effectiveness. This may be empirically questionable (i.e. it is open to question whether *in fact* British governments have been effective), but it is accepted broadly as a normative position. Americans, by contrast, have convinced themselves for the most part both that limited government is normatively preferable to fused government and also that the American variant has been effective.

If one central feature of democracy is that rulers should be directly accountable for their actions, the American system offers some problems. As far as the executive branch is concerned, only one individual exercises power as a direct result of popular participation in an electoral process, the President, and Presidents are only elected indirectly. What is more, in their second term Presidents can never be accountable directly for their performance (since they cannot constitutionally stand again for election). Additionally, the remaining major figures in the executive branch are all patronage appointments and are neither elected to positions of authority nor subject to popular recall.

Furthermore, national government policy, expressed in the form of laws, is a shared responsibility, so that it is unclear precisely who is to be held responsible for legislation. Laws are nearly always compromises — compromises between the two houses of Congress, compromises between the Congress and the President — so that it is unclear who precisely is to be held responsible for what. Democratic accountability is thus a somewhat random affair in which electors may well punish officials for outcomes for which they were not in fact responsible.

The making of the budget illustrates this point well. The executive branch, through the Office of Management and the Budget, takes the initiative and offers to Congress in the President's name a package of proposals. These proposals, whether concerned with spending or revenue, are then considered in detail by committees in both houses of Congress and will be amended, often substantially. Much negotiation will then ensue, between the House of Representatives and the Senate and also between congressional leaders and the White House. Sometimes, indeed, these negotiations do not result in a brokered deal and the law-makers are forced, if government is to continue at all, to pass a resolution continuing the expenditure decisions of one financial year into the next. More often, a bargain is struck. The degree of difficulty in reaching an acceptable compromise depends upon the extent to which the President and Congress are ideologically opposed. A moderate Republican like President Eisenhower could reach an accommodation with a relatively conservative Democratic Congress in the 1950s in a way which a more inflexible George Bush could not with an assertive Congress controlled by Democrats in the late 1980s. Democrats blamed the Republican President; Republicans blamed the Democratic Congress.

This is inevitable in a system where the separation of powers genuinely allocates power to different branches of a government system. The events of the 1970s and 1980s brought the normative arguments about the separation of powers, which had concerned for the most part only academics and intellectuals, much more into the open. The empirical argument about whether the system actually worked thus became more immediate as politicians, commentators and then ordinary people began to consider the unthinkable: failures in the United States (to manage the economy, to combat poverty, to provide proper welfare services, to protect the dollar) began to be explained in terms of system failure. As Lloyd Cutler was to argue, the system of separation of powers, certainly as it operated in these decades, if it did not actually cause governmental failure, encouraged it. Members of the Congress were obsessed by the need to curry favour with the most articulate and well-resourced members of their districts and were consequently driven by parochial, and thus by definition minority, interests. The President, elected in a different way but with no hierarchical power over legislators, reflected a different set of popular wishes, often symbolic and concerned with style as much as with substance, and normally dominated by foreign policy issues. In such a situation, it was difficult to 'form a government' capable of carrying through a single coherent and internally consistent set of public policies in the national interest. As the two branches of government consequently pulled in different directions, there was altogether too much checks and balances and not enough effective government.

Many of the normative arguments supporting the principle of the separation of powers have already been rehearsed in the context of the division of powers. Fear of an over-powerful government, belief in the variety of ways in which 'the people' ought to be represented in a democracy, and the assumption that good policy emerged from negotiation, bargaining and civilized argument, all play their part. While critics accept that these are important arguments, especially in the context of *democratic* theory, they argue that of still greater importance is the extent to which the governmental system is *efficient* at its primary task of making public policy to enhance the well-being of the American people (see, generally, Goldwin and Kaufman, 1986).

They tend to see the President as the central figure in an efficient policy-making system. This is particularly true in the field of foreign relations where the Constitution, practice and common sense have granted the President the dominant authority. Such has been the case for a long time, but it was strengthened as a result of the Cold War antagonism between the US and the Soviet Union and the threat of nuclear war. From time to time the Congress or the courts would check the more extravagant claims of a President, as happened in 1953 when the Supreme Court found President Truman's seizure of the steel mills during the Korean War unconstitutional (*Youngstown Sheet and Tube Co. v. Sawyer*) or in 1974 when Congress passed legislation purporting to limit the President's use of the armed forces. The ideal conception of balanced authority, in which Congress plays its constitutionally empowered role and Presidents theirs and the courts manage the disagreements, rarely holds for long (see Koh, 1990). The President soon regains the upper hand.

From the perspective of the White House, the separation of powers is clearly an unwelcome institutional limitation on effective diplomacy. President Carter could sign a Strategic Arms Limitation Treaty with the Soviet Union, but he could not be certain that his signature would be upheld by the Senate, which is given the constitutional authority to ratify all treaties. In the event, he failed to obtain the Senate's approval. This is an extreme case, but the principle of shared power spills over into the whole range of relationships (trading, military, diplomatic, cultural) with which the United States is involved and for which the day to day responsibility lies with the executive branch. Hence, Congress's autonomy is an unwelcome restraint and the committee system within Congress, which emphasizes the local concerns of Representatives over and above a broader assumed national interest, yet further reduces the possibility of the President governing efficiently. Such a view is not new; but it became more stridently expressed in the 1970s and 1980s when the President was, for all but four years, a Republican and the majority of the House of Representatives was composed of Democrats throughout this period. Hence, a natural institutional competition between legislature and executive was made worst by the party competition between Republican and Democrats.

This introduces the importance of how popular demands and interests are articulated and mediated in the political world. Parties have been the traditional way in which competing views about public policy have been aggregated and presented, in a simplified form, to the electorate. The ideal 'party model' presupposed a coherent ideological rationale to each party's policies and a commitment to that ideology (and therefore collection of policies) by its supporting voters. Sometimes called the 'responsible party model', many American academics hankered after it in the 1950s as a way of making governments more obviously accountable in the US (*American Political Science Review*, 1950). But American political parties and American voters have obstinately refused to behave as the model demands. The links between voters and candidates are of many kinds: ideology, specific policies, personality, and loyalty, all play a part. The end result is that the party label, although important, does not provide the glue to hold together members of the same party within each chamber of the Congress, or between members of Congress and President, or between the elected and electors. On each political issue a separate majority coalition has to be negotiated.

The significance of the party system, which is discussed in much greater detail in Chapter 4, is that any empirical evaluation of the separation of powers must take into account the American way of politics as it is. Critics have argued that recent changes in the way Presidents are selected have had deleterious consequences (e.g. Polsby, 1983) and many look to electoral reform to resolve the problem of bifurcated politics in Washington (Robinson, 1985; Shafer, 1988). In other words, the problem is not so much the principle of the separation of powers as the electoral politics which feeds into the institutional structure. Many look back to the 1930s when, it seemed, the system 'worked'. Then the American electorate chose an overwhelmingly Democrat Congress, eager to work with a Democrat President, Franklin Delano Roosevelt, who was thought to have a clear and coherent set of policies by which to advance the general welfare of the American people. This is mythologizing. The Democrats were not as united as often imagined; Roosevelt to a large extent developed his policies as he went along; the ties between local electorates and Representatives regularly constrained what the President could do.

It is clearly the case in the United States that cohesive and disciplined parties do not exist and that it is not sensible to imagine that they could be made to exist. On the down side, this means that a Democrat in the White House cannot take Democrat support in the Congress for granted but must bargain and negotiate on every policy issue. President Clinton, therefore, has much work to do to ensure congressional support for his politics. On the up side, this means that each brokered policy ought to reflect fairly accurately public opinion on that unique policy and that even a Republican President can do a deal with a Democrat Congress and therefore govern. It is within this context that the principle of the separation of powers must be evaluated.

The separation of powers, like the division of powers, raises several quite different sets of questions. The normative issues revolve around the relative advantages of centralized and unified government and checks upon any government; and around the difficulty of representing a demi-continent with a myriad of conflicting interests except through a system in which no single coalition of interest can dominate the whole over time and across most issue areas. The empirical issues relate to practicalities of co-ordination between legislature and executive, to the possible advantages of compromise and negotiation, and to the price Americans pay for their weak political parties.

SUMMARY

In thinking about the separation of powers, three points need to be considered:

- The principle of the separation of powers presumes that liberty is best protected where three different sets of people are responsible for rule making, rule application and rule adjudication.

- In fact, the needs of modern government and the consequences of the United States' status as a superpower have shifted the responsibility for most proactive measures towards the executive branch, a shift which the flexibility of the Constitution has permitted.

- Precisely how the competition for power between the Congress and the presidency works out depends ultimately upon political factors, upon the skills and willingness to compromise of the parties involved, and on the ideological distance between the legislative and executive branches.

4 THE SUPREMACY OF THE CONSTITUTION

The United States Constitution has survived for more than 200 years. What is especially remarkable is the extent to which the formal document has altered so little. If the first ten amendments are considered as part of the original constitutional structure (and ratification depended to some extent on the promise that a Bill of Rights would be added as soon as possible), there have been a mere 17 amendments in over 200 years. Some of these are of minor significance; and one (the eighteenth), that which declared the manufacture, sale and transportation of alcohol unconstitutional, was itself reversed (by the twenty-first). The shape of the Constitution has barely altered; what has changed has been the degree of democratic participation mandated by the Constitution (Grimes, 1978). And yet the Constitution quite obviously operates now in a very different way from 200 years ago (see, generally, Schechter, 1986; Hodder-Williams, 1988). How could this be?

The answer to this conundrum is the Supreme Court. What has happened is that the meaning of certain parts of the Constitution has developed and changed over the years as successive Justices have faced new sets of facts and new claims (see McCloskey, 1960). The Court is composed of nine Justices, all of whom participate in all cases (unlike the situation in the UK where the Judicial Committee of the House of Lords sits in panels). It takes just five votes to decide a case and so to define the current meaning of the Constitution. This authority is not found in the Constitution itself. Indeed, in the early years of the Republic other political actors, Presidents or members of Congress, felt that they were as legitimate an authority as to the Constitution's meaning as was the Supreme Court. In time, however, with a few remarkable and visible exceptions, the supreme position of the Court came to be accepted.

The Court itself claimed this right in 1803 in the case of *Marbury v. Madison*. Chief Justice John Marshall then observed that the Constitution was the fundamental law of the land and that any act of the legislature repugnant to it was void. Moreover, he wrote, 'it is emphatically the province and duty of the judicial department to say what the law is'. In commonsensical terms, Marshall was surely correct; but he certainly had no explicit constitutional command to rely upon. Since that date, the Court has assumed the responsibility of defining the applicability of each clause of the Constitution when called upon to do so.

Practice has ensured that the Constitution *is* supreme and that nobody, however significant, can act outside the rules it lays down and have the claim to be acting legally taken seriously. The problem at issue is its interpretation. Whoever controls that manifestly wields immense power since different applications of its often very general phrases (such as 'commerce among the states', 'equal protection', 'due process', etc.) will inevitably produce different results. Because the Supreme Court is the body which applies the Constitution to the disputes generated by the United States' litigious society, Nathan Glazer dubbed it the 'imperial judiciary'. Chief Justice Hughes once went so far as to assert that 'the Constitution is what the judges say it is', but this is something of an over-simplification. When a constitutional question comes before the Court and is decided (when, for example, the Court decided in *Goldman v. Weinberger* that the First Amendment's protection of religious freedom did not permit a rabbi to wear his yarmulka indoors against military regulations), then that is indeed what the Constitution means.

But usually it generates further litigation or action in another part of the political system which in time produces a new set of facts. Let us continue with *Goldman v. Weinberger*. Many members of Congress did not like the Supreme Court's judgement and they introduced a bill, which permitted members of the armed forces to wear religious apparel indoors if the item was neat and conservative. The bill also permitted the Secretary of Defence to prohibit the wearing of an item of religious apparel if it interfered with the performance of military duties. The bill was passed into law in 1987. This is a classic example of what Louis Fisher has called a 'constitutional dialogue' (Fisher, 1988). His argument is that, although the Court's judgement is final at the moment of its utterance, it immediately spawns a host of actions aimed at refining it, or enhancing it, or overturning it altogether. There is, in effect, a continual dialogue between the judicial branch and state governments, or the federal government, or state courts. The law does not stand still.

In the political world, however, the conception of constitutional dialogues has not been widely accepted. The common assumption is that the Supreme Court, through its authority to declare the meaning of the Constitution, is the final arbiter of the Constitution's meaning and can thus wield consider-able power of the kind normally associated with directly elected govern-ments. A major democratic dilemma is then exposed. These unelected and unaccountable Justices — indeed, only five of them — can establish new rights (the right to a lawyer, the right to an abortion, the right to publish obscene material) which elected politicians, reflecting popular opinion, reject. The liberal decisions of the Court during the 1960s, when Earl Warren was Chief Justice, generated considerable political antagonism to its actions in conservative quarters. When Richard Nixon became President in 1969, he was determined to ensure that the Justices he nominated would not 'make law' but be restrained in their exercise of judicial power. Despite his attempts the Court continued in the 1970s and into the 1980s to exercise its power regularly and often in areas of considerable sensitivity (see Blasi, 1983).

In the 1970s, for example, the Court began to evolve a jurisprudence that virtually ended discrimination on grounds of gender, that established affirm-ative action as a constitutional response to racial or gender discrimination, that created the right to an abortion, that (for a short while) banned capital punishment, and that continued to demand a strict separation between church and state as well as a high level of fairness in trials. By the time Reagan entered the White House, the conservatives were becoming frus-trated that the Republican Party's virtual control of the presidency since 1969 had failed to change the Court's way of thinking. The Court, and thus the meaning of the Constitution, became a major political issue in the 1980s. Attempts were made to introduce constitutional amendments to reverse the abortion and separation of church and state decisions and the administration took every opportunity to express its disagreement not only with those decisions but with several others. Not since Franklin Roosevelt had threa-tened to increase the size of the Court in 1937 in order to change its juris-prudence had an administration so openly attempted to alter the Court's output (see Schwartz, 1988, and O'Brien, 1986, on the court packing; Caplan, 1987, on the Reagan Administration's arguments before the Court; and Hodder-Williams, 1990, generally).

The argument over the Supreme Court's role in the US governmental sys-tem has, as you would now expect, both a normative and an empirical aspect. The normative argument basically relies upon two propositions. The first holds that the Court is intrinsically undemocratic, since it is unaccount-able to any electorate, and thus lacks legitimacy when it adjudicates on dis-putes in such a way that major public policy outcomes occur. The second holds that the responsibility in a democracy for public policy lies exclusively with the political branches and that the Court ought, therefore, refrain from entering what Justice Felix Frankfurter once called 'the political thicket'.

Of course, these arguments are appealing. But they need to be examined with some care. A starting place is the Constitution itself as envisaged by the Founding Fathers in Philadelphia. It was not considered to be an un-equivocally democratic document; and it clearly is not. Indirect voting, qualification for voting to depend upon the states, the treatment of slaves, all are explicit examples of a suspicion of democracy. The whole structure of government, encapsulated in the divided sovereignty of federalism and the separation of powers, was intended to constrain elected politicians. Read again James Madison's marvellously realistic appraisal of the human condition in *The Federalist* No.51, with its realization that men, not being angels, needed to have their powers constrained. Over the years, it is true, the least democratic parts of the Constitution have been democratized; the vote can no longer be withheld from potential electors because of their colour, their gender, or their failure to pay taxes, but the political culture which underpins the political system still firmly believes that power may be misused and that it is the possible misuses of power which need checking.

Furthermore, the immediate and deliberate addition to the Constitution of the Bill of Rights suggests that eighteenth-century Americans felt the Constitution could be improved by the addition of provisions which consciously protected individuals against the government. And there is no sign that Americans have any wish to remove these amendments; on the contrary, to the majority of Americans the Constitution *is* the Bill of Rights. These rights can only be protected if courts are prepared to deny elected officials the fruits of their electoral victories. A rights-based culture is, almost inevitably, anti-majoritarian and those who uphold this culture — the Supreme Court — can easily be painted as anti-majoritarian and anti-democratic. But democracy is a great deal more than a system of crude majority rule. It contains within it a set of assumptions about how the majority should, and should not, behave and thus a justification for a system which holds the majority to account. The Supreme Court, in this perspective, thus enhances democracy.

"Oh, yeah? Well, I just happen to have a copy of the Bill of Rights with me."

It is, in any case, something of an over-simplification to deny the Justices of the Supreme Court any democratic legitimacy. Prospective Justices are nominated by a President who has been elected by the American people and they are confirmed (or rejected) by Senators, who have also been elected by the American people. Inevitably, because of their life tenure, there can be a lag between Court values and national values when there is a dramatic political realignment and any dominant coalition will fail to reflect the policy preferences of *some* regions or groups or classes in society. But, over the years, the members of the Court come to reflect the dominant coalitions in Washington (Dahl, 1957).

There is also among many critics an empirical misunderstanding. The Supreme Court, like any court of last resort in any country, exercises the power of judicial review. That is to say, its fundamental task is to review appeals made on a point of law and to decide whether the challenged action does, or does not, comport with the law. Most of the Supreme Court's work is devoted to interpreting the laws passed by Congress. This is called statutory interpretation (i.e. interpreting a statute). If the Court should judge in a way of which the law-makers disapprove, the law-makers can pass an amendment to that statute which makes plain what the Congress intended to convey. In the late 1980s, the Supreme Court did interpret several laws, especially some sections of the Civil Rights Act, in a restrictive way, which a majority in Congress felt to be in error. Consequently, a new Civil Rights Act was passed in 1991 specifically to 'reverse' the decisions of which the Congress disapproved. This was a high profile instance of the legislature's ability to constrain the Court when it is involved with statutory interpretation, but in every year there is normally a handful of instances when the Court is, as it were, 'put right' through congressional action.

Constitutional adjudication is different. Despite the reality of constitutional dialogues, it is difficult to reverse most of those cases which have been based upon an interpretation of the Constitution. Since the Constitution enjoys a special status, tampering with it is generally thought improper. Furthermore, the logic of a Bill of Rights is that elected governors will, from time to time, be confounded. Only when there is genuine national commitment to a change (as with the Twenty-Sixth Amendment granting voting rights to eighteen-year-olds) or where an issue unites élites without raising any popular interest and therefore opposition (as with the Twenty-Fifth Amendment, setting out procedures to be followed when a President is incapable of carrying out the duties of the office) does an amendment usually succeed.

There are two ways of amending the Constitution. One originates in Congress, where two-thirds of each house must approve a proposal. This is then referred to the states for ratification and it becomes an amendment when three-quarters of the states have given it their approval. These are stiff conditions when, in addition to the principled opposition to a proposal, there is also a widespread feeling that the Constitution should not be amended except when absolutely necessary. Whereas in India the political culture finds nothing amiss about regular amendments to the national constitution, the American political culture has placed the Constitution on a kind of pedestal which makes alteration to it symbolic of an attack on its virtuous status. All amendments have, therefore, been originated at the centre and have, with rare exceptions like the post-Civil War amendments, been technical or democracy-enhancing. It is possible to originate an amendment from the grass roots, however, but no amendment has yet been proposed successfully via that route. States may call for a convention to consider an amendment and it is perhaps a sign of the wide concern over the national budget that the number of states which have proposed the calling of a convention to consider an amendment requiring that the national budget be balanced (several state constitutions have such requirements) is only two short of the necessary number.

The Constitution thus permits the people to propose amendments to their system of government, through their representatives either in Washington or in their home states. But this possibility is rarely taken up. The Constitution is in fact amended as a result of judicial action. And this can present difficult questions for democrats. Judicial review is not a matter of dispute; all political systems require courts to adjudicate on the application of the laws of the land. Judicial supremacy is. Once again, there is a normative side to the argument as the logic of limited government is set against a rather crude conception of democracy and democratic accountability. There is also an empirical side. The exercise of judicial power does generate considerable disquiet on occasions. The decisions which outlawed segregated schooling, or forbade prayer-reading in schools as a form of religious imposition, or established a right to an abortion, all galvanized articulate sections of the public into action and criticism of the Court. It is important, however, to remember two things. First, these cases are relatively rare and most of the major political decisions (dealing with war and peace, with budgetary priorities, with the principles of economic and social policy) are entirely outside the reach of judicial power. They virtually never raise constitutional issues which can be litigated in the federal courts. Hence, notions of an 'imperial judiciary' are overstated.

Secondly, the assumption that there is a direct relationship between a decision by the Supreme Court and its full implementation needs careful scrutiny. The two decisions outlawing segregated schooling and requiring states to proceed 'with all deliberate speed' to effectuate the end of segregation did not, in fact, result in desegregated schools for at least a decade and a half (Wilkinson, 1979). Even then, it needed the Congress to pass the 1964 Civil Rights Act and an enthusiastic executive branch to implement the Act. Much has been made by conservatives of the Court's liberal effect on social policy and the Court's appropriateness in this area is widely questioned. What is given less emphasis is the more significant point, from an empirical stance, that the impact of many of the Court's decisions in the area of social policy has not been great (Rosenberg, 1991).

But this does not, and cannot, answer the enduring question about the principles on which the Justices ought to exercise their power in those instances where the Constitution is rightly in need of interpretation. The dispute here is unresolved and probably unresolvable. What Americans have to rely upon is the wisdom and integrity of their nine Supreme Court Justices and it is the case, of course, that not all the Justices are always the epitomes of wisdom and integrity.

SUMMARY

In thinking about the supremacy of the Constitution, three points need to be considered:

- When the supreme law is vested in a written document, the importance of those who interpret and apply it gives them a very significant role in the political process.

- There is an inevitable (and probably irreconcilable) conflict between crude democratic principles and limited government protected through a justiciable Constitution.

- The importance of the Justices of the Supreme Court reflects the paradoxical nature of American democracy which combines both a populist tradition which holds that public policy should be legitimated through the consent of the governed and an anti-government tradition which seeks to protect (through the division of powers, separation of powers and the supremacy of a written Constitution) the people from the excesses of government.

5   CONCLUSION

We must address the Constitution in two distinct ways. First of all, there are the normative questions about how the US government *ought* to be structured. However, in dealing with an abstract issue of this kind, it is essential not to divorce the answer from practical possibilities. The context in which the debate takes place involves an acceptance of the dominant values of the

American élites and of the ordinary American people. These involve a general suspicion of strong government, a populist instinct to check élites, and a belief in multiple centres of power. Even more significant is the widespread attachment to the Constitution as one of the central, if not *the* central, symbols of Americanism (Corwin, 1936; Baas, 1980). Within this context, radical alterations to the Constitution seem highly unlikely.

The second focus is empirical. But even here a clear judgement has to be made on what would count as efficient government and what would count as democratic government. In the last analysis, it is likely that institutions and practices which enhance efficiency might well limit democracy. It is important, however, not to assume that these two values operate in opposition to each other; a system which is legitimized by a democratic process will almost certainly be more effective than one based upon authoritarian principles. Few scholars believe that the American constitutional system is currently operating perfectly; many believe that it cannot be set right in the current climate of democratic assumptions. As Robert Dahl expresses it, 'the problem is so profoundly built into the interaction between the constitutional framework and democratic ideology that it cannot be solved without a fundamental alteration in one or the other' (Dahl, 1990–1, p.372). This pessimistic conclusion may nevertheless be realistic.

REFERENCES

Abraham, H. (1988) *Freedom and the Court: Civil Rights and Liberties in the United States*, New York, Oxford University Press (5th edn).

American Political Science Review (1950) 'Towards a more responsible two-party system: a report of the Committee on Political Parties', vol.44, supplement.

Baas, L.R. (1980) 'The Constitution as symbol: patterns of meaning', *American Politics Quarterly*, vol.8, pp.237–56.

Blasi, V. (ed.) (1983) *The Burger Court: the Counter-Revolution that Wasn't*, New Haven, Yale University Press.

Bowen, C.D. (1966) *Miracle at Philadelphia: the Story of the Constitutional Convention*, Boston, Little, Brown.

Caplan, L. (1987) *The Tenth Justice: the Solicitor-General and the Rule of Law*, New York, Knopf.

Corwin, E. (1936) 'The Constitution as instrument and symbol', *American Political Science Review*, vol.30, pp.1071–85.

Cutler, L.N. (1980) 'To form a government', *Foreign Affairs*, vol.59, pp.126–43.

Dahl, R.A. (1957) 'Decision-making in a democracy: the role of the Supreme Court as national policy maker', *Journal of Public Law*, vol.6, pp.279–95.

Dahl, R.A. (1967) *Pluralist Democracy in America*, Chicago, Rand McNally.

Dahl, R.A. (1990–1) 'Myth of the presidential mandate', *Political Science Quarterly*, vol.105, pp.355–72.

Fisher, L. (1988) *Constitutional Dialogues: Interpretation as Political Power*, Princeton, Princeton University Press.

Glazer, N. (1975) 'Towards an imperial judiciary', *The Public Interest*, vol.41, pp.104–23.

Goldwin, R.A. and Kaufman, A. (eds) (1986) *Separation of Powers — Does it Still Work?*, Washington, DC, American Enterprise Institute.

Grimes, A. (1978) *Democracy and the Amendments to the Constitution*, Lexington, Heath.

Hodder-Williams, R. (1988) 'The Constitution (1787) and modern government' in Bogdanor, V. (ed.) *Constitutions in Democratic Politics*, Aldershot, Gower.

Hodder-Williams, R. (1989) 'Redefining federalism: the primacy of politics over the Constitution' in Maidment, R. and Zvesper, J. (eds) *Reflections on the Constitution: the American Constitution After Two Hundred Years*, Manchester, Manchester University Press.

Hodder-Williams, R. (1990) 'Ronald Reagan and the Supreme Court' in Hogan, J. (ed.) *The Reagan Years: the Record in Presidential Leadership*, Manchester, Manchester University Press, pp.143–63.

Koh, H.H. (1990) *The National Security Constitution: Sharing Power After the Iran Contra Affair*, New Haven, Yale University Press.

Laski, H. (1949) *The American Democracy: a Commentary and an Interpretation*, London, Allen & Unwin.

Lerner, M. (1945–6) 'Constitution as court and symbol', *Yale Law Journal*, vol.46, pp.1290–1319.

Lipset, S.M. (1964) *The First New Nation*, London, Heinemann.

Lobel, J. (ed.) (1988) *A Less than Perfect Union: Alternative Perspectives on the US Constitution*, New York, Monthly Review Press.

McCloskey, R.G. (1960) *The American Supreme Court*, Chicago, University of Chicago Press.

Maidment, R. (1992) *The Judicial Response to the New Deal: the US Supreme Court and Economic Regulation, 1934–36*, Manchester, Manchester University Press.

Marshall, B. (ed.) (1987) *A Workable Government? The Constitution After Two Hundred Years*, New York, Norton.

Meese, E. (1985) 'The Attorney-General's view of the Supreme Court: towards a jurisprudence of original intention', *Public Administration Review*, vol.45, pp.701–5.

O'Brien, L. (1986) *Judicial Roulette*, Cambridge, Mass., Twentieth Century Fund.

Polsby, N.W. (1983) *Consequences of Party Reform*, New York, Oxford University Press.

Robinson, D.L. (ed.) (1985) *Reforming American Government: the Bicentennial Papers of the Committee on the Constitutional System*, Boulder, Westview.

Rosenberg, G.N. (1991) *The Hidden Hope: Can Courts Bring About Social Change?*, Chicago, University of Chicago Press.

Schechter, S.L. (1986) 'Amending the United States Constitution: a new generation on trial' in Banting, K.G. and Simeon, R. (eds) *The Politics of Constitutional Change in Industrial Nations: Redesigning the State*, London, Macmillan.

Schwartz, H. (1988) *Packing the Courts: the Conservative Campaign to Rewrite the Constitution*, New York, Scribners.

Shafer, B. (1988) *Bifurcated Politics: Evolution and Reform in the National Party Convention*, Cambridge, Mass., Harvard University Press.

Spaeth, H.J. and Smith, E.C. (eds) (1991) *The Constitution of the United States*, New York, HarperCollins (13th edn).

Sundquist, J. (1986) *Effective Government and Constitutional Reform*, Washington, DC, Brookings Institution.

Welch, S., Gruhl, J., Steinman, M. and Comer, J. (1992) *American Government*, St. Paul, West Publishing Co. (4th edn).

Wheare, K.C. (1963) *Federal Government*, Oxford, Oxford University Press.

Wilkinson, J.H. (1979) *From Brown to Bakke: the Supreme Court and School Integration, 1954–1978*, New York, Oxford University Press.

Wright, D.S. (1982) *Understanding Intergovernment Relations*, North Scituate, Duxbury (2nd edn).

FURTHER READING

There is, of course, no better way of examining this topic than reading the Constitution with care. *The Federalist Papers* remain an excellent contemporary defence, but you should perhaps look at criticisms made at the time. A good source is Herbert Storing's *The Abridged Anti-Federalist*.

In the 1980s there were many reviews of the Constitution, some of which are mentioned in the reference list, e.g. Marshall (1987), Robinson (1985) and Sundquist (1986). A particularly readable collection is Jack David and Robert McKay's *The Blessings of Liberty*. A more British perspective is Simmons (1989). There is, in the end, no rival to reading a few case studies to get an understanding of how institutions function in practice. The two by Bernard Schwartz (1986, 1988) give a good picture of how the Supreme Court deals with difficult constitutional issues. Finally, because the Supreme Court is so closely involved in political matters, it is important to be quite clear about its 'political role'. This is a matter I deal with in Hodder-Williams (1992).

See Marshall (1987), Robinson (1985) and Sundquist (1986) in the references.

David, J. and McKay, R. (eds) (1989) *The Blessings of Liberty: an Enduring Constitution in a Changing World*, New York, Random House.

Hodder-Williams, R. (1992) 'Six notions of "political" and the United States Supreme Court', *British Journal of Political Science*, vol.22, pp.1–20.

Schwartz, B. (1986) *Swann's Way*, New York, Oxford University Press.

Schwartz, B. (1988) *Behind Bakke*, New York, New York University Press.

Simmons, R.C. (ed.) (1989) *The United States Constitution: the First 200 Years*, Manchester, Manchester University Press.

Storing, H. (1985) *The Abridged Anti-Federalist*, Chicago, University of Chicago Press.

INDEX

Fiorina, M.P., 62, 71, 75, 76
Fisher, Louis, 233
Flag Protection Act (1989), 113–14
Foley, M., 16, 21
Food and Drug Administration (FDA), 80
Food Safety and Inspection Service, 80
Ford, Gerald, President, 42, 107, 133
Ford, Henry Jones, 41
foreign affairs: role of President, 47, 229, 230
Founding Fathers, 2, 12, 216, 234–5
    political parties, 41
    separation of powers, 3, 16, 38, 75, 227
Fowler, E.P., 145
Fox, K., 147
France, 92, 185
Frankfurter, Felix, Justice, 123, 234
Franklin, Benjamin, 9, 15–16, 32, 116
Franklin, G.A., 78
Frazier, E. Franklin, 166
Free, L.A., 61
Freedman, J.O., 80
freedom, 17, 227
    of religion, 233
    of speech, 113, 135–6
    see also liberty; rights
Freedom of Choice Act, 134
Friedman, M., 197
Friedman, R., 197
Frisch, M., 15
frontier, 24
Fuchs, E., 148
Fukuyama, Francis, 7, 8, 163

Galveston, Texas, 143
Garcia v. San Antonio Metropolitan Transit Authority, 142, 225, 226
Gates, J.B., 119, 121
gender: welfare, 187, 192, 204, 205
Germany, 92, 101, 185, 187
Gettysburg Address, 21
Ginsberg, B., 42
Ginsberg, Ruth Bader, Justice, 133
Ginsburg, N., 199, 200, 208
Gitlow v. New York, 222
Gladstone, William, 3
Glazer, N., 218, 233
GNP (Gross National Product), 62, 63–4, 184, 194
Goldberg, Arthur, Justice, 127
Goldman v. Weinberger, 233
Goldwin, R.A., 230
Gordon, David, 138–9
Gordon, L., 186
Gosnell, H., 143
Gottdiener, M., 145
government, 9, 11–13, 29, 38, 225, 228
    overload, 61–85
    see also cities; federal government; local government; separation of powers; state government
government,
    divided, 42–3, 62, 75–7, 89, 229, 230
    parliamentary, 56–7
    prerogative, 46
    public opinion of, 16, 29, 61, 67–8
governors, state, 91, 100, 108
Graham, H.D., 175, 176, 177, 180
Great Depression, 8, 25–6, 121, 141, 189, 190, 220
Great Society programme, 26, 29, 37, 51,

151, 192–6, 223
Greider, W., 62
Grentzke, J.M., 73
gridlock, 2, 3, 16, 26, 62, 75
Griffith, D.W., 21
Griffiths, E.S., 144
Grimes, A., 9, 232
Grimshaw, W., 154
Gross National Product (GNP), 62, 63–4, 184, 194
group rights, 177–8
growth coalitions, 151
growth machine theory of urban politics, 150, 151
Gurr, T.R., 138, 140, 141–2, 150, 151, 153, 154
Guterbock, T., 154

Haber, S., 144
Hamilton, Alexander, 9, 12–13, 16, 116–17, 127
Hamilton, Charles V., 170–1
Hardin, C.M., 56
Harlan, Justice, 163, 167
Hart, J., 45
Hartmann, E.G., 162
Hartz, Louis, 19, 30–2
Harvey, D., 150, 151
Health and Human Services, Department of, 80
health care, 66, 72, 79, 148, 194–5, 207–10
Health Maintenance Organizations (HMOs), 208, 209
Heclo, H., 79
Hispanic Americans, 164
    city mayors, 154
    health care, 66
    House of Representatives, 103
    poverty, 200
    racial segregation, 146
history, end of, 7, 8, 163
HMOs (Health Maintenance Organizations), 208, 209
Hodder-Williams, Richard, 215–41
Hofstadter, Richard, 30
Holt, M.G., 144
homicide, 201
Hoover, Herbert, President, 40
hospitals, 208
House of Representatives, 14, 39, 53, 103, 216, 229
    elections, 73, 90, 108, 226
housing, 146–7, 149
Housing and Urban Development, Department of, 149
Hughes, Charles Evan, Chief Justice, 120, 233
Humphrey, Hubert, 105
Hunter, A., 198
Hunter, Floyd, 138, 152
hyper-pluralism, 62, 70–4, 80, 81

ideology, 7, 27, 30, 31
    political parties, 230–1
    welfare, 188, 197, 204–5
Ikenberry, J., 190
ill health, 185, 190, 191
Illinois, 132
immigration, 120, 137, 139, 140
    policy, 161–4
Immigration and Naturalization Service v. Chadha, 41, 115

imperial judiciary, 218, 233, 237
imperial presidency, 26, 28, 29
imperialism, 24, 32
India, 236
Indians, American see Native Americans
indirect primary elections, 108
individual rights, 17–18, 177, 217, 227, 235
individualism, 30, 221, 227
industrialization, 120, 139
inherent powers, 46–8
initiatives, 68
insurance, health care, 208–9
insurance, social, 189, 190–1, 192
integration, 167–8, 170–1, 181, 211
interest groups, 2, 4, 70–1, 84
    abortion, 130–1
    amicus curiae briefs, 82
    class action suits, 82
    election campaigns, 73, 102, 111
    health care, 66, 79, 208–9
    iron triangle, 78–9, 179
    rule making, 81
interest groups, minority, 57, 126, 229
Iran: arms sales (Irangate), 32, 51
Ireland, 92, 185
iron triangle, 78–9, 179
issue networks, 79, 179
Italy, 185

Jackson, Andrew, President, 91
Jackson, Jesse, 178
Japan, 185
Jefferson, Thomas, President, 7, 9, 13, 15, 16, 24, 26–7, 32–3
Jencks, C., 144, 153
Jim Crow (segregation) practices, 173, 176
Johnson, Gregory Lee, 113–14, 136
Johnson, James Weldon, 168
Johnson, Lyndon B., President, 50, 175
    civil rights legislation, 126, 179
    emergency powers, 48
    Great Society programme, 26, 29, 151, 192, 223
    War on Poverty programme, 141, 194
Jones, B.D., 143
Jones, C.O., 79
Jones, Charles, 50
Jordan, A.G., 71
judges see justices
judicial activism, 122–35
judicial restraint, 123
judicial review, 18, 113–21, 123, 127, 135, 236, 237
judiciary see justices; separation of powers; Supreme Court
judiciary, imperial, 218, 233, 237
Judiciary Act (1789), 118–19
justice, 159–60
    social, 205
justices, 118, 233, 237
    appointment, 81, 128, 132–4, 217, 235
    Court-packing plan, 121–2, 234
    see also Supreme Court

Kaczorowski, R., 20–1
Kallen, Horace, 164
Katz, J., 191, 192–3, 194, 195–6, 203
Katznelson, I., 138, 139–40, 150, 151
Kaufman, A., 230

ACKNOWLEDGEMENTS

Grateful acknowledgement is made to the following sources for permission to reproduce material in this book.

TABLES

Table 3.4: Courtesy of The Gallup Organization; Table 5.1: Gates, J.B. (1992) *The Supreme Court and Partisan Realignment*, Westview Press; Table 5.2: adapted from Rosenberg, G. (1991) *The Hollow Hope: Can Courts Bring About Social Change*, University of Chicago Press; Table 6.1: Gurr, T.R. and King, D. (1987) *The State and the City*, University of Chicago Press, also by permission of Macmillan Education, London; Table 6.2: Landis, J.D. (1987) 'The future of America's central cities', *Built Environment*, vol.13, The Alexandrine Press; Tables 6.3 and 6.7: adapted from Savitch, H.V. and Thomas, J.C. (1991) 'Conclusion: end of the millennium big city politics', *Big City Politics in Transition*, Sage Publications Inc.; Table 8.1: Courtesy of the Organization for Economic Co-operation and Development (1985); Table 8.2: adapted from Esping-Andersen, G. (1990) *The Three Worlds of Welfare Capitalism*, Polity Press; Table 8.4: Katz, J. (1986) *In the Shadow of the Poorhouse: a Social History of Welfare in America*, Basic Books.

FIGURES

Figures 2.1 and 9.1: Reprinted by permission from *American Government*, fifth edition, by Welch *et al.* Copyright © 1994 by West Publishing Company. All rights reserved.

CARTOONS

p.45: Burt Thomas/Reproduced by kind permission of the publisher of *The Detroit News*; p.235: Drawing by C. Barsotti; © 1981. The New Yorker Magazine, Inc.; p.238: Copyright Sidney Harris.

ILLUSTRATIONS

p.23: Courtesy of the National Archives, Washington, DC/Photo: Stephen R. Brown, 1986; pp.26 and 31: Popperfoto; p.50: Photo Yoichi R. Okamoto/ Courtesy of the Lyndon Baines Johnson Library Collection; p.75: Architect of the Capitol/Photo: National Graphic Center; p.100: UPI/Bettmann; p.105 (left): Copyright Raymond Depardon/Magnum; p.105 (right): AP/Wide World; p.114 (left): UPI/Bettmann Newsphotos; p.114 (right): UPI/Bettmann; p.133: P.J. Griffiths/Magnum; p.144: Burt Glinn/Magnum; p.169 (top): Eve Arnold/Magnum; p.169 (bottom): Bruce Davidson/Magnum; pp.178 and 190: AP/Wide World Photos; p.210: Popperfoto/Reuter/Photo by Joe Giza; p.216: Courtesy, Winterthur Museum.